HIERARCHY
IN
ORGANIZATIONS

An International Comparison

Arnold S. Tannenbaum

Bogdan Kavčič

Menachem Rosner

Mino Vianello

Georg Wieser

FOREWORD BY DANIEL KATZ

HEIRARCHY
IN
ORGANIZATIONS

Jossey-Bass Publishers

San Francisco • Washington • London • 1974

HIERARCHY IN ORGANIZATIONS
An International Comparison
    by Arnold S. Tannenbaum, Bogdan Kavčič, Menachem Rosner,
    Mino Vianello, and Georg Wieser

Copyright © 1974 by: Jossey-Bass, Inc., Publishers
    615 Montgomery Street
    San Francisco, California 94111
    &
    Jossey-Bass Limited
    3 Henrietta Street
    London WC2E 8LU

Library of Congress Catalogue Card Number LC 73-20963

International Standard Book Number ISBN 0-87589-219-1

Manufactured in the United States of America

JACKET DESIGN BY WILLI BAUM

FIRST EDITION

Code 7414

The
Jossey-Bass
Behavioral Science Series

FOREWORD

In the ebb and flow of social science research, where it is difficult to detect a forward current among the eddies and tides, *Hierarchy in Organizations* and the program of research it represents are an encouraging indication of a significant scientific advance in the field of organizational psychology. Progress in this area of study has been slow in that, on the one hand, the good ideas in general have been illustrated rather than researched and, on the other hand, quantitative research lacking the guidance of theory has provided descriptive data of very limited utility. The research of Tannenbaum and his associates—the systematic gathering of data in many settings about a central set of propositions—is an exception to these trends.

The importance of this volume can be understood more fully in the context of different historical approaches and developments in the field. These approaches—the anthropological (or case study) method, the emphasis upon small groups, and traditional industrial psychology—have overlapped both historically and substantively. Many hope they will converge in a social-psychological system approach, and Tannenbaum's research program illustrates how such an integration can be achieved.

The case study approach of the anthropologist, with its depth understanding of a given social unit, is still probably the best source of information about organizations. In a series of studies most of which appeared in the decade of the fifties, an older generation of sociologists provided a rich background of materials for the formulation of hypotheses. Among the better known are Selznick's study of the Tennessee Valley Authority (1949), Gouldner's account of a coal mine (1954), Stanton and Schwartz's investigation of a hospital psychiatric ward (1954), Blau's comparison of two government agencies (1955), Lipset's study in collaboration with Trow and Coleman of a labor union (1956), and Sykes' graphic account of a prison (1958). Though we have moved away from this tradition, it fortunately persists in the insightful work of a number of investigations such as W. Brown's *Explorations in Management* (1960), and Stotland and Kobler's *Life and Death of a Mental Hospital* (1965).

Valuable as this approach is in the first stages of a science, it attempts little in the way of measurement of variables and quantification of relationships. Hence it provides small opportunity for the confirmation of findings from one study to another or for determining the relationship between variables. It is still too early in the development of the field to abandon this approach, but progress will come when we combine it with more sophisticated methods.

The small-group approach, which began with the work of Elton Mayo and his followers, is still one of the main streams in the field and has been refreshed by the concepts and experiments of the group dynamicists in the United States and the Tavistock researchers in Great Britain. The Mayo investigators rediscovered the informal group as it operated in the context of the factory setting. These early researchers were not interested in organizational variables but in group processes at the level of interpersonal relations. Having discovered that organizations do not function as described in formal organization charts, they abandoned large system variables for the specifics of personal relationships. This change in focus led readily to a fusion with what is sometimes called the human-relations approach. The small group, moreover, was the major concern of the group-dynamics people, and their experiments on group decision-making, communication, and cohesion were seen as related to the functioning of the work groups in organizations. In fact in some instances researchers actually tested the group-dynamics concepts in industrial settings, as did Seashore in his work on cohesion, group norms, and productivity (1954). In general, however, in the United States the group dynamicists, like their Mayo predecessors, took no account of organizational variables. In England, however, the Tavistock followers of Kurt Lewin pursued a rather different line of investigation, still consistent with the master theorist, which opened the door to a consideration of system variables. They conceived of the organization as a sociotechnical system and as a system dependent upon the character of the social environment (Trist and others, 1963). But in their research they did not move beyond the sociotechnical system of the work group into the managerial and institutional systems of the higher levels of the structure. They gave their major attention to process and structure of the small group.

The Mayo work and the subsequent emphasis upon interpersonal processes were revolts against the traditional industrial psychology of adapting man to the system. Taylorism, which exemplified the traditional approach, was the study of how to make men more productive within the framework of the factory system. System variables were taken as givens, not as variables to be studied and manipulated in their own right. In fact the Western Electric experiments were inspired by Frederick Taylor's so-called scientific approach; the objectives of these experiments were to find the optimum level of illumination for productivity in winding reels and the optimum relationship between rest and work periods for attaining greatest productivity. The finding that social rather than physical factors were critical determinants of productivity led the investigators to drop their interest in physical conditions of work and to emphasize group factors. The conventional approach of the industrial psychologist continued, however, in studies of conditions of work, of time and motion, of training methods, of personnel selection and placement. The objective remained the same, fitting the individual to the work role. This approach has now broadened somewhat in its analysis of individual morale and in the man-machine emphasis of human engineering. But man-machine system refers to a small segment of the total industrial system, and no attempt is made to deal with social-system variables. For example, the notion of giving a team responsibility for assembling an engine and thus revising the role system of the factory goes beyond the logic of man-machine technicians.

There is now a movement within departments of psychology and sociology toward a social psychology of organizations. Both conventional industrial psychology and the small-group approach grossly neglected the organizational structures with which they were dealing. The older anthropological approach had a much more adequate view of the total picture, and researchers in this tradition pointed out the relationships between formal structural variables and psychological processes, as in Sykes' description (1958) of the factors leading to prison riots. But, as has been noted, these early researchers attempted no systematic measurements of the processes they investigated. The new organizational psychology attempts to provide research design and specification of variables and their measurement in relating psychological process to aspects of organizational structure.

The movement toward an organizational psychology received impetus from the development of older approaches. Some of the Tavistock group began to look at systemic aspects of industrial enterprises as they noted their dependence upon environmental conditions. Sociological theorists gave consideration to organizations as subsystems of society. Social psychologists applied open-system theorizing to the functioning of organizations (Katz and Kahn, 1966). Likert (1967), starting out as an exponent of interpersonal processes, gave added thrust to the new movement by theoretically tying group process to the functioning of an organizational hierarchy. Whether Likert's normative theory acquires research support in all its specifices is not as important as the fact that we at last have a theory which attempts to tie together organizational structure and group process.

Tannenbaum's research on control in organization is an excellent example of the social-psychological approach. It selects a critical set of variables in organizations based upon system analysis and then relates these characteristics to the pychological processes at the interpersonal and individual level. It thus embraces the thinking about participation and group decision-making from the small-group approach in the context of social structure.

The propositions with which Tannenbaum is concerned are, moreover, pursued systematically in repeated studies in a variety of settings. In scientific research one cannot do everything at once and give answers to all the problems of the universe. But the necessary limitation of any single research program to a small piece of the picture should not be an excuse, as it sometimes is, for shying away from important variables and tough problems and settling on trivia. This is not the case with the work of Arnold Tannenbaum. He takes as his major concern the problem of power and its distribution in organized structures. After all, this is what social organization is all about (Yuchtman and Seashore, 1967). If spontaneous cooperation could achieve coordinated collective effort as some Utopians have it, or if technology could ensure the automatic running of social systems as many of the technocrats and Taylorites believe, this would be a simple world without strife, industrial conflict, boycotts, political machinations, economic threats and reprisals, cold and hot wars. Social organization does not remove the struggle for economic rewards, psychological gratifications, and power as a means to these rewards and as an end in itself. Rather it institutionalizes the distribution of power, channels it, and in some instances restricts its use and in others exaggerates it. Problems of power and control in society have not been wholly neglected in organizational studies, but they have not received attention commensurate with their importance, especially in the Mayo approach and the industrial-psychological approach.

They are somehow not supposed to be there, or their treatment in present institutional forms is accepted as a solution and not inquired into. However, people interested in serious social change, unless wearing the blinders of individually oriented psychology, inevitably turn to issues of power distribution. For its part, the establishment, like some industrial psychologists, does not talk about power. It uses power. There seems to be almost an inverse correlation between talk and practice, with the rebels high on the talking side and the authorities high on the side of practice.

One reason Marxian theory is still alive is its clear and explicit and, sometimes, even accurate formulation of power issues. Though more sophisticated in dealing with psychological complexities, most social science theories have still not caught up with the Marxian conceptualization of power as a function of social structure. (It should be mentioned in passing that the historical dialectic of Marx could well be considered another approach to the study of organizations.) Marx was concerned not with organizations in themselves but with their functions as subsystems of society. In this one respect his point of view resembles that of Parsons (1960). But while the Parsonian approach is bland in its assumptions about value consensus, Marxism is relentlessly bitter about the internal contradictions in society. Parsonian theory assumes stability and evolutionary change; Marxian theory, sudden change and revolution. True to its theoretical assumptions the Marxian method calls for thorough study of historical processes, for constant examination of systemic changes. Marx and Engels were continuously analyzing the failures and successes of the labor and radical movements in various countries to revise and refine their conceptualizations of the specific dialectic processes. Such a historical approach, in which social, economic, and technical changes are the key set of variables and in which theory has to be validated and revised against practice, has not been utilized in the study of organizations. Perhaps this failure will be remedied in the future if and when historians and behavioral scientists join forces in an attack on common problems. The present volume, in its examination of the same type of organization in different countries at different developmental stages, suggests an alternative procedure.

The studies in Tannenbaum's program also illustrate how methodological difficulties can be overcome in social-psychological research. Tannenbaum (1968a) developed standardized scales for getting at organizational members' perceptions of the amount of control exercised by their peers and by those at other levels of the hierarchy. By averaging individual perceptions, Tannenbaum derived measures of the organizational variables of amount and distribution of power. These indices could then be related to measures of communication, motivation, and satisfaction. The accuracy of these measures of perceived power remained in question however. They could, for example, reflect the individual's favorable attitude toward his organization, and the same favorable attitude could be expressed in his reports on communication and motivation. This type of objection has to be met in any study attempting to relate system variables to attitudinal variables when all the measures are obtained from the perceptions and attitudes of the same population. One direct but difficult way of handling the problem would be controlled observations of behavior of conforming to others and of influencing others in various role settings. Tannenbaum's interest in cross-cultural research gave him another criterion for assessing the system variable of distribution of power in objective fashion. He worked in countries and settings in which organizational control is known to have different degrees of centralization and distribution. Thus at the one extreme are the kibbutzim factories, in which power is widely distributed, at the other extreme are factories in Italy and Austria, with a high degree of centralized power. The measures of distribution of control based upon individual perception were clearly supported in these cross-cultural comparisons.

The cross-cultural approach exemplified by this volume deserves comment in another context, that of research methodology. Too often what passes for comparative national research consists of studies with no sampling design and with research objectives imposed by the American investigator collecting data

here and there at his convenience. The research reported here
involved native investigators in five countries who worked out
the design and objectives as a cooperative enterprise.

Tannenbaum's major findings bear upon the analytical
problem of power as a zero-sum concept and upon the normative problem of the effects of power distribution on organizational effectiveness and member gratification. His earlier work
attacking the zero-sum concept of power had been criticized for
not differentiating sufficiently between organizational situations
in which there is a community of interest and those in which
there is a conflict of interest. With a community of interest,
where A and B are working toward the same goals, they can
mutually influence one another, and the total influence is greater
because A's power is not at the expense of B's. With a conflict
of interest, the more A controls a given decision the less control
B has. In the studies reported in this volume the authors deal
directly with socialist factories, like the kibbutzim plants in
Israel and socially-owned factories in Yugoslavia, and with
capitalistic factories in Italy, Austria, and the United States.
The commonality of interest should be greater in the socialist
than in the capitalistic factories. The findings do indicate the
significance of common ownership; the socialist factories do
show the flatter control curves. But the findings also indicate the
multidimensional character of power distribution. Participative
practices employed in the small-group approach appreciably
mitigate the negative effects of hierarchy in capitalistic countries.
Community and conflict of interest are not all-or-none affairs.
Even where there is collective ownership of a factory, hierarchy
exists and can have negative effects unless accompanied by supportive interpersonal relationships.

The work reported in *Hierarchy in Organizations* thus
is not only a major contribution to substantive knowledge and
theory development in organizational psychology and sociology
but provides new input into a most critical social issue: What
direction should the organization of collective effort take in the
future? This book does not give us the full answers to questions
of how we achieve equity of return in collective effort, citizen

equality in the setting of goals, and humanitarian relations in a role system, but it suggests that some of these normative issues are also research questions which can have operational answers.

DANIEL KATZ
Institute for Social Research
The University of Michigan

PREFACE

Hierarchy is designed to solve
a universal problem of organization, the need to coordinate the
efforts of many persons performing a variety of tasks. But
hierarchy in turn creates problems of its own—division between persons of different rank and the seeds of disaffection and
conflict inherent in that division. *Hierarchy in Organizations* is
about such problems.

We have chosen to study industrial organizations from a
number of societies that differ from one another in their approaches to solving the problems of hierarchy. Twenty of the
industrial plants included in this study are in Israeli kibbutzim
and in Yugoslavia, where organizations are formally designed
on a socialist ideological basis. Thirty plants, matched to the
socialist ones, are in the United States, Austria, and Italy. In
the socialist factories private ownership has been abolished, and
a high degree of formal participativeness and equalitarianism
among members has been established. We explore in *Hierarchy
in Organizations* the general proposition that these conditions

reduce if not eliminate the unintended and dysfunctional effects of hierarchy.

We have employed the methods of survey research to collect data from persons at all levels in these fifty industrial plants, and we have utilized statistical procedures to help evaluate the data. Our concern is not with methodology however, and *Hierarchy in Organizations* should be understandable to readers who have only a casual acquaintance with the techniques of social research. We have written the book for those who are interested in the adjustment of individuals in organizations and who are concerned also with questions of ideology, culture, and political system that have implications for the design of organizations and consequently for the adjustment and welfare of members. The book therefore concerns issues relevant to a number of disciplines. It is addressed to psychologists, sociologists, political scientists, students of public and business administration, and historians with an interest in quantitative social research. We think it will be of interest as well to managers and administrators who are curious about life in organizations radically different from their own.

Acknowledgements

The research described was undertaken in a spirit of close collaboration. It could not have been done otherwise. The data are from five countries, each represented by one of the authors. We had to deal as a group with five cultures, five languages, and radically different political systems. But this research required a good deal more than the curiosity and spirit of collaboration that motivated the authors; we were helped substantially by others who, for better or worse, must share some responsibility for what we have done.

The work was initiated under a grant from the National Science Foundation, and the Ford Foundation provided additional support that permitted us to enlarge the collection of data and to do analyses that otherwise would not have been possible. We are grateful to the officers of these foundations for their faith and for the substantial financial support they provided.

We offer *Hierarchy in Organizations* as a report to them of what we have done.

We were assisted by many persons during the several years of this project. Workers and managers in more than fifty industrial plants in five countries participated. The data of this research are their data, and we are much indebted to them. We do not name the companies because of our commitment to maintaining anonymity.

During the course of our work we held a number of meetings for which we relied on the facilities of host institutions: the Institute of Advanced Studies in Vienna, the University of Rome, the Central Slovenian Trade Union Organization in Ljubljana, and the Study Center in Florence of the Italian Confederation of Free Trade Unions (CISL). The United States National Institute of Mental Health provided counterpart funds in support of meetings in Ljubljana; Gerhard Eichinger helped with our computer work in Vienna; Piero Merli Brandini generously arranged for our use of the facilities in Florence.

One of the authors spent a year on leave at the Institute of Industrial Relations, the University of California, Berkeley, were colleagues Raymond Miles and George Strauss offered outstanding hospitality and support during a period when substantial analyses and writing were being done; and Linda Dayton, Joan Lewis, and Barbara Porter went considerably beyond the call of duty to see that the typing and administrative assistance needed were efficiently rendered. During this period, Frank Many of the Survey Research Center, University of California, did the computer work, which was substantial and complex. At the Institute for Social Research, The University of Michigan, we relied on David Warren and Gregory Eurich and the OSIRIS and MIDAS program packages. Leslie Kish, Graham Kalton, and Laura Clem of the Institute for Social Research provided consultation concerning sampling and statistics as did Kenneth Guire of The University of Michigan Statistical Research Laboratory.

The Kibbutz Industries Association supported our effort to obtain the collaboration of the kibbutz plants, which, as the reader will see, make a vital contribution to the data of this study. Mihal Palgi helped administer the research and collect the data in the kibbutz plants, and the Givat Haviva Social Research Center on the Kibbutz put its facilities at our disposal. Naphtali Golomb and Uri Leviatan of the center provided suggestions important to the analysis and interpretation of the data, and we offer our thanks to them.

We were also fortunate in having the advice and moral support of friends and colleagues who offered incisive critiques of an early draft of this book and, more soothingly, suggested ways to create a more reasonable and readable statement of our project. We therefore thank Robert Kahn, Edward Lawler, George Strauss, Henk Thierry, and Ernst Zahn, and we plead that they be absolved for any misapplication by us of their generous and much appreciated advice.

Marian Mittendorf and Kuniko Tsuchiyama prepared the draft and revisions of the draft, and Kuniko Tsuchiyama also attended to the many fine points of preparing the final version for the publisher. We much appreciate their help and the spirit in which they gave it.

Ann Arbor, Michigan	ARNOLD S. TANNENBAUM
Ljubljana, Yugoslavia	BOGDAN KAVČIČ
Kibbutz Reshafim, Israel	MENACHEM ROSNER
Rome	MINO VIANELLO
Vienna	GEORG WIESER
February 1974	

CONTENTS

I

HIERARCHY
IN ORGANIZATIONS

At the very highest level there is very little knowledge. They do not understand the opinion of the masses. They are very busy from morning until evening, but they do not examine people and they do not investigate matters. Their bureaucratic manner is immense. They beat their gongs to blaze the way. They cause people to become afraid just by looking at them (Mao, 1970).

This book is about some of the effects of hierarchy in organizations. Research in the United States suggests that persons at different levels in an organizational hierarchy differ predictably in important aspects of adjustment. Organization members at upper echelons, more than those at lower levels, are likely to experience greater motivation, involvement, and interest in their jobs; stronger identification with and loyalty to the organization; and the satisfaction of needs for self-esteem,

self-actualization, and exercise of authority. Significant percep-
tual, ideological, and cognitive differences, along with differences in symptoms of mental and physical illness, also distinguish
persons of different rank.

Most if not all work organizations are structured hierarchically, although the character of hierarchy may differ from
one organization to another. Some organizations are tall (having many levels) and others are flat. Some have ambiguous
lines of authority and others have a clearly defined system of
ranks. Some organizations contain a single, simple chain of
command; other organizations may be more complicated, having "line" and "staff" as well as other hierachies. Nonetheless,
despite these variations, hierachy comes as close as any social
characteristic does to defining a basic and universal dimension
of organization.

Hierarchy, however, raises issues that are not unique to
organizations, issues that are related to society itself. Hierarchy
means inequality in the distribution of valued goods whether
in the form of power, money, prestige, or other social com-
modities. Sociologists from the very beginning have asked such
questions as, "Why is there inequality among men? Where do
its causes lie? Can it be reduced, or even abolished altogether?
Or do we have to accept it as a necessary element in the structure of human society?" (Dahrendorf, 1970, p. 4.)

Need for Hierarchy

Division of labor provides one explanation for why hierarchical differentiation may develop:

> The maintenance of any social system requires
> the continuous and successful performance of a variety
> of activities. There is no known social system in which
> every member performs exactly the same pattern of
> activities. . . . The development of social differentia-
> tion is of central importance to our understanding of
> social stratification because every axis of the former
> is at least a potential dimension of the latter. Given
> that one or more properties of social objects are uti-

lized to distribute them to various groups, there is always the possibility that the features used to distinguish one object from another will become not just distinguishing marks, but marks of distinction. In this event, the objects, and the groups into which they fall, will be both differentiated and differentially valued. Thus social differentiation *may* be transformed into social inequality [Laumann, Siegel, and Hodge, 1970].

Yet the relationship between social differentiation and social inequality is not simple, and it is apparent that the magnitude of this relationship differs from one society to another. Nor is the relationship entirely a matter of chance. Societies define implicitly if not explicitly how much of a relationship should exist between differentiation and inequality and whether the gap between those who have power, money, or prestige and those who do not is great or small.

According to classical theories, the gap is great and it is inevitable in organizations. Hierarchy is a part of the system of authority that is essential to the maintenance of order. Organization is a system of rules and commands, and organizations cannot function without a line of authority to assure that the decisions of leaders at the top are carried out reliably by members at the bottom. Not only do leaders have the legitimate right and the superior knowledge to justify their authority, according to classical views, but lower ranking members lack industriousness and must be supervised closely in a tight chain of command if they are to be induced to perform on the job. This places great responsibility on leaders and requires unusual talent. Leaders must therefore be rewarded accordingly, not only as a matter of just compensation but also as a means of assuring that the very best persons are attracted to and remain in positions of leadership.

These traditional arguments have not been without critics, chief among them the Marxists. Hierarchy, in the Marxian view, is a means of exploitation based on class rule. Workers do not lack industriousness and they need not be supervised closely except in a capitalist labor market, which creates opposition in workers and the consequent need for hierarchical control. Marx recognized the division of labor as a basis of hierarchy, but he saw the root cause as private property. Exploitation will disappear, according to Marx, and the character of hierarchy will be radically altered, with the abolition of capitalism and the creation of a society based on the voluntary association of free producers. Division of labor will continue to be an essential component of organization, but privileges of income, status, and power will not be attached to different positions in this new, equalitarian society and the deleterious impact of social differentiation on the lives of members will be eliminated.

The promise of the Marxian revolution has not been realized, in the view of some authors, because Marxian theory has not been *really* tried in practice and, in the view of others, because the theory itself has inherent weaknesses. Dahrendorf (1970), for example, has raised questions about the importance of property as a basis for social differentiation:

> In the Soviet Union, in Yugoslavia, in Israel, and wherever else private property has been reduced to virtual insignificance, we still find social stratification. Even if such stratification is prevented for a short period from manifesting itself in differences of possessions and income (as in the kibbutzim of Israel), the undefinable yet effective force of prestige continues to create a noticeable rank order. If social inequality were really based on private property, the abolition of private property would have to result in the elimination of inequality. Experience in propertyless and quasi-propertyless societies does not confirm this proposition. We may therefore regard it as disproved.

But this "disproof" is not entirely convincing to many sociologists, and the effect of the abolition of private property on stratification and hierarchy is still an open question.

Contemporary organization theorists, including many psychologically minded behavioral scientists have, like the Marxists, raised questions about the classical assumptions underlying hierarchy, but they have proposed a different solution to some of the problems hierarchy creates (Argyris, 1964; Likert, 1961; Follett, 1942; Mayo, 1945; Roethlisberger and Dickson, 1964). Hierarchy based on the classical assumptions creates alienation, conflict, and frustration, along with other dysfunctional effects. It is is necessary therefore to introduce techniques of human relations, including forms of participative management, in order to mitigate these undesired consequences. Supervisors, for example, must behave in supportive and sensitive ways toward subordinates, deemphasizing status differences, expressing confidence and trust, taking an interest in their people as human beings, listening to their ideas and suggestions and involving them in decisions concerning work matters. These techniques, according to theory, enhance the sense of personal worth and importance of all members and increase their mutual trust and feeling of identification with the organization. They therefore reduce the conflict and divisiveness that hierarchical differentiation might otherwise cause.

Human relations approaches, too, have been criticized. They are said to be superficial, impractical, manipulative (Bendix and Fisher, 1950; Strauss, 1963; Wilensky, 1957. Basic power and property relations remain unchanged and the psychology of interpersonal relations provides only a thin sugar-coating for the bitter conflicts inherent in hierarchy. Some authors nonetheless see conditions emerging in industry, and in society generally, that are leading to less rigid hierarchical arrangements consistent in principle with human relations and participative approaches. (Katz and Georgopoulos, 1971; Kerr and others, 1962; Tannenbaum, 1968b). These conditions are not a direct result of the human relations movement but rather a result of changes in industrial technology and the character of the industrial environment. For example, the division of labor, which is the root of hierarchy in the classical organization, brings into the modern, technologically advanced organization highly trained specialists who may be more expert in a particular area of technology than their superior. These subordinates will necessarily have a good deal of autonomy and will make decisions that in the classical organization would be reserved for the superior (Mechanic, 1962). Furthermore, the accelerated rate of change that is said to characterize modern society requires adaptable, "organic" organizations and "temporary systems" that have ambiguous and changing lines of authority (Burns and Stalker, 1961; Bennis and Slater, 1968). Organizations that must continually react to a turbulent environment must continually create task forces composed of members who possess as a group the mix of skills needed to cope with the problem of the moment. Such groups bring together persons of different rank from different parts of the organization—and a member's influence in the group depends not on his formal position but on his expertise. With the problem solved, the group disbands and members move to other groups and other problems. Hierarchy in such a system lacks the stability and rigid authoritarian character of the classical model.

Thus hierarchy in its simple, traditional form is being challenged from a variety of sources. Yet in one form or another hierarchy remains, and it is likely to remain a manifest and important element of organization structure. The universality and importance of hierarchy therefore suggest it as a topic for comparative research. Furthermore, organizations in a number of societies, while sharing with those in the United States the element of hierarchy, have formal systems of authority differing radically from those in this country. We have chosen to study a number of such organizations, including industrial plants in Yugoslavia and in Israeli kibbutzim, that are formally designed on a socialist ideological basis, along with comparable plants in the United States, Austria, and Italy, in order to learn something about how the formal structure of authority in organizations, and the formal ideologies upon which they are based may modify the effects of hierarchy.

The following illustrate the general categories of effect we have investigated: satisfaction with and attitudes toward the enterprise; sense of responsibility and motivation in the plant; adjustment, including feelings of self-esteem, resentment, alienation; perceptions and ideals concerning aspects of the enterprise and the member's role in it. Differences in some of these reactions and adjustments between organization members at different ranks that have been documented through research in the United States can be explained in part by several formal gradients that ordinarily accompany hierarchy.

Explaining Hierarchical Differences in Reaction and Adjustment

First, authority is distributed hierarchically in organizations.* Individuals at upper levels have more power and exercise more control than those at successively lower levels. This distribution of power in the hierarchy has an important impact on job satisfaction. Studies of organizations are reasonably consistent in showing a positive relationship between job satisfaction and the amount of control a person exercises in his work situation (Blauner, 1960). Having some say in the affairs of the work situation contributes also to a member's sense of involvement in his work and in the organization, as well as to his identification, personal commitment, and feeling of responsibility on the job (Likert, 1961; Morse and Reimer, 1956; Tannenbaum, 1966). Part of the explanation for these relationships is that members generally prefer exercising influence to being powerless—although there are individual differences in this regard. Results from a number of studies show that workers, supervisors, and managers are more likely to feel that they have too little authority than too much (Katz, 1954; Porter, 1962; Tannenbaum, 1962b; Zupanov and Tannenbaum, 1968a). Furthermore, this felt deficiency decreases with hierarchical ascent (Porter, 1962).

Second, persons at higher levels are formally assigned greater status in the organization than persons at lower levels. Accordingly, persons at higher levels are considered more important and have greater responsibility, official respectability, and recognition. They also receive higher pay and enjoy greater privileges and perquisites: stock options, longer vacations, and

---

* The documentation for the following is based on research done in the United States and some of the material presented here is from Tannenbaum, *Social Psychology of the Work Organization* (1966).

paid sick leaves. The responsibility, respect, and recognition, along with the greater material rewards associated with status, contribute significantly to the satisfaction of important needs— and to a sense of self-esteem. There are indications that status and self-esteem (which accompanies status) affect not only the satisfactions of organization members, but also their mental and physical health (Kasl and French, 1962).

Third, by and large jobs at higher levels are intrinsically more interesting or challenging than those at lower levels and working conditions are more congenial. At higher levels jobs are generally less repetitious, routinized, and fractionated; and they allow greater discretion and choice to organization members. Accordingly, these jobs permit greater individuality to members and a greater sense of self-fulfillment or self-actualization. At lower levels, however, a worker may experience serious frustrations because his job fails to provide sufficient opportunity for him to use his abilities or to realize his potentials (Argyris, 1957; Allport, 1933; Walker and Guest, 1952). Not all persons prefer varied and challenging rather than routine and simple work (Hulin and Blood, 1968; Blood and Hulin, 1967; Turner and Lawrence, 1965; see also Shepard, 1970); but the preponderance of research evidence suggests that job satisfaction tends on the average to be greater among persons performing jobs that require discretion and skill than among those doing jobs that are routine and repetitive.

For these reasons hierarchy, in American plants at least, represents to many organization members the path to achievement; movement or lack of movement along the hierarchy implies personal success or failure. Thus, hierarchy, which is a basic *organizational* characteristic, has profound *psychological* implications for members. Related as it is to power, status, success, and important satisfactions, hierarchy touches upon some of the deepest human sensibilities. It is not surprising therefore to find that hierarchy is frequently associated with conflict, both within and between organization members.

Intrapersonal conflict may be associated with hierarchy in a number of ways. For example, the exercise of authority may be a mixed blessing because of the seriousness of the decisions that are sometimes made by persons in authority. A "right" decision can mean important organizational as well as personal success; a "wrong" decision can lead to failure. Furthermore, the deeper involvement and commitment of persons at upper levels, and their greater stake in the organization, may lead to worries that persons at lower levels do not experience. Gurin, Veroff, and Feld (1960) found that while managerial and professional personnel were more likely than lower-ranking persons to experience ego satisfactions through their work, these managers and professionals were also more likely to experience ego frustrations stemming from their greater commitment to their work.

Power, which is a basic correlate of hierarchy, has deep and sometimes conflicting emotional connotations for those who exercise this power as well as for those who are subject to its exercise (Adorno and others, 1950). Some organization members also can be expected to feel ambivalent about hierarchical roles that imply contradictions between success and equality ideologies (Seeman, 1953). Furthermore, the striving for success in the hierarchy may imply competitiveness, about which some persons feel conflicted (McClelland and others, 1953). The formation by industrial workers of informal groups that regulate production is partly the result of the workers' desire to minimize the emotional costs of competition. Similarly, some of the psychological appeal of unions in the United States has been the avoidance of competition among workers (Barkin, 1953). The ambivalences associated with hierarchical advancement are apparent when workers are promoted to foremen; such promotions are sometimes viewed by other workers as betrayal. Union stewards who accept promotion in a company are especially likely to elicit the emotions associated with status and competition in the hierarchy, as the following quotation illustrates: "Must be something wrong with a man to do that. Brown was offered the foreman's job but he refused. He's a good man. They (foremen) only get ten to fifteen cents more than a workingman. They get no protection. When Holt became a foreman I said to him, 'Rat, aren't you?' He said, 'What do you mean?' I said, 'You always were a union man; now you're going to push the men around. How far you going to get pushing?' " (Tannen-baum and Kahn, 1958). A second worker saw "envy" as the reason for some workers' opposition to such promotions.

The ambivalence associated with status and achievement in the hierarchy may lead to interpersonal conflict, as illustrated by the previous quotation. Many of the interpersonal conflicts in the hierarchy derive from the fact that in the hierarchy persons work together but are rewarded and motivated differ-ently. Organization implies a kind of class society in the sense that, psychologically and economically, some members are more advantageously situated in it than others. Symptoms of inter-personal conflict, or of the potential for conflict, can be seen in three general differences between echelons in addition to the gradients discussed above: differences in perceptions and cognitions; differences in ideals and norms; and differences in loyalties.

Differences in Perceptions and Cognitions. Research suggests that persons in different hierarchical positions perceive and interpret important events in the organization quite dif-ferently. These differences derive partly from the differences in "self-interest" and in motivations of persons at different ranks. These persons also have different sources of information and vantage points from which to view organizational events. Moreover, their immediate social and psychological environ-ments are strikingly and systematically different. For example, the president interacts frequently with his vice-presidents and others at the executive level who share his relatively positive view of organizational life. These highly involved and inter-ested persons feel relatively little dissatisfaction regarding au-thority, self-esteem, and self-actualization (Porter, 1962). On the other hand, persons at the bottom of the hierarchy live in a psychologically depressed area, and each of them has consid-erable support from his fellow workers for his relatively jaun-diced view of organizational life.

A number of research studies have documented some of the different perceptions and cognitions that are a function of hierarchical position. For example, studies have shown that superiors and their immediate subordinates differ in their perceptions of the following things: (a) how persons get ahead in the organization, whether through merit or "pull" (Morse, 1953); (b) the obstacles that stand in the way of the subordinates doing a good job (Maier and others, 1961); (c) the similarities between the subordinates' and supervisors' jobs, and the abilities required for these jobs (unpublished data); (d) the extent (and freedom) of communication between subordinates and supervisors (Mann, 1953); (e) the motives of subordinates and their attitudes toward their jobs and toward their superiors (Stouffer and others, 1949; Kahn, 1958).

Differences in Ideals for the Organization. Persons express different ideals for their organization. In crucial respects, the kind of organization that workers want is a different kind from that preferred by their supervisors and managers. On the question of authority, for example, a compilation of results from a number of studies reveals that employees, on the average, want to exercise more control over what goes on in the work place than they perceive themselves to exercise. However, in almost none of these organizations do *supervisors* want employees as a group to exercise more control than they are perceived to be exercising. (Exceptions are found in some Yugoslav organizations, Zupanov and Tannenbaum, 1966, and in American voluntary organizations where the ideals of officers were compared to those of members, Smith and Tannenbaum, 1963.) Simply put, employees are likely to want a more democratic organization than supervisors want. The classic study of the American soldier documented some of the striking attitudinal and ideological differences that exist between ranks (Stouffer and others, 1949). Persons at different ranks express quite different preferences regarding how social relations between noncommissioned officers and enlisted men should be conducted and how discipline and supervision should be carried out. Discipline that implies emphasis on "spit and polish" and "military courtesy" was generally regarded as desirable by most officers but as undesirable by enlisted men. Such differences are not suprising but they are nonetheless significant in reflecting the underlying bases of conflict within the organization. In small ways and in large, rank-and-file members prefer one kind of organization, and officers prefer another.

Differences in Loyalty and Support for the Organization. Superiors are more likely than their subordinates to identify with the organization and to support it psychologically; organizational policies and actions are more likely to seem to them morally correct, fair, and just. Superiors are more likely to take the view that what is good for the organization is good for *all* its members. The ideals for the organization held by officers are therefore likely to correspond more closely than those of rank-and-file members to the official ideals of the organization, although the operation of the organization may in some respects conform more closely to what rank-and-file members want than to the wishes of officers. For example, a study of productivity and attitudes of workers and their foremen (Likert, 1961) showed that: (a) the level of productivity considered reasonable by workers is below that considered reasonable by their foremen; (b) the level considered reasonable by foremen is below that officially considered reasonable by the company; (c) most workers are producing at levels considerably below the official norm and below the level considered reasonable by their supervisors; and (d) the actual level of production corresponds more closely to what workers consider reasonable than to what their foremen or higher company officials consider reasonable.

A member's attitudes of support for the organization and its policies are likely to change as his position in the hierarchy changes. Workers who become foremen are likely to adopt attitudes similar to the attitudes of other foremen, and different from the attitudes of workers. For example, in one study, workers promoted to foremen were compared to a matched group of non-promoted workers (Lieberman, 1956). Although both groups showed essentially the same attitudes toward the company and its policies before promotion, one year after promotion foremen had changed to greater agreement with and support for the organization and its policies. The foremen felt that the company was concerned about the welfare of workers; they saw the union as an impediment to the organization, they changed markedly in their support for the controversial company incentive system; and they showed some shift in the direction of adopting the company's point of view rather than the union's on the issue of seniority as the basis for promotion.

These differences in perceptions, ideals, and loyalties need not imply interpersonal conflict except that these differences occur among persons who are highly interdependent. The vital interests and welfare of each depend in some degree on the actions of the others. A supervisor, for example, is responsible for directing the behavior of his subordinates. The supervisor, however, is impeded in exercising control over his subordinates when his information about them is in error, and when his actions and theirs are based on seriously differing perceptions (Bennis and others, 1958). At the very least, discrepancies in perceptions and cognitions make the job of control and coordination more difficult; at worst, they contribute—in the context of differences in rewards, satisfactions, ideals, involvements, and loyalties—to resentment, distrust, hostility, and opposition.

The Research

A good deal is known through research in the United States about hierarchy and its effects, as the foregoing review suggests. A base is therefore laid for a comparative investigation that can contribute to the refinement of our knowledge about this universal feature of organization. We have attempted to achieve some of this refinement by replicating aspects of the research reviewed above in organizations based on ideologies that differ importantly from those prevailing in the United States. These ideologies, which we discuss in the next chapter, help define the norms and rules concerning ownership of the enterprise, rights and prerogatives of leaders, distribution of rewards, and character of the decision-making structure. In some of the organizations private ownership has been abolished and a high degree of formal participativeness and equalitarianism among members has been established. We shall explore the general proposition that these conditions reduce if not eliminate the unintended and dysfunctional effects of hierarchy.

Selection of Plants. We selected ten industrial plants in each of the five places: Israeli kibbutzim, Yugoslavia, Austria, Italy, and the United States. Kibbutz plants are owned by the kibbutz as a whole. Formally, these plants are highly participative. They operate within an ideology of equality among all members, and a number of institutionalized procedures, including formal decision-making meetings as well as the election and turnover of all managerial and supervisory personnel, are established to assure the realization of the formal ideology (Darin-Drabkin, 1962). No one in the kibbutz receives monetary payment and all share according to their needs the material rewards available.

The organizations from Yugoslavia are also socially rather than privately owned, and they operate within an ideology of workers' self-management. Like the kibbutz plants, they are formally very participative. Workers' councils are established to assure that the workers, through elected representatives, are the most powerful group in the organization (by comparison, for example, to managerial groups). The councils are the final authority on many basic decisions, such as setting prices of products and allocating profits. They have the formal power to fire managers (Blumberg, 1968; Kolaja, 1965; Pateman, 1970; Sturmthal, 1964).

All of the Yugoslav plants in our study are located in Slovenia, which in a number of ways is culturally akin to its neighboring country, Austria. Organizations from Austria and Italy are included in the study in order to provide a more "conventional" European frame of reference within which the data from Yugoslavia and Israel can be interpreted. Austrian and Italian organizations conform to traditional ideologies, resembling (more than those in kibbutzim and in Yugoslavia) the ideologies in many Western nations. The Italian and Austrian organizations may be family-owned, but their formal structure of authority conforms essentially to the non-participative, bureaucratic pattern. American organizations, which are also included in the research, resemble in their ownership and formal system of authority the Italian and Austrian plants; they are privately owned and ultimate authority resides with the person at the top. Organizations from these three "private economy" systems nonetheless differ among themselves in managerial style and in their degree of informal participativeness—and these variations are relevant to the effects of hierarchy that we are studying.

We established a plan for matching plants among the five countries so that meaningful comparisons might be made, but we were forced to compromise this plan in several ways. Two main criteria were employed in matching: number of employees and type of industry. Except for the kibbutz plants, which are located within agricultural communities, most of the plants are in urban areas of moderate size. The Italian plants are in the industrial north; the Yugoslav plants are in Slovenia, which is the most industrialized part of Yugoslavia. The American plants are located in four Midwestern states, with the exception of two plants in North Carolina. Workers in the American plants include Blacks and Mexican Americans.

We chose five industries—plastics, nonferrous foundry, food canning, metal works, and furniture—because these were among the limited possibilities available in kibbutzim. We intended to select two plants, a small and a large within each industry in each country, except in the Israeli kibbutzim, where all of the plants were to be small. Two plants were not always available in each industry within kibbutzim, however. We therefore have among kibbutz plants one cannery, one furniture plant, four plastics factories, and two plants in foundry and metal work. We attempted insofar as possible, where factories were to be matched, to select them so that their technologies and work processes were identical, but we cannot claim to have achieved this with a high degree of precision. For example, one furniture plant may manufacture upholstered sofas and chairs while another makes cabinets and window frames. Likewise, "matched" plants may differ among themselves on such characteristics as skill level, education, and sex ratio of work force, and in some structural characteristics such as number of hierarchical levels and average span of control, although we tried wherever possible to equalize matched plants on these characteristics. While these variables could not be controlled precisely in the design, some of them will be controlled statistically in the analyses to follow.

Table 1 presents the sizes of the plants in the five industries in the respective countries separately for plants categorized as small and as large. In Chapter Four we present data about age, sex, and education of the sampled membership in the respective countries.

Although the organizations categorized as small in Table 1 are small in absolute terms, they are not much different in size from the average of all American manufacturing organizations, which is about fifty-six persons (U.S. Bureau of the Census, 1971). There are obvious differences in size between the plants of the respective countries, yet the differences are relatively small and do not prevent meaningful comparisons. Because we have both small and large organizations it will be possible to evaluate the effect of size on the hierarchical gradients being studied. Hence we shall have some indication of how much the difference in gradients that we observe between countries might be explained by the small differences between countries in size of plant.

Selection of Respondents Within Each Plant. Thirty-five persons were selected in each organization. The sampling procedure was addressed to the following two objectives: first, maximizing the number of uninterrupted hierarchical chains from the bottom to the top of the organization (where a hierarchical chain is defined as a series of persons that includes one, and only one, immediate subordinate of each person, with the exception of the person at the bottom for whom there is no subordinate); and second, equalizing (insofar as possible) the number of persons drawn from each hierarchical level.

The first objective implies that each respondent is paired with an immediate superior or subordinate or both, and that this pairing extends from the bottom to the top of each organization. Because of the pyramidal nature of organizations, supervisory and managerial personnel may belong to

Table 1. Sizes of Plants (Persons Employed)

Plant Type	Italy	Austria	United States	Yugo-slavia	Kibbutz
SMALL PLANTS					
Plastics	83	43	48	57	42, 43, 62, 76
Foundry	62	34	80	62	46, 75
Canning	88	107	47	62	33
Metal Works	111	30	66	127	38, 41
Furniture	76	41	58	110	59
Average	84	51	60	84	52
LARGE PLANTS					
Plastics	343	242	215	167	—
Foundry	1081	1133	1354	1496	—
Canning	650	405	499	164	—
Metal Works	529	668	362	324	—
Furniture	540	299	590	576	—
Average	629	549	604	545	—

several chains as defined; the manager belongs to all chains. The second objective implies that the sampling rate is greater at the top of the organization than at the bottom. For example, a sample of 35 persons in an organization of five levels would, ideally, include seven persons at each level. However, since the organization is likely to have only one manager, this person would be selected with certainty, the remaining 34 respondents to be distributed equally among the remaining four levels. However, there might be only five persons immediately subordinate to the manager. All of these persons, then, would be selected, the remaining 29 respondents to be distributed equally among the remaining three levels, and so forth. The choice of a supervisor at one level determines the possible choice of subordinates; subordinates were eligible for the sample only if their superiors were selected. Eliminated from the sample are infirmary, cafeteria, and kindergarten employees as well as personal secretaries, chauffeurs, and others who might perform personal services for managers.

Table 2 presents the number of respondents at different levels in the plants of the respective countries and the average level of these respondents. Level 1 defines the position of the

Table 2. Number of Respondents at Different Levels in Plants

Level	Italy	Austria	United States	Yugo-slavia [a]	Kib-butz [b]	Total N
SMALL PLANTS						
1 (top)	5	5	5	5	10	30
2	9	17	21	13	59	119
3	52	44	32	61	160	349
4	80	71	61	35	78	325
5	22	5	54	61	9	151
6	6	—	—	—	—	6
Average Level of Respondent	3.7	3.4	3.8	3.8	3.0	
Total N	174	142	173	175	316	980
LARGE PLANTS						
1 (top)	5	4	5	4	—	18
2	8	21	33	11	—	73
3	19	42	44	33	—	138
4	44	37	44	66	—	191
5	56	33	31	50	—	170
6	31	9	13	9	—	62
7	13	12	5	2	—	32
Average Level of Respondent	4.6	3.9	3.8	4.0		
Total N	176	158	175	175	—	684

[a] Due to error in sampling, respondents were selected exclusively from the production department of the large foundry in Yugoslavia; personnel from administrative, sales, and research departments were excluded along with the director.

[b] Ten small plants are included from kibbutzim and five from each of the other countries.

top person; level 2 is immediately below level 1, and so on. The differences in numbers of respondents among the countries reflects in part differences in the way the plants are organized hierarchically, although the sampling procedure was designed to minimize these differences. (For example, we attempted insofar as possible through our standardized sampling procedure to obtain equal numbers of persons from each level in all plants.) The kibbutz plants tend to be "flatter" and therefore respondents tend on the average to be closer to the top (as well as to the bottom) in these plants than do the respondents in the small plants of the other countries. One small

Italian plant has as many as six levels; none of the other small plants has that many levels. Among the large plants, those in Italy and the United States differ the most. This difference reflects the relatively large proportion of managerial personnel in the American, compared to the Italian plants, and the likelihood that the top men in the sampled Italian plants have a narrow span of control. In four out of five large Italian plants (and in three out of five small ones) the director has only one immediate subordinate. In only one small American plant does the top person have only one subordinate.

Differences between countries also reflect differences in response rate (the rate is especially low in Austria), as well as several errors in carrying out the sampling procedure. However, the errors are relatively minor and they do not vitiate seriously the comparability of the data. It does not seem likely that the substantial differences in the data between plants that we discuss in the remainder of this book are to be explained in terms of these minor errors.

Defining Hierarchical Position. Figure 1 shows an abbreviated, hypothetical organization chart. The position of an individual in this chart can be defined by the number of persons directly above him in the chain of command. Thus the hierarchical position of individual a is 0; the position of b and c is 1, d and e is 2, and f and g is 3. Each member is defined by his "distance" from the top—which is a function of the number of persons intervening between him and the top. Individuals who are at the same distance from the top may, however, differ in their distance from the bottom. Persons b and c, for example, are equidistant from the top, but because they are located in chains of different length, they are not equidistant from the bottom of their respective chains.

Individuals are therefore assigned a second score, defined by their distance from the bottom. Individuals f, g, e, and c are all at level zero by this method. For chains of a given length, distance from the bottom is simply the complement of distance from the top, and a person's score on one index in effect defines his score on the second. Because chains may differ in length, however, as in Figure 1, distance from the top does not auto-

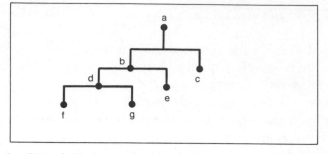

Figure 1. Hypothetical organization chart.

matically define distance from the bottom. In the fifty plants of this study the average correlation between these two measures of position is —.82. The highest correlations occur within the Yugoslav plants where the average is —.92. The Yugoslav plants are structured quite symmetrically, with most if not all chains within a plant being the same length. The lowest correlations occur in the kibbutz plants, where a number of plants have chains with as few as two levels as well as chains with as many as five levels. The average intercorrelation between the two measures of position within kibbutz plants is —.69.

Thus persons who are near the top of their hierarchical chains are in general relatively distant from the bottom—but the correlation is not perfect. These two definitions of hierarchical position are therefore conflicting in some degree. In order to avoid some of the confusion created by these conflicting definitions, in the analyses to follow we shall hold constant the length of chain. Under these conditions distance from the top is simply the complement of distance from the bottom.

One further complication should be considered. Some individuals may be in a number of hierarchical chains. For example, the top person is in all chains. Person *b* is in three chains, *abdf, abdg* and *abe*. The first two of these chains contain four levels and the last contains three. We have assigned a score or several scores to each respondent according to the length of the sampled chain or chains in which he is located. Respondent *b* in Figure 1, for example, would receive two scores, one identifying him in a chain (or chains) of length 4, and one identifying him in a chain of length 3. In certain analyses to follow, an individual may enter the data more than once, because he is in a number of chains of different length. Approximately 5 percent of respondents, most of them at or near the top of their organization, belong to sampled chains of differing length. Thus 95 percent of the respondents belong to only one chain, or to a number of chains all of which are the same length. Of the remaining 5 percent most of these belong to chains of only two or three different lengths.

The Measuring Instrument. The data of this study were obtained primarily from a questionnaire administered to 35 persons at all levels in each of the organizations. The questionnaire items were drawn largely from questionnaires used in earlier research, but many of these items were modified so that they might translate well into four languages and so that comparable meanings could be maintained in all countries. A number of questions that were initially chosen were subsequently eliminated because they did not meet these criteria. The questionnaire was pretested in one plant in each country and a number of questions were improved as a result, or they were eliminated because they were found to be frequently misunderstood.

The translations, done in the respective countries, were retranslated into English by a group of independent translators not familiar with the questionnaire, and improvements were made as a result. The final questionnaire therefore had the benefit of a good deal of preliminary work involving a high degree of collaboration between the authors at all stages.

Each respondent was interviewed briefly before filling out the questionnaire. One important function of the interview was to get from the respondent his own view of his position in the hierarchy. We knew his *official* position from the organization chart, but in some cases respondents did not agree with the chart. Such disagreements were recorded and coded, but in the analyses that follow we rely on the official definition of the respondent's position. The interview also helped to establish rapport with the respondent, and provided us an opportunity to explain the scientific purpose of the research (without describing this purpose in terms of hierarchy). We assured the respondent that his anonymity would be maintained, we illustrated how the questionnaire was to be filled out, and answered questions that the respondent might have. Someone on the research team was available while the respondent answered the questionnaire, in the event he needed help.

Interpreting the Data. In the following chapters we make comparisons between the five countries, separately for small plants and large. We shall refrain, however, from making comparisons between small and large plants except in special cases where certain controls are applied, since the sample in the large plants contains a substantially larger proportion of managerial personnel than does the sample in small plants.

Data based on the responses of the organization members are subject to a number of errors, both random and systematic. Systematic errors associated with country are a serious risk in cross-national studies. For example, questions may differ subtly in meaning from country to country and identical responses may therefore have different meanings in different countries. Furthermore, culture may predispose persons to answer questions in certain ways, and differences in response between countries may reflect these cultural predispositions. We have tried to guard against some of these errors by formulating and selecting questions that would translate well and that would have, as best we could judge collectively and with the help of a pretest, comparable meaning. Many questions were rejected because they did not meet this test. Nonetheless, we cannot rule out the possibility of bias, and we shall therefore consider at points along the way how our interpretations might be qualified because of possible errors inherent in the research design and in the measures.

A further qualification is necessary in considering the results of this research. The plants that we have chosen are a very small and select group within their respective countries. We chose the plants, and the countries from which they come, in order to have organizations that vary widely in ideological base and system of authority. We are able to achieve this wide variation by choosing matched plants in such disparate places as kibbutzim, Yugoslavia, Italy, Austria, and the United States. But the plants that were available to us and which fit our design in terms of size and technology, are restricted to a relatively small and select group. We offer these plants simply as illustrations of organizations operating on the bases of different ideological assumptions and authority structures, not as representative of plants in the respective countries. We believe the plants are good illustrations in the sense that they are all reasonably successful and viable organizations within their respective societies. We hope that they are good illustrations in the sense that they manifest the ideological principles upon which they are purportedly based. Data presented in the following chapters offer some justification for this hope.

Plan of the Book

Chapter Two describes some of the historical and ideological bases of management in the five countries. These bases are the source of differences between countries in the character of hierarchy and its impact on members. Ideologically, the Israeli kibbutz and the Yugoslav systems are more participative and equalitarian than the Italian, Austrian, and American systems. Industrial plants in these groups of countries therefore differ in their formal system of reward and in the way decisions are made and control exercised. Chapter Three presents data based on members' responses to the questionnaire that document some of the differences between countries in decision making and control in plants suggested by the ideological distinctions discussed in Chapter Two. They also illustrate how plants may not function entirely according to ideological prescription, at least as this functioning is reported to us by members.

Chapter Four examines how the hierarchical distribution of authority and reward (such as pay or opportunities associated with one's work) differ among the plants of the five countries. This chapter presents evidence that hierarchy is emphasized more in some systems than in others, implicitly or explicitly, and that some systems are therefore more hierarchical than others. Differences between systems in emphasis on hierarchy correspond in some degree to differences in their formal participativeness. Chapter Five explores the proposition that participativeness and the associated deemphasis on hierarchy reduces the hierarchical gradients of satisfaction, attitude, sense of responsibility, and other criteria of the adjustment of members. It also examines how the correlates of hierarchy, including authority and reward, along with certain demographic characteristics, help explain the impact of hierarchy on members.

Chapter Six considers the plant itself as the unit of analysis (in previous chapters the data are aggregated by country), and it explores how the hierarchical distribution of reaction and adjustment is related to other characteristics of the plant, such as the composition of the work force or the degree of participativeness reported by members. It also examines the superior-subordinate pair as the unit of analysis and explores how the superior's style of leadership as reported by subordinates may be related to the gradient of adjustment between him and his subordinates. This chapter examines relationships within countries as well as between them, and it therefore holds culture and political system constant in some analyses.

In Chapter Seven we discuss our conclusions as well as the disagreements between us and the doubts, where they exist, about the meaning behind the data of this research. We share a commitment to the scientific method as an approach to exploring facts and testing hypotheses about people, organizations, and societies, and we have tried within the limits of the technology available to us to conduct this research in the spirit of that method. We therefore share a reasonable confidence in the data presented in this book. But we do not always share interpretations of the data, and we sometimes disagree about their implications from a value standpoint. These disagreements are not primarily differences between those of us from socialist and those from capitalist societies; they occur perhaps even more within these two "camps" than between them. They grow as much out of differences in outlook due to culture, and they are related as much to methodological and abstract theoretical preferences as to differences in political ideology. We sublimated these differences during the earlier chapters by keeping close to the data or by restricting ourselves to interpretations that were mutually agreeable. We were able to exercise this discipline only because we anticipated the opportunity taken in Chapter Seven to present interpretations that more freely express our values and more fully reflect our experiences as members of five societies.

II

MANAGEMENT
IN FIVE COUNTRIES

$\mathbf{M}$anagerial practice differs between countries a good deal more than it differs within them, and cross-national research provides an opportunity to observe contrasting systems that cannot otherwise be compared. One would be hard put, for example, to find industrial plants in the United States where workers elect superiors on a rotating basis or where a council composed of workers and managers makes basic policy decisions. But in the kibbutzim of Israel members do elect their superiors, who after a term rotate out of office, and in Yugoslavia the workers' collective comprised of all members is the supreme authority in the enterprise.

We have selected plants in this study that differ sharply in ideological base and in related principles of organization. Some are formally a good deal more equalitarian and participative than others. In this chapter we shall describe features of these systems—including the way plants are owned and controlled, the recruitment of leaders, and the prevailing philosophy of management—that have implications for participation and hierarchy. We describe first the Yugoslav and kibbutz systems, each of which illustrates in its own way certain features of a Marxian-socialist approach to industrial organization. We turn then to the United States, Austria, and Italy, which illustrate variations within a capitalist or "free enterprise" framework.

The Yugoslav System

Self management has been associated traditionally with the ideology of socialism and with a number of social movements starting with the Utopians. Workers' control of enterprises has also been an ideal of revolutionary labor movements. In Yugoslavia an attempt is being made to realize this ideal. Three general facts help to explain the introduction of self management in Yugoslavia.*

(1) The ideology of the Yugoslav Communists is based on the concept of society as expressed in the works of Marx, Engels, and Lenin. According to this ideology the appropriation of political power through the dictatorship of the proletariat is only the first phase of the socialist revolution. Dictatorship of the proletariat does not mean control *by* the workers but rather control *on behalf of* the workers. This dictatorship must therefore be replaced if the revolution is not to lose its socialist character. Power used on behalf of the workers must be modified into power exercised by the workers. This means management of enterprises by employees.

The leaders of the Yugoslav Communist Party were heavily committed to the ideal of workers' self management partly because of circumstances of the Yugoslav revolution,

---

* The legal and institutional framework of the system of workers' self-management is described by Gorupic and Paj (1962), Burt (1972), Hunnius (1973). For social studies, see Adizes (1971); Kolaja (1965); Sturmthal (1965); Dunlop (1959). For general background information and views, see Hoffman and Neal (1962); Maclean (1957); McVicker (1957); Kralj (1969).

which was part of a war of national liberation. This war entailed great suffering by Yugoslavs, who fought without significant help from foreign personnel. Such slogans as "abolition of exploitation" and "power to the workers" were important mobilizing slogans which many partisans in the war came sincerely to believe. The extremely high price of the war—nearly 11 percent of the population was killed—was implicitly seen by many partisans as a price paid in advance for liberation, the abolition of exploitation, and the other goals stated in the revolution. Redemption required fulfillment of the promise.

(2) The political system of Yugoslavia after the war was copied from the Soviet pattern. Enterprises were managed by the state, represented in the enterprise by the director. Workers were represented primarily by labor unions, which like the state itself were under the influence of the party. This system of centralized control was highly inefficient, partly because it was cumbersome, ignored market demand, and failed to provide appropriate incentives. Furthermore, the government bureaucracy which held power on behalf of the workers and which controlled the enterprises began to develop into a governing class in its own right. As the centralized bureaucracy grew and became more powerful, the influence of the workers diminished. This did not conform to the promise of the revolution, and strong opposition to the bureaucracy began to develop even within the party.

(3) The political dependence of Yugoslavia on the Soviet Union after World War II led to economic dependence, which Yugoslavia tried to undo in 1948 by breaking with Stalin. A consequence of this rupture was the isolation of Yugoslavia from its former trading partners. A severe economic crisis and a general scarcity of goods followed. Conditions in the country were desperate, and Yugoslav leaders saw the need for a practicable and appealing program to rally the people. The answer was self management.

The first law of self management was introduced in 1950, and was based on approximately one year of experience in several hundred experimental workers' councils. Since 1950 self management has been progressively extended from production organizations to other sectors of social activity (such as educational and health organizations), and in 1963 a special form of self management was introduced into government administration. The formal power of the councils has also grown since 1950. Initially, workers' councils were consultative bodies with limited jurisdiction. Today practically all important decisions in plants are made by workers' councils or other self managerial bodies.*

Ownership. Yugoslavia was an underdeveloped country before World War II, with peasants comprising about 75 percent of the population. Industrial plants were small and not highly mechanized. Many of these small plants were owned by Yugoslavs, but big companies, such as those in the mining industry, were owned by West Europeans. The revolution abolished private ownership.

Yugoslavs distinguish between social ownership and state ownership. State ownership is ownership by the government on behalf of the people. Social ownership is ownership of the enterprise by society as a whole, and the management of an enterprise is delegated to the workers' collective—those people who work in it. State ownership implies that all enterprises have a common owner, the state. Yugoslav enterprises are socially owned. The prerogatives of such ownership are limited by law only in that the workers' collective is responsible for maintaining and enhancing the value of the enterprise. Social ownership, according to the Yugoslav view, is a necessary condition for self management.

Organization Structure and Decision Making. Self management implies direct participation of all workers in basic decisions of the enterprise. Because direct participation is not always feasible, especially in very large enterprises, means have been developed for indirect forms of participation as well.

Direct participation may occur through meetings of the entire workers' collective, meetings of work units, or through referenda. Meetings of the entire collective are held once or

* The Yugoslav system of workers' self management has undergone change since its inception in 1950, and important constitutional changes have been introduced in 1974. The description here applies to the period of this research, which occurred prior to 1974.

twice a year to evaluate the financial status of the enterprise
and to discuss other important issues. Meetings of a work unit
are called more frequently to decide about issues relevant to
the unit. Referenda may be held to decide such questions as
merger with another enterprise, major investments, changes in
product, or the liquidation of the enterprise.

Because direct participation is not possible in all of the
decisions that must be made, the workers' collective delegates
part of its authority to several elected groups or persons, thus
creating the basis for indirect participation. The 1950 Federal
Law prescribed three such groups or persons: the Workers'
Council, the Managing Board, and the Director. The Workers'
Council consists of ten to fifty persons, depending on the size
of the enterprise. Candidates for the Council are nominated
by the trade union or by the workers, but they are elected by
all employees. The Managing Board is elected by the Workers'
Council and it consists of five to fifteen persons. Members of
the Managing Board may be members of the Workers' Council
or they may be experts or managerial personnel not on the
Workers' Council. The Board is designed to advise the council
as well as to interpret and expedite on a day-to-day basis the
decisions of the Council. The Director is an ex officio member
of the Council, and does not have a vote, but he is nonetheless
likely to be very influential in the Council. Like the Managing
Board, the Director is elected and discharged by the Workers'
Council.

The Council is the supreme operative authority in an
enterprise; it is responsible only to the collective as a whole,
and it makes decisions concerning such issues as: approval of
annual and long-term production plans; prices of products;
investments; allocation of profit; distribution of wages and
salaries; use of enterprise's funds; hiring and firing of employees, especially managerial and staff personnel; verifying
and approving the annual balance; discipline. Relevant information and proposals concerning these issues are prepared
for the Council by the Managing Board, the Director, staff personnel or by subcommittees of the Council.

Changes were introduced by a Federal Law in 1968 in

order to overcome problems of the self-management structure. Councils were not able to handle effectively all of the issues brought before them. The excessively long and frequent meetings that were necessary to handle all of the Council's business proved impractical, and in many cases the Managing Board made decisions in its own right rather than as an executive arm of the Council. The 1968 law therefore permitted Councils to create one or more executive groups or "boards" to facilitate decision making. For example, separate boards might be created to handle problems of division of income, investment, and production planning. Small plants might have two or three such boards, and large plants might have as many as twelve. These boards are elected by the Council and they can be dissolved by the Council.

Recruitment of Managerial Personnel. Industrial plants are required by law to announce all job openings publicly. Announcements are usually made through local newspapers. Open recruitment minimizes the chances that hiring and firing will be used as a personal basis of power over people. Hence, all employees including managerial personnel are recruited through public announcements. The decision to hire is usually made by an elected executive body of the Workers' Council, but the Director is elected by the Workers' Council itself. Decisions about firing are made through the same bodies.

Top managers are elected, usually for a period of four years, but they may be reelected at the end of each period. Nonetheless, a public announcement is made and candidates may apply for the position when it becomes available at the end of each period of office.

Philosophy of Management. The formal Yugoslav philosophy of management is implicit in the ideology of self management. The essential purpose of such management is the resolution of class conflict through the abolition of classes. Private property is seen as the root of the class structure, and hence the abolition of private property is a necessary step in the abolition of classes and of class conflict. Profit of the enterprise should therefore be taken only by those who contribute to the work of the enterprise and on the basis of their specific contribution. Ownership, as in the private enterprise system, or position in the state bureaucracy is not a criterion. This principle concerning the disposal of profit is a central moral norm of the self-management philosophy.

In addition to eliminating class conflict, the Yugoslav system is designed to humanize work and to create conditions for the development of human personality. Authority relations are therefore an important issue in the formal Yugoslav philosophy of management. Emphasis is placed on mutual respect and equal rights of all employees; there must be no superiority or inferiority. An implication of this emphasis is that supervisors and managers do not formally exercise authority over others, but rather are said to coordinate or organize the work. Hence they are called organizers of work. This aspect of the Yugoslav managerial philosophy resembles the impersonalization of authority proposed by Weber, and its intent, like Weber's, is to eliminate the abuse of power by eliminating the personal bases of power. It is also consistent with the formal emphasis in the Yugoslav system on equalitarianism and participativeness and therefore differs from the bureaucratic model in this respect.

The Kibbutz System

Kibbutz plants resemble the Yugoslav in ideological base, but there are differences. Kibbutz plants are located in rural communal settlements varying in size from about forty members in newly founded ones to as many as one thousand in the older communities. The kibbutz community is run as an economic unit composed of several autonomous branches. Most of the branches are agricultural, but recently a growing number of kibbutzim have added one or two industrial plants like the ten included in this research.

There are no individual household accounts in the kibbutz, and members receive no wages beyond a small annual cash allowance for personal expenses. The main meals are eaten in the communal dining room, and members' needs are provided for by communal services on an equalitarian basis. All income goes into the common treasury.

The kibbutz is governed by committees and by a general assembly which is convened weekly. Each economic branch is headed by an elected branch manager who is replaced every two to three years. An economic coordinator is responsible for coordinating the different branches and for implementing the production and investment plans.

The kibbutz movement was founded sixty years ago as a form of agricultural settlement, but in the past ten years an emphasis has been put on industrialization. The number of industrial plants in kibbutzim grew from 108 in 1960 to 197 in 1972. The pace of industrialization is rapid, even relative to that in Israel generally, and the kibbutz contribution to total Israel industrial output grew from 3.1 percent in 1955 to 6.6 percent in 1972.

Two social factors made the fast pace of industrialization possible. First, the educational and cultural level of kibbutz members is relatively high. Most founders of kibbutzim and all members born there have at least a secondary education. The kibbutz movement set up a vast network of adult education and vocational training institutions. Kibbutz members entering industry from agricultural work usually have a technical background because of the advanced technological and agro-technical level of kibbutz agriculture. Second, the democratic principles of the kibbutz have lead to a relatively wide distribution of managerial ability. Every year about 50 percent of kibbutz members acquire managerial experience because of the participation on a rotating bases in a variety of committees and organizational roles. Furthermore, training for various social and managerial functions is integrated into the general system of kibbutz education and managerial skills are therefore widely shared.

The socialist ideology of the kibbutz prohibits the employment of hired workers, and kibbutz plants are therefore limited in size since plants must draw workers from the kibbutz itself. In 1971, 79 percent of the plants had less than fifty workers. Only 15 plants out of 174 employed more than 100 workers. Nor is industry very diversified. Of 174 industrial plants in kibbutzim in 1971, 146 were in five industries: metal works, 58; plastics, 32; electronics, 22; food, 20; furniture-wood, 14.

The structure of kibbutz plants has been influenced by the equalitarian and democratic principles of kibbutz ideology and by practical considerations. Plants were therefore created with a concern for ideology but also on the basis of practical experience gained in other work branches and with the guidance of production engineers. As kibbutzim became more industrialized, a formal model for the industrial plant was developed. This model specifies a participative system of decision making. Participation is direct, through a worker's assembly, and indirect through the election by workers of committees and of the management board. The model proposes the establishment of committees for professional and technical problems, marketing, and other functions such as the nomination of plant officers and the selection of workers for vocational training. The management board typically includes: (a) the central officeholders in the plant, such as the plant manager and the production manager; (b) the central officeholders of the kibbutz, such as the economic coordinator and treasurer; and (c) workers' representatives not holding managerial office. The workers' representatives, like the plant officeholders, are elected by workers, while the kibbutz officeholders are elected by all members of the kibbutz. Some decisions, such as election of the plant manager and approval of the investment plan, are usually made by the general assembly of the kibbutz as a whole, where the plant-workers participate along with all other kibbutz members. The management board makes final decisions only on technical and professional matters. In almost all other matters the role of the management board and of the different committees in decision making follows the formal model. The board prepares proposals for decision by the worker assembly or the kibbutz general assembly.

The role of the plant and kibbutz institutions in different areas of decision making is presented in Table 3 which shows that some issues are discussed both by plant committees and by kibbutz committees. Usually the plant committees ascertain the needs of the plant, such as the need for investments or for training of workers. The worker assembly reaches a tentative decision that is again discussed by the kibbutz com-

mittees, bearing in mind the kibbutz investment plan or training plan. The decision will then be given final approval by
the kibbutz general assembly. The election of the plant manager works differently. The candidates are discussed by the
committee of the kibbutz dealing with appointments to all
kibbutz offices and this committee nominates one candidate.
After discussion by the plant management and the workers'
assembly, the final appointment is made by the kibbutz
assembly. The plant manager is elected by the larger assembly
because any kibbutz member who has managerial experience
may be chosen as plant manager, whether or not he is a member
of the plant. All other candidates for plant office, including
first-line supervisors, are selected from among members of the
plant and are elected by the workers' assembly.

Table 3. The Role of Plant and Kibbutz Institutions
in Areas of Decision Making

| | INSTITUTIONS | | | | |
Areas	Plant committees	Plant management	Workers' assembly in the plant	Kibbutz committees	General assembly of kibbutz
Production plan	—	Proposal	Decision	Discussion	Approval
Investment and development plan	—	Proposal	Decision	Discussion	Approval
Organization of work	—	Proposal	Decision	—	—
Technical-professional problems	Discussion	Decision	Information	—	—
Vocational training	Discussion	Proposal	Decision	Discussion	Approval
Election of management team	—	Discussion	Discussion	Suggestion	Decision
Election of other officers	Suggestion	—	Decision	—	—

Table 3 shows how decisions formally should be made in kibbutz plants. There are deviations from this model in practice, however. Data collected in 37 kibbutz plants, for example, reveal that in some plants the workers' assembly does not exercise as much authority as it should concerning the production plan, although it exercises a good deal of authority concerning work organization and work arrangements. In conformity with the intent of the model, all officeholders in all plants are brought into office through elections.

The system of organization in kibbutz plants contrasts strikingly with the classic bureaucratic model. This is nowhere more clearly illustrated than in the selection of leadership. All officers, from the first-line supervisor to the production manager, are elected by the workers, and their tenure is usually limited to two to three years for the supervisor, and four to five years for the production manager. Persons are asked by a nomination committee to run for office. They may refuse, but if they are elected, they usually serve. Furthermore, officers do not have the impersonal, legitimate authority of the bureaucratic leader, nor can they fall back on techniques of coercion or reward that go with a leader's power in other systems. The rights and duties of officers are *not* precisely defined and the way an incumbent fulfills his responsibilities depends largely on his personal characteristics and ability to relate to others. Most officeholders, especially first-line supervisors, engage in production work, and only a part of their time is dedicated to supervision and other managerial functions. Furthermore, relations between members in different positions are not limited to formal working relations in the plant but are a part of a more general network of relations in the larger community. Thus participation by workers in decision making is the result of the participative ideology which governs plant operations, but it is also consistent with a larger philosophy of life and pattern of relations that all members share.

The Italian, Austrian, and American Plants

Industrial plants in Italy, Austria, and the United States differ radically in ideological base from those in kibbutzim and

in Yugoslavia, and they are formally less equalitarian and participative than kibbutz and Yugoslav plants. These "private
enterprise" nations nontheless differ among themselves in the
way plants are owned and controlled, in the recruitment of
leaders, and in the prevailing philosophy of management, and
these differences have implications for participativeness and
hierarchy in industry.

Ownership. The nature of ownership of industrial firms
in these countries, in sharp contrast to plants in kibbutzim and
in Yugoslavia, may be owned by a single individual, by two or
more persons in partnership, by many stockholders, or by other
institutions including in some cases the government itself. The
owners are legally entitled, by virtue of their ownership, to
direct the enterprise, but in large companies substantial control
is delegated to professional managers. Thus, management and
ownership are often separated. In cases of separation, managers
may nonetheless acquire some ownership interest through the
purchase of stock. Some companies in the United States en-
courage such purchases by providing attractive options, or they
may pay bonuses in the form of stock. In smaller firms, the
owner is more likely to play a direct role in the management
of the enterprise, and family members may be brought in to
help manage the business.

The American plants in this study illustrate a range of
ownership principles, all within the private enterprise framework. Three of the five large plants are parts of corporations
that sell shares to the public. The managers do not own the
plants except that they may have some stock in the company.
In four of the five small plants, and in one of the large, the
owner is the chief officer, and in some of these, members of
his family are part of the managerial group.* These family-
connected persons are nonetheless trained professionally. For
example, the son of the owner-director of the small foundry,

* The small foundry, which we classify as family-owned, was acquired by a holding company shortly before the data were collected. The
management, however, remained unchanged and the plant continued to
function essentially as it had prior to the acquisition. The acquisition
provided financial benefits to the former owners, as well as to the acquir-
ing company, without changing the essential character of the plant's administration.

who has a responsible managerial post in the plant, is trained as an engineer. In the small plastics company the owner's son, who is second-in-command in the plant, has a degree in business administration.

Private ownership prevails also in Austria, although a great proportion of the very large corporations are controlled by three federally owned banks. Furthermore, all of the utility companies and coal mines and nearly all of the steel mills are run by the federal or state government. The legal structure of these companies, however, is like that of a private corporation except that the government and other public institutions rather than private individuals own the shares. Family ownership is very common among small and medium-sized industries.

Of the five large Austrian plants in our sample, one is part of an international corporation that sells shares on the market, one is owned by the government, one is owned by an agricultural co-op, and the remaining two are family-owned. Of the small plants three are family-owned and two are partnerships.

Italy also has private and state-controlled enterprises, although family ownership is dominant among enterprises of the type included in this study. Italian capitalism is in large measure family capitalism, and even most large corporations are owned by family interests (Ferrarotti, 1959). All but one of the enterprises selected in the Italian sample are family-run.

Recruitment of Leaders. In general, supervisors and managers are appointed by their superiors (or the owners) rather than elected by subordinates, as in the kibbutz plants. Furthermore, the director's tenure (if he is not the owner) depends on the judgment of superiors rather than of all employees, as in Yugoslavia.

The three countries differ in their emphasis on professional training as a criterion for the selection of managers. This emphasis is clearly greater in the United States than in the other two. Family ties play an especially important role in Italy, and consequently few good managerial positions are open to outsiders. Partly for this reason and for reasons we will consider below, industrial employment has low value in Italy, and many educated persons who are potential recruits avoid such employment. A smaller proportion of companies is family-owned in Austria than in Italy, and in-plant mobility is less restricted by family ties. Professionals do not avoid industry for reasons of prestige as in Italy, but Austria, like Italy, lacks training facilities for managers and the supply of professionals is therefore limited.

Organization Structure and Decision Making. The plants included in this study are, with respect to their administrative structure, like many others in the same size and industry categories. They are in general reasonably well structured in the formal administrative sense; departments are clearly delineated and roles are specified. The chain of command conforms to the bureaucratic and traditional administrative science models. Subordinates, in general, have only one formal superior and authority is defined by one's relative position in the chain of command. In practice, there may be cases of ambiguity where a formally designated superior does not in fact function as the superior, or where a member reports to more than one superior. But these are more the exception than the rule.

The formal system therefore implies a decision-making structure in which policy is determined by persons at or near the top of the organization. While decision-making conforms essentially to the oligarchic pattern, trade unions interject an element of participativeness and workers may formally and indirectly participate in some decisions through collective bargaining. The scope of decisions, however, is limited.

The approach of unions to collective bargaining differs between the three countries. In the United States, more than in Italy and Austria, collective bargaining occurs at the plant level and focuses on issues of immedaite concern to workers such as wages and working conditions. In Italy and Austria, bargaining is likely to take place at the national level. Italian and Austrian unions are closely linked to political parties and are influenced by social ideologies, including Catholic, Communist, and Socialist. The philosophy of "simple pragmatism" that underlies the American union movement contrasts sharply with the Italian approach, and expresses itself in the almost exclusive concern for the immediate "bread and butter" objectives of workers and in the effort to achieve these objectives through shop stewards, and through grievance and bargaining committees in the plant (Tannenbaum, 1965; also, 1974). As a result, American unions have more impact than the Italian and the Austrian within the plant. Four of the large plants in the American sample and two of the small ones are unionized, but trade unions have an implicit effect even in non-union plants because of the industry-wide norms regarding wages and working conditions they help to establish and the industrial relations climate they help to create.

Although Austrian and Italian unions place greater emphasis than American unions do on political action, these two countries differ in the political orientation of their unions and in the results unions achieve. In Austria, for example, efforts by unions have led to the legal establishment of councils elected by workers in each plant. These councils, which do not compare in formal power to the Workers' Councils of Yugoslavia, have limited authority concerning some personnel decisions such as the firing of an employee. The councils also oversee working conditions that are regulated either by law or through union agreements, and they have the right to be informed about policy decisions. Beyond this right to be informed, the role of the council in economic decisions is negligible. Nonetheless, these features of the industrial system in Austria indicate some participativeness at least in the values officially expressed by government and by unions. They also imply a degree of cooperativeness between management and labor, and a national committee consisting of union and employer representatives with equal votes has been created to advise the government on economic matters such as the price of goods that are not regulated by market influences.

The relatively cooperative approach to industrial relations and participative values in Austria, though limited in scope, distinguish the Austrian industrial climate from the Italian. Unions in Italy also advocate participativeness, sometimes in Marxist and revolutionary terms, but management for the most part has avoided participative practices, even of the modest varieties found in Austria. For many Italian unions, relations with management are part of the class struggle.

Thus workers, more in the United States than in Italy and Austria, exercise some control in their plants through unions, and these unions act to constrain some managers in the unbridled pursuit of efficiency and profit without regard for the interests of employees. Government, too, imposes restraints such as minimum wage laws, child labor laws, and safety regulations, and it supports the right of workers to organize into unions and to strike. These restraints do not mean that workers have formal control of their plants as do the workers in kibbutzim and in Yugoslavia. But they do mean a less abusive and exploitative industrial system than that of the earlier years of laissez faire capitalism.

Philosophy of Management. The "free enterprise" and socialist systems differ in the extent to which political ideology bears directly and explicitly on the governance of the factory. Marxist ideology as expressed in the Yugoslav and kibbutz constitutions, for example, has clear implications for ownership and control of the factory. American political ideology, on the other hand, like the Italian and Austrian ideologies, is a good deal more ambiguous in this regard. Indeed, there is no unitary and formalized ideology relevant to the factory in these countries. An American enterprise, for example, can in principle be owned and controlled by its workers without contraditing the constitution or the ideological precepts on which the constitution is based. Nor does such ownership seriously contradict values that prevail in the society. In Yugoslavia or in the kibbutz, however, ownership of a major enterprise by an individual, a family, or by stockholders would be a clear breach of the Marxist ethic.* While a unitary ideology of industrial

---

* A number of socialist countries do permit private entrepreneurship on a limited scale. Most of Yugoslav agriculture is private, as are some small businesses, restaurants, and tourist enterprises. But the number of employees permitted in each such economic unit is carefully limited. Foreign companies have established factories in some of the socialist countries, Yugoslavia included. All of these arrangements, nonetheless, do represent a compromise of the ideological interdiction against private ownership and the employment of others for private gain. In kibbutzim, too, one finds occasional compromises: for example, some kibbutz plants (not included in this study) hire workers from outside the kibbutz. Unlike the kibbutz worker, hired employees receive a wage for their labor.

governance does not exist in the "free enterprise" systems, certain values and rationalizations relevant to industrial leadership prevail and these help explain the way enterprises are run.

"The more frequent managerial philosophy," in the United States, according to Harbison and Myers, "is one that asserts top management's primary responsibility for decision-making and for directing the efforts of subordinates, motivating them, controlling their actions, and modifying their behavior to fit organizational needs" (Harbison and Myers, 1959). This is the core of managerial belief in Austria and Italy as well as the United States, but these countries differ between themselves in the degree of "liberalism" which managers apply in interpreting this general and essentially authoritarian core. Of the three countries, Italy and the United States provide the clearest contrast, with Austria falling between the two on many of the issues discussed below.

In Italy the developing entrepreneurial class tried to emulate the traditions and life style of the nobility which it replaced as a ruling class. Family ownership fits this aspiration since control of the business, like rule of the dukedom, passes on through inheritance. The reputation of the family, which is a paramount consideration in Italy, is identified with the reputation of the firm and the continuity and unity of the family are connected to the continuity and security of the enterprise. Economic success is not valued in itself, as it is in the United States. Business is only an instrumentality for the family—and an unpleasant one at that, since commercial activity is really not compatible with the idealized, aristocratic life style to which the owners aspire. Management is not imbued with a business-success or achievement-oriented ideology as in the United States. Managers are therefore conservative and cautious; risk is avoided because profit is not as important as security. Bankruptcy means more than economic failure, it means shame for the family.

Family ownership sets a tone in Italian industry that has clear implications for hierarchy and (lack of) participativeness; this is well described by Ferrarotti:

The rigidly hierarchic pattern of the family-centered and -motivated society reflects itself in the management structure and in management-labor relations. . . . In general, Italian enterprise authority is highly centralized and personalized and reflects the paternalistic orientation of the patrimonial business elite. This means that Italian managers are reluctant to delegate authority and they tend to think of their authority in terms of personal power rather than in terms of a necessary function related to, and coordinated with, other equally necessary functions within the enterprise. The enterprise is seen as some sort of private kingdom. . . . In fact, the logical outcome of the refusal to delegate authority is the unwillingness or the inability to train junior executives and young assistants. . . . Again as a consequence of [the manager's] practice of power centralization, he is too busy with too many things and he wants to do everything himself. In Italian industry the manager who feels hurt if anything has been done without his direct knowledge and participation is a familiar character [Ferrarotti, 1959, pp. 239–40].

Given this system of organiztion, the Italian manager is not likely to be very participative, and a study by Haire, Ghiselli, and Porter (1966) suggests that he is less likely than the American manager to endorse "democratic" attitudes in most of the areas of superior-subordinate relations that the authors investigated. Harbison and Burgess (1954) see in Europe generally, and in Italy in particular, that:

The social distance between management personnel and workers is much greater than it is in the United States, as . . . are the differences in education and income. Consequently, development of understanding between workers and management, which is a problem even in America, is far more difficult in France, Italy, and Belgium. Management-labor communication tends to be from the top down and to be dictatorial. This does not make it easy for management to enlist loyalty and interest on the part of workers in the enterprises, nor does it lead to participation among workers in lowering costs and improving efficiency. Workers in European plants seldom "talk back" to their bosses. Upward communication is neither expected nor encouraged.

Nonetheless, some tempering of the Italian system is occurring as industrialization develops and family ownership in its traditional form declines. Professionalization is on the increase even in family-controlled firms, and managers are beginning to adopt some of the pragmatic approaches to managerial control that imply a softening of the traditional autocratic form.

The early American entrepreneurs, unlike their Italian counterpart, had no aristocracy to replace but a vast unexploited land to conquer. The businessman was portrayed as a pioneer, an adventurer, a hero. His goal was easy to define: economic success; enlargement of the business; and the amassing of wealth, which anyone could achieve regardless of his station at birth, providing only that he was sufficiently capable. This at least provided a rationalization to help justify the wealth acquired by some and the poverty suffered by others in a society where democratic and equalitarian values were extolled.

R. Bendix (1956) describes the growing ideology of business success at the turn of the century, an ideology that contrasts sharply with that prevailing in Italy and in Europe generally:

> College presidents spoke of the increasing opportunities for young men which business success had brought about, one of them declaring that "there are more successful men in every calling today than ever before." In 1900 the Rev. M. D. Babcock declared that "Business is religion, and religion is business." Even *The Nation,* a liberal journal, maintained in 1888 that the capitalists of today are the workingmen of yester-

day, just as the workingmen of today are the capitalists of tomorrow. Many public spokesmen, it seems, agreed with the editors of one journal who declared that wealth was "a sociological blessing, not a sociological danger." "Everywhere," states A. W. Griswold, from whose study these quotations have been selected, "honor was being done the captains of industry and the kings of enterprise [pp. 257–258].

This opportunity-success philosophy fit the prevailing notions of democracy and equality in America in the sense that opportunity was presumed open to all and that each man was to be judged on the basis of what he personally accomplished—not on the basis of his social status at birth.

The United States grew up as an "achieving society" (McClelland, 1961), and love of work, the so-called Protestant ethic, glorified the effort that led naturally to success. Work was not a necessary evil, as in the Italian value system, but a worthy and desirable effort justifiable for its own sake and also instrumental in promoting the great economic success to which many persons aspired. The approach of management was therefore pragmatic and rational in the pursuit of success: do what works in the context of what is possible. Tradition, life style, and other sentimental commitments were of secondary importance—unlike the Italian approach. Old ways were expendable if new and better approaches to success could be found. And, in fact, new ways were being found. American industry was a good deal more experimental and risk-oriented in its search for better ways. Research and development became a prominent part of the business organization in America long before R & D was considered by European industry, and it has continued to play a more substantial role in American industry than in Europe. Personnel departments, too, grew up as management realized the need for better ways of handling the human problems of organization, and the skills of the psychologist were added to those of the engineer and the accountant. The business school, which until recently was an exclusively American institution, served to provide further bases for professionalizing management and for rationalizing the pursuit of success.

The philosophy that asserts top management's primary responsibility for control of the enterprise applies no less in the United States than in Italy except that the American manager is more pragmatic in his approach to controlling. Results, not rituals, are what count and if this requires a modification of past ways, the American manager is prepared, at least more than his Italian and Austrian peer, to modify his ways. The search by managers for effective means of control has led to an interest in applications of the behavioral sciences and in techniques of human relations. Professional managers, in particular, are prone to consider these applications as part of a growing set of science-based techniques of effective management, especially since these applications fit values that are broadly advocated in American society. These techniques stress morale as well as efficiency, self-fulfillment as well as profit. They attach importance to the individual and his motivation in the enterprise. Such approaches view organization members as resources, with skills and knowledge as well as energies that can be put at the disposal of the organization (Miles, 1965). Mobilizing such resources requires that members participate in decisions where their skills and knowledge apply. Such participation is premised on some degree of trust by management in workers, and it supposes that the trust will be reciprocated, that harmony and cooperativeness will be enhanced, and that all members share a common interest. These approaches therefore imply some degree of participativeness, although this participativeness is usually restricted to operational problems rather than to issues of policy, which in the Yugoslav and kibbutz plants are subject to the control of the total membership of the enterprise. Participative schemes based on behavioral science are not widespread, but these schemes imply a philosophy of human relations that is attractive to many managers, and managerial practice is moving, if only informally and incipiently, toward the realization of this philosophy. Such movement together with cultural values that in principle extol democracy and equality should mitigate in some degree the effects of hierarchy that we are studying.

Summary and Conclusions

There is, of course, variation within each of the five countries in the way managers approach the job of management. The foregoing descriptions are idealizations in that they do not portray this variability and do not stress the important changes that are occurring and that are likely to make some of these countries more alike in the future than they have been in the past (Kerr and others, 1962). The descriptions nonetheless provide an image of differences between the countries that have implications for differences in participativeness and in emphasis placed on hierarchy. Table 4 summarizes some of these differences. Chapter Three presents data that help define aspects of participativeness in the plants of the respective countries as the members see it.

Table 4. Management Principles in Plants in the Study

Illustrating principles of	Kibbutz	Yugoslavia	U.S.	Austria	Italy
Ownership	Enterprise owned by the kibbutz of which the employees are members.	Enterprise owned by Society which delegates responsibility to the workers' collective consisting of all members of enterprise.	Enterprise owned by single individuals, by partners, or by shareholders.	Same as U.S. plus some state ownership.	Same as U.S. with more emphasis on family ownership.
Recruitment of managerial personnel	Elected, usually from among plant members.	Appointed and/or approved by the Workers' Council or an executive arm of the Council.	Appointed by superiors; emphasis on technical competence.	Same as U.S.	Same as U.S. with some concern for loyalty to family of owners.
Formal philosophy of management	Highly equalitarian based on socialist conception.	Highly equalitarian based on principle of self management and the definition of management as "technical coordination."	Bureaucratic and traditional tempered by human relations concerns and equalitarian cultural values.	Mostly bureaucratic and traditional with some human relations concerns.	Traditional, patrimonial, bureaucratic.

Table 4—continued

Illustrating principles of	Kibbutz	Yugoslavia	U.S.	Austria	Italy
Organizational structure	Departmentalization; specialization; unity of command; scalar principle modified by participative principles and informal interpersonal relations.	Departmentalization; specialization; unity of command; scalar principle modified by principle of "self management" including Workers' Councils.	Departmentalization; specialization; unity of command; scalar principle; bureaucratic modified by informal "human relations."	Departmentalization; specialization; unity of command; scalar principle; bureaucratic.	Same as Austria with more personalized, patrimonial control.
Formal decision making	Ultimate decision making power resides with the total membership.	Same as Kibbutz.	Ultimate decision making power resides with owners, tempered by restraints such as unions, and legal requirements.	Same as U.S.	Same as U.S.
Reward system	Complete equality, with small financial allowance to all members. Some benefits distributed according to need.	Monetary rewards distributed according to rank and function. Medical and other benefits available to all.	Highly differentiated system of monetary rewards distributed according to rank and function. Other benefits also graded according to rank.	Same as U.S.	Same as U.S. with greater emphasis on status differentials.

III

DECISION MAKING
AND CONTROL

The ideological differences between the systems in this study have clear implications for differences in the way industrial plants are controlled. Some of the plants are a good deal more participative than others. This chapter presents data that help describe participativeness and related aspects of control as members in the plants of the five countries report it.

By participation we refer to a system in which all members determine in some degree the decisions of the organization. Different amounts and kinds of participation can be distinguished, including formal and informal. Formal participation is a system in which rules explicitly establish decision-making structures through which all members contribute to decisions. The implicit if not explicit assumption underlying these rules is that members should and will contribute to the decisions, and unless they do the organization of course can not

50

be said to be participative in practice. Members may participate directly, entering personally into the deliberations that lead to binding decisions, or they may participate indirectly through representatives. Furthermore, the decisions can concern system-wide issues such as the distribution of profits, investments, or the pricing of products; or they may concern operational details of a work group such as who should be selected as a leader of the group or how the work of the group should be done. In this formal sense plants in kibbutzim and Yugoslavia are clearly more participative than plants in the other countries.

By informal participation we refer to the receptivity and responsiveness of managers and supervisors to the ideas and suggestions of subordinates. Such informal participativeness may grow out of an explicit commitment to human-relations managerial approaches, or it may be a natural and spontaneous outgrowth of the values of members. It may also be the result of strong unions. Informal participation implies leadership that is supportive of subordinates and sensitive to their needs, but such leadership may occur in an otherwise conventional, oligarchic organization. If lower-ranking persons have influence in such a system it is through their immediate superior—and this influence is usually limited to operational questions of the work group. While formal participativeness is defined in terms of legally established decision-making structures, informal participativeness is defined in terms of style of management and sharing by superiors of their authority with subordinates. Formal and informal approaches to participation need not be mutually exclusive in practice, however, and we shall see evidence of plants that function with elements of both.

Decision Making in the Plants

Figure 2 presents data obtained in response to six items adapted from an index developed by Likert to measure the participativeness of organizations. Likert's scheme implies a continuum of organizations from "authoritative" to "partici-

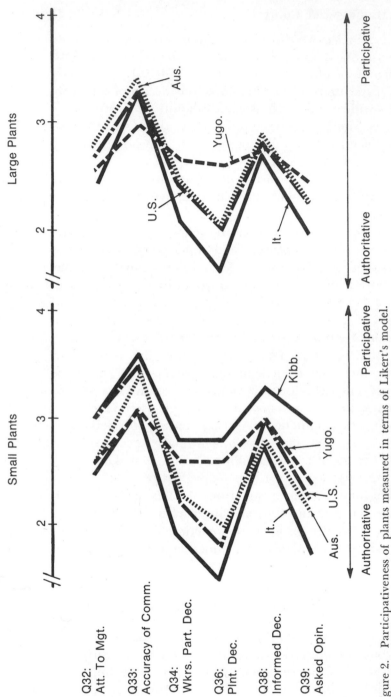

Figure 2. Participativeness of plants measured in terms of Likert's model.
Note: Each of the points in this figure and each of the averages and percentages shown in subsequent figures and tables are based on between 150 and 175 respondents except in the kibbutz plants, where the number of cases is between 300 and 350 unless otherwise indicated.

pative." Three of the questions in the following index (34, 36, and 39) * are directly concerned with decision making aspects of participation; the other questions measure some of the predicted effects of participation on attitudes and communication. Likert has found a high degree of correlation between these items:

32. What are the attitudes of the company members toward plant management?
  [1 Attitudes are strongly opposed to the management. . . .
   4 Attitudes strongly support the management]

33. What do workers communicate to their superiors?
  [1 They communicate all relevant information accurately. . . .
   4 They distort all information]

34. Do workers participate in making important decisions related to their work?
  [1 Not at all. . . .
   4 They jointly decide about all important things concerning their work]

36. Do workers participate in making important decisions related to general plant problems?
  [1 Not at all. . . .
   4 They jointly decide about all important things concerning general plant problems]

38. In this plant, are decisions made by the persons who have the most adequate and accurate information?
  [1 Rarely. . . .
   4 Always]

39. When decisions are being made, are the people affected asked for their opinions and suggestions?
  [1 They are almost never asked for their opinions and suggestions. . .
   4 They are almost always asked for their opinions and suggestions]

* The question numbers correspond to the numbers in the questionnaire, which is available from the senior author. Although the participative response is placed at the extreme right for all of the items shown in Figure 2, the direction of the scales were varied in the questionnaire so that a high score on some items implies a low value on participativeness.

The data of Figure 2 do not show a completely consistent relationship between the items that concern participative decision making (34, 36, 39) and the items that concern attitude and communication (32, 33, 38); countries that rank high on the former are not necessarily high on the latter. Nonetheless, for the decision-making items as a group, the kibbutz and Yugoslav plants are clearly more participative than the remaining plants; the Italian plants are the least participative. The differences between countries on these items are highly significant statistically.

To what extent does the participativeness reported by our respondents in the five groups of plants correspond to the ideals expressed by these respondents? Three questions parallel to the decision-making questions in the Likert index were asked in order to answer this question:

35. *Should* workers participate in making important decisions related to their work?
    [1 Not at all. . . .
     4 They should jointly decide about all important things concerning their work]
37. *Should* workers participate in making important decisions related to general plant problems?
    [1 Not at all. . . .
     4 They should jointly decide about all important things concerning general plant problems]
40. In your opinion, when decisions are being made *should* the people affected be asked for their opinions and suggestions? . . .
    [1 They should never be asked for their opinions and suggestions.
     4 They should almost always be asked for their opinions and suggestions]

The aspirations expressed by the kibbutz and Yugoslav respondents are higher than those expressed by the other groups, consistent with the higher level of participativeness reported by kibbutz and Yugoslav personnel—and with the formal ideological requirements for participativeness in these systems. The ideals expressed by the American respondents, however, are lower than those of the Italian and Austrian respondents even though the American respondents report as much participative decision making in their plants as do the Austrian respondents and more than do the Italian. Nonetheless, all the groups show a discrepancy between the level of participativeness that they report and the ideals that they propose. The average respondent in each group prefers that his organization were more participative than he judges it to be—which is consistent with a good deal of prior research, including a study of managers in fourteen countries by Haire and others (1966).

The data of Figure 3 show the discrepancies between "ideal" and "actual" participativeness for the plants in each country. These data were obtained by subtracting the results for each question concerning participativeness from the corresponding question concerning the ideal. The Italian and American organizations make an interesting contrast since both groups, illustrating "private economy" systems, are relatively low on participativeness as measured by the decision-making items, but the discrepancy between the ideal and actual levels of participativeness differs considerably between these countries, being small in the American plants and large in the Italian. The kibbutz and American plants also contrast well since they differ from each other substantially in their "actual" and "ideal" levels of participation—yet they are almost identical with respect to the *discrepancy* between the ideal and actual levels. In both sets of plants the actual level of participation, whether low or high, corresponds relatively well to the ideal. For whatever reasons, the kibbutz members and the American workers are relatively close to having the level of participative decision making they want, even though what they want is quite different in the two places.

Interpersonal Participativeness

Aspects of participativeness can be gauged by a number of questions designed to measure the participativeness and sup-

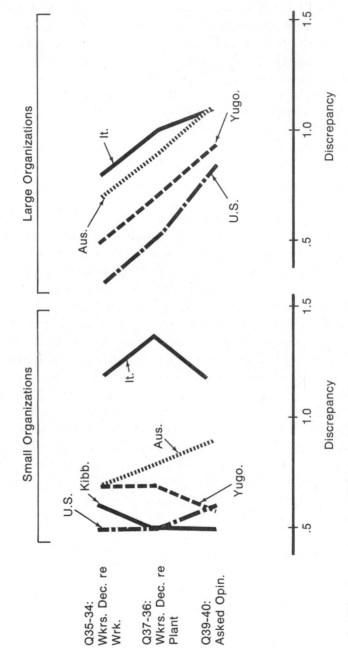

Figure 3. Discrepancy between "ideal" and "actual" participativeness.

portiveness of the respondent's superior. These questions provide one indication of informal participativeness in the plants:

41. Does your immediate superior ask your opinion when a problem comes up that involves your work?
    [1 He always asks my opinion. . . .
    5 He never asks my opinion] *
42. Is your immediate superior inclined to take into account your opinions and suggestions?
    [1 Not at all. . . .
    5 Very much]
43. Is your immediate superior friendly and easily approached if there are problems?
    [1 Not at all. . . .
    5 To a very great extent]
44. Does your immediate superior make people under him feel free to take their complaints to him?
    [1 He makes them feel completely free. . . .
    5 Not at all free]
46. Do you have trust in your immediate superior?
    [1 Never. . . .
    5 Always]

Table 5 shows the results separately for the small and the large organizations.

The kibbutz plants rank first and the Italian plants last on these questions, as on the decision-making items. The American small plants, however, are very close to the kibbutz, and among the large organizations the American plants rank first. If we take these items to reflect aspects of informal participation, and the earlier decision-making items to represent formal participation, the following picture emerges. The kibbutz plants are participative, formally and informally. The Yugoslav organizations are participative formally and the American informally while the Italian and Austrian organizations are participative neither formally or informally with the Italian being the least participative on all counts.

* The scale of this item and of item 44 was reversed for purposes of calculating the means shown in Table 5, so that a high score would represent a high degree of participativeness or support.

Table 5. Participativeness and Supportiveness of Superior

Superior Behavior	Q.	Italy	Austria	United States	Yugo-slavia	Kibbutz
SMALL PLANTS						
Participative	41	3.0	3.1	3.5	3.4	3.9
	42	2.7	3.2	3.4	3.1	3.5
Supportive	43	3.5	3.1	4.0	3.6	4.0
	44	3.4	3.6	3.9	3.4	4.3
	46	3.7	3.9	4.3	3.9	4.3
Average		3.3	3.4	3.8	3.5	4.0
LARGE PLANTS						
Participative	41	3.4	3.6	3.8	3.6	
	42	3.1	3.7	3.6	3.3	
Supportive	43	3.8	3.5	4.1	3.8	
	44	3.6	3.9	4.0	3.3	
	46	3.8	4.0	4.1	4.0	
Average		3.5	3.7	3.9	3.6	

Note: In order to simplify this and subsequent tables, the N's are not presented. See note to Figure 2.

Control in the Plants

Figure 4 presents data in response to the following question concerning the distribution of control:

26. How much influence do the following groups or persons actually have on what happens in this plant? (Circle one number on each line across.)

	Very little influence	Little influence	Some influence	Quite a lot of influence	A very great deal of influence
(a) Plant manager and his executive board	1	2	3	4	5
(b) All other managerial or supervisory personnel	1	2	3	4	5
(c) The workers as a group	1	2	3	4	5

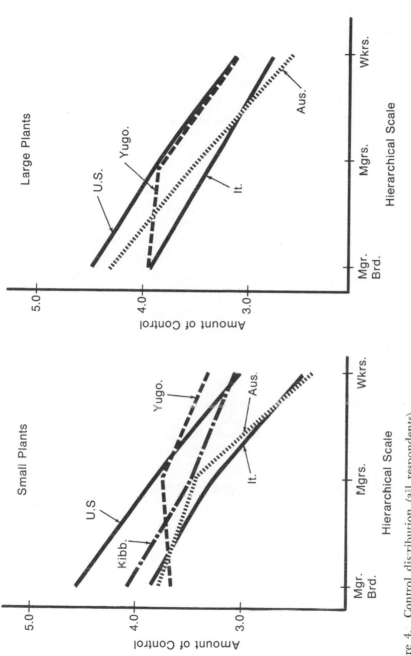

Figure 4. Control distribution (all respondents).

These data provide only a rough indication of distribution of control in the plants, but the differences between countries in Figure 4 are nonetheless meaningful. The Yugoslav and kibbutz plants have flatter, more "power-equalized" curves than do the other plants, consistent with their more participative structures. An implication of the flat curve in the Yugoslav plants, however, is that the top managers exercise less control than do the managers in any other group of plants, while the workers exercise more control than do workers in any other group (Adizes, 1971; Mozina, 1969; Rus, 1970). The "weakness" of the Yugoslav manager in the context of the responsibilities he faces has been noted as a problem for managers by previous observers of the Yugoslav industrial scene.

The slopes of the curve in the three "private economy" countries are almost identical, showing rather steep negative inclinations, but these countries are nonetheless distinguishable in terms of the height of their curve, suggesting that the American plants are the more highly controlled of the group. But the American plants are not, in terms of the data of the previous sections, the least participative; the Italian plants are, and they are also the least controlled. Furthermore, the participative kibbutz and Yugoslav plants are moderately high in amount of control according to this measure, which may appear ironic in the context of the "permissiveness theory" of participation that assumes participation to be a system of very little control. On the contrary, these data add credence to the contention that the participative organization may be more highly controlled than its less participative counterpart (Tannenbaum, 1968a).

In general, these data are consistent with our understanding of differences in control between the formally participative and non-participative systems although they diverge from our expectation in some details. Should not the data show, for example, that workers in the kibbutz plants exercise more control than workers in the corresponding American plants? We think that they probably should and that these deviations illustrate a possible weakness in the data—a weakness, however, that does not override their larger consistency and the meaningful relationships they demonstrate, as we shall see in later sections. In the meanwhile we can speculate about why members attribute as much control as they do to workers in the American plants.

Control in a plant is probably viewed pragmatically by respondents in terms of issues that are important to them (Tannenbaum, 1962a). The argument of Bell (1958) may help explain the meaning of control to American respondents. "If there is any meaning to the idea of workers' control, it is control—*in the shop*—over the things which directly affect his work-a-day life: the rhythms, pace, and demands of work; a voice in the equitable standards of pay; a check on the demands of the hierarchy over him."

Although American workers do not have authority concerning broad policy issues, they do have informal influence through superiors concerning aspects of their daily work life. And, more formally, they exercise a degree of control in some plants through their union with respect to immediate, "bread and butter" issues and working conditions. A British trade-union committee reporting their observation of American unions, for example, saw them playing a role similar in some respects to the British joint consultative committees that were created to achieve formal participativeness in British plants. "To a large extent matters dealt with by . . . [these] committees in Britain are in the U.S.A. written into union-company agreements" (British Trade Union Congress, n.d.). Ross Stagner (1957, quoted in Ferrarotti, 1959) reports an incident which illustrates the difference between the control that workers exercise through unions in American plants compared to the control exerted in Italian plants. While touring an Italian plant, he writes: "I noticed a considerable number of what seemed to be fairly serious accident hazards. In talking with workers, I discovered that one of them was a representative of CIGL [the union]. . . . I commented on the accident hazards, and he agreed that they had a fairly high accident rate. When I asked him what action the union was taking with respect to this, he said, 'None. We are busy organizing for the revolution.' " The data of Figure 4 of course show that American workers (as well as kibbutz and Yugoslav workers) exercise more control in their plants than Italian workers exercise in theirs.

The kibbutz and Yugoslav plants do distinguish themselves predictably from the American plants with respect to the *"ideal"* amount of control that members advocate for workers, if not the "actual" amount of control they perceive workers to exercise. Members in the former, ideologically participative plants, both large and small, advocate more control by workers than that advocated by American respondents. These data, shown in Figure 5, are based on this question:

27. In your opinion, how much influence *should* the following groups or persons have on what happens in this plant?

The discrepancy between the "ideal" and "actual" curves is very much alike in all countries and it corresponds to that found through earlier research in a variety of organizations (Smith and Tannenbaum, 1963). The "ideal" control curve roughly parallels the "actual," but in each case it is higher and more nearly horizontal than the "actual." This discrepancy between "ideal" and "actual" is apparently very general, occurring as it does under such a variety of conditions. Nonetheless the kibbutz and Yugoslav plants show a more positively sloped "ideal" curve than do the other plants, consistent with their more participative ideology.

Reward and Sanctions

Two questions were asked concerning the rewards dispensed for good work and the sanctions imposed for bad work, in order to understand better how control is exercised in the plants. The question to measure rewards was posed as follows:

12. What happens if a member in this organization does an especially good job in his work?

Respondents were asked to check as many responses as applied among a list of possible answers. Table 6 shows the percent of

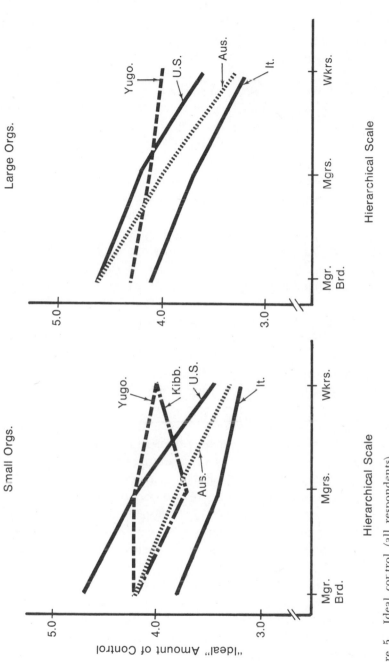

Figure 5. Ideal control (all respondents).

respondents who checked each of the possible answers to this question. These data suggest a number of striking facts, some of which can be seen by comparing the relative frequency with which the rewards are checked within each country separately. In the kibbutz plants as a group, the high opinion of co-workers is checked more frequently than any other reward, but by way of contrast, this is one of the two least checked items in the Italian plants. "Praise by coworkers" as well as "the high opinion of superiors," and "opportunities for advancement" are also relatively important in kibbutz plants. The Yugoslav plants, small and large, show a pattern of rewards resembling that in the kibbutz plants, although the high opinion of co-workers does not stand out so strikingly and opportunity for advancement is not among the most prominent items checked. A relatively high proportion of respondents in the small Yugoslav plants say that "nothing" will happen when a worker does a good job.

In the American plants great prominence is given to the opinion and praise of superiors as well as to the opportunity for advancement, hinting at the importance attached to upward mobility in these plants. The high opinion of co-workers, however, is not unimportant, ranking fourth among the items in the American plants, large and small. The Austrian plants, like the American, rely heavily on superior opinion and praise. However, in the small Austrian plants as many respondents say that nothing will happen as say that the superior will have a high opinion of a person who does a good job, suggesting a somewhat indifferent attitude toward good work—if not toward bad work. A relatively large proportion of Italian respondents also say that nothing will happen when a worker does a good job. This item ranks first among the items in the Italian small plants, and third in the large plants. Furthermore, although the percentage is low, the Italian respondents in small plants rank ahead of respondents in the other countries in reporting that a member will be *criticized* by co-workers if he does a good job. Among the large plants, Italian respondents share first place with the Austrian respondents on this "reward" for good work, although only 10 percent of the respondents check this item. Nonetheless, supervisory praise has some prominence in the Italian plants.

Table 6 intimates several facts and a principle for which we shall see further support in later sections, and Table 7 helps make these intimations more explicit. This table presents correlations between countries in the pattern of rewards for good work. In deriving these correlations, the rewards of Table 6 were ranked within each country according to the percent of respondents who checked each. For example, the "high opinion of co-workers" ranks first among the "rewards" in kibbutz plants. In the Italian plants this "reward" ties for last place. These rankings were then correlated between countries.* The correlations, shown in Table 7, were computed separately for small plants and for large plants (shown in parentheses).

Most, although not all, of the correlations are positive, indicating in general more similarity than dissimilarity between countries in the way good work is rewarded. Some distinctions can be made however. The Italian plants, both large and small, resemble the Austrian more than they resemble the plants in any other country. On the other hand, the Italian plants are *least* like the kibbutz, and they are rather dissimilar to the American plants too. The kibbutz plants show about equal likeness to the Yugoslav and American plants in these patterns. Thus the Italian and kibbutz plants describe extremes in pattern of rewards, with the small Yugoslav and American plants resembling in some degree the kibbutz, and the Austrian showing some similarity to the Italian, as well as to the American and the Yugoslav.

But these data suggest a fact that may have more profound and enduring significance than the differences and similarities between countries. With one exception, the correlations for the large plants are greater than those for the small, and we wonder whether it is reasonable to think that large organizations are generally more alike than small ones in pattern of rewards. Such a principle is by no means at odds with the "logic

---

* Item 8 of Table 6 was dropped from all countries when computing the correlation with kibbutzim since this item is not included in the kibbutz data.

Table 6. Percent of Respondents Who Indicate Rewards for Good Work

REWARD	SMALL PLANTS					LARGE PLANTS			
	Italy	Austria	United States	Yugo-slavia	Kibbutz	Italy	Austria	United States	Yugo-slavia
1. His superior will have a high opinion of him	15	24	50	31	25	24	40	61	46
2. His superior will praise him	31	42	48	30	20	28	45	65	51
3. His coworkers will have a high opinion of him	11	15	35	28	51	14	16	28	43
4. His coworkers will praise him	15	16	23	31	25	14	17	25	35
5. His coworkers will criticize him	16	8	3	4	2	10	10	8	6
6. He may be offered a better job at the same level	11	7	16	9	4	14	12	16	20
7. He will have a better opportunity for advancement	14	11	39	13	25	28	38	59	24
8. He will be given a bonus or higher wage	23	15	23	17	—[a]	20	33	19	24
9. Nothing will happen	33	24	11	30	21	26	21	7	20

[a] This category was not included in the questionnaire administered in kibbutzim because of its inapplicability.

Table 7. Rank Order Correlations Among Countries
for Rewards Dispensed for Good Work

Country	Austria	United States	Yugo-slavia	Kibbutz
Italy	.62 (.89)	—.15 (.52)	.27 (.45)	—.35
Austria		.51 (.73)	.86 (.71)	.29
United States			.52 (.90)	.55
Yugoslavia				.55

Note: Correlations in parentheses apply to large plants; all others apply to the small plants.

of industrialization" suggested by Kerr and others (1964); advancing industrialization, which implies among other things the growth of large-scale organization, introduces into the work organization technological and administrative imperatives that increase the similarity of organizations in various nations despite differences in culture and economics: "Technology is . . . a unifying force. At one moment of time there may be several best economic combinations or social arrangements, but only one best technology. The technology can be up to date or antiquated, but there is no question which is which, and the modern is constantly replacing the ancient" (pp. 228–229). Investment in technology as well as in personnel is greater in the large organization, and the large organization more than the small one may resemble the organization of the future. More complex administratively and more advanced technologically, large plants conform to a general logic of industrialization that does not apply so definitively to simpler and technologically less sophisticated small organizations.*

* The sample of respondents in large plants includes a larger percent of managerial personnel than does the sample in small plants (see the section concerning selection of respondents in Chapter One). The difference in correlation between small and large plants in Table 7 is not attributable to this sampling difference, however. Analyses done separately for rank and file respondents and for managerial show that the correlations based on the responses of managers are not in general larger than those based on the responses of rank-and-file members.

Reward for good work has its counterpart in sanctions for bad work, and these sanctions were measured by asking:

14. What happens if a member in this organization does a very poor job?

The results are tabulated in Table 8. Criticism by a superior is the most frequently checked reaction in all countries, with the exception of the United States. In that country, "less good opportunity for advancement" is more prominent, although supervisory criticism ranks a close second. In the kibbutz plants a relatively large proportion of respondents indicate that co-workers will criticize and have a low opinion of a member who does a poor job. Low opinions and criticism by co-workers as a reaction to a poor job is also relatively frequent in Yugoslav plants. Such peer control is entirely consistent with the participative mode of operation. In the United States plants, the low opinion of superiors and co-workers ranks third and fourth among the reactions to poor work. The data from the Italian plants again suggest uniqueness. Although the percentages are small, more respondents in the Italian plants than in any others say that workers will support a member against criticism or that nothing will happen if a member does a poor job. These data, along with those of Table 6, are consistent with the low level of control ascribed to the Italian plants by respondents (Figure 4).

The data of Tables 6 and 8 suggest that a member is more likely to be criticized when he does a poor job than he is likely to be praised when he does good work—except in the American plants. This exception may reflect the supportiveness by superiors in the American plants, suggested in Table 5. Kibbutz superiors are supportive too, according to Table 5, and although they are more likely to criticize for poor work than to praise for good, the likelihood of overt criticism (or of praise) is not very great. The support provided by kibbutz superiors apparently does not depend on the quality of the subordinate's work. In the kibbutz, as in the Yugoslav plants, the superior has some help from the subordinate's own peers in criticizing poor work and praising good.

The priority of criticism over praise occurs in one form or another in most of the countries. Note especially the reticence of a superior or peer in kibbutz plants to praise members even when the former have a high opinion of the latter (Table 6). Although 25 and 51 percent of respondents say that superiors and peers respectively will have a high opinion of a member who performs well, only 20 and 25 percent indicate that a superior or peer will actually praise the high performing member. This hesitancy may be due to equalitarian norms in the kibbutz. A high level of praise of those who do exceptional work can lead to a form of adulation that is inconsistent with equality. Sincerity is also an important norm in the kibbutz, and praise may be inhibited in order to avoid any semblance of flattery.

On the other hand, kibbutz superiors and peers do not appear as reluctant to translate their low opinion of a member into overt criticism. Some 26 and 30 percent of members indicate that superiors and peers respectively have a low opinion of a poor performer, but the likelihood of criticism is indicated by as many as 49 and 36 percent of respondents (Table 8). Superiors in the other countries are also likely to express overtly their low opinion of a poor performing worker. In all cases, the percentage indicating that the superior will criticize is greater than the percentage indicating that the superior merely has a low opinion of the worker. But, strangely, a reversal of the tendency to inhibit *praise* occurs in the Italian and Austrian plants. For example, while only 15 and 24 percent of respondents indicate that a superior will have a high opinion of a high performing worker in the Italian and Austrian plants respectively, larger percentages, 31 and 42, say that superiors will actually praise a high performing subordinate. It is as if some superiors offer praise even though they may not have a high opinion of the person they are praising.

Nonetheless, some punitive reaction, whether it be criticism by a superior or peers or a reduction in chances for promotion, is very likely to follow from a member's failure to perform well. Positive effects for good work are not so forthcoming in most countries. In each country the likelihood that

Table 8. Percent of Respondents Who Indicate Sanctions for Poor Work

Sanction	SMALL PLANTS					LARGE PLANTS			
	Italy	Austria	United States	Yugo-slavia	Kibbutz	Italy	Austria	United States	Yugo-slavia
1. His superior will have a low opinion of him	27	28	39	34	26	30	50	51	51
2. His superior will criticize him	56	63	49	66	49	51	75	62	78
3. His coworkers will have a low opinion of him	10	13	31	29	30	12	28	33	35
4. His coworkers will criticize him	16	26	19	37	36	16	24	25	52
5. His coworkers will support him against criticism	18	6	7	8	1	15	7	11	11
6. He will be given an inferior job	16	8	6	16	12	14	14	15	31
7. He will have less good opportunity for advancement	26	19	56	23	27	31	53	68	47
8. He will be fined	29	13	2	8	—a	21	23	—	20
9. Nothing will happen	13	4	6	6	11	15	6	8	8

a This category was not included in the questionniare administered in kibbutzim because of its inapplicability.

nothing will happen is greater when one does well than when one does poorly. *Something,* therefore, is more likely to happen in response to poor work than in response to good. The differences on item 9 between Tables 6 and 8 suggesting that "nothing" is the more likely response to good work than bad are not great in each country but they occur consistently and are probably not to be explained by chance. Even though it may not be rationally justifiable (Skinner, 1971), this preeminence of punishment is understandable as a reaction to the manifest threat to the organization created by substandard performance. Chronic poor work is obviously intolerable and it is likely to arouse anxiety on the part of those who are committed to the organization's survival. Attack is a natural (if not the most effective) reaction to this threat. Good performance, on the other hand, does not have the emotionally provocative implications of poor performance, since members are supposed to perform well and good performance can have a balming effect on those responsible for organizational well being: all is well, urgent reaction is not required. Furthermore, to those who administer them, sanctions may appear less costly than rewards, and sanctions may be preferred consciously or unconsciously for this reason. For example, even praise by a superior, which is a reward that can be dispensed without immediate cost, may carry implications for a pay raise or a promotion. Criticism, however, appears to entail neither immediate nor future cost. On the contrary, it suggests reduction in cost since it implicitly warns the recipient that he could suffer loss of pay or of rank.

One might wonder, too, whether there are psychological bases (in addition to the causes suggested above) that lead people to an asymmetry in the dispensing of rewards and sanctions. Are some of the roots of this asymmetry to be found in the general life-adjustment of members and in predispositions that they bring to the organization? Does this asymmetry occur outside the work organization as well as within? An especially interesting case in point is the informal sports team, because it typically illustrates a balance of praise and criticism very different from that suggested above. Teammates are full of cheers and warm praise for good performance and they rarely criticize a fellow player for committing an error. A player of course risks not being asked into the game if his performance is poor, but the strong overt support for good performance and the subdued reaction to poor performance stand in contrast to what we suspect prevails in many organizations. Through games men behave in ways that may not be possible otherwise.

The correlation between countries in the pattern of sanctions for poor work is like that indicated in Table 7 concerning rewards. The large plants again, with one exception (the Yugoslavia-Austria correlation), show bigger correlations than the small plants, suggesting again that large plants are more alike than small plants in these patterns. But none of the correlations is negative, as in Table 7. Is it possible not only that sanctions are a more likely reaction than rewards but also that the pattern of sanctions is more universal in human affairs than that of rewards? Is this a reason why organizations from diverse systems are therefore more alike with respect to sanctions than reward?

Peer and Superior Control

Sanctions are intended as a means of control, but the effectiveness of criticism as a technique of control depends in part on the recipient's sensitivity to the criticism—on the extent to which he finds it an "aversive stimulus." Obviously a superior can exercise little influence over a subordinate through criticism if the subordinate is indifferent to the criticism. We therefore asked:

30. Suppose your immediate superior told you that you did some job badly. How much would it bother you?
31. Suppose some of your co-workers told you that you did some job badly. How much would this bother you?

Both questions were answered by checks on a scale from 1 (not at all) to 5 (very much). The data, shown in Table 9, indicate that workers in different countries differ (significantly) in their response to criticism by superiors and by peers. American plants rank first in the disturbance felt by members when they are criticized by superiors; Italian plants rank last. Thus criticism by superiors in the Italian plants may not have as much implication for control as does criticism in the American plants, even though there may be more criticism in the Italian plants than in the American—which is consistent with our assertion that American managerial and supervisory personnel exercise more control in their plants than do their Italian counterparts.

Table 9. Effect of Superior and Peer Criticism

| | RESPONDENT WOULD FEEL TROUBLED BY | | |
Country	Criticism by Superior	Criticism by Peers	Average
SMALL PLANTS			
Italy	3.3	2.9	3.1
Austria	3.7	3.0	3.4
United States	4.1	3.4	3.8
Yugoslavia	3.7	3.7	3.7
Kibbutz	3.7	3.5	3.6
LARGE PLANTS			
Italy	3.8	3.3	3.6
Austria	3.9	3.0	3.4
United States	4.1	3.3	3.7
Yugoslavia	4.0	4.0	4.0

Criticism by peers elicits the greatest reaction in the Yugoslav plants and second in the kibbutz plants, and in fact the *likelihood* of criticism by peers appears also to be greater in these plants than in the others (Table 8). The participative model would suggest such peer-generated influence and a corresponding sensitivity to criticism by peers for doing a bad job. The relative lack of concern by the Austrian and Italian members, indicated by the measure combining criticism by superior and peers, implies less involvement and greater indifference in the work situation on the part of these members compared to others, a fact for which we shall see further evidence in later sections. These plants therefore resemble, more than the others, a laissez faire system of operation. On the other hand, the American, Yugoslav, and kibbutz plants are relatively high on the combined effect of superior and peer criticism, and the ranking of countries on this measure is similar although not identical to that for total amount of control suggested in Figure 4. The difference between the results of the two measures need not imply inconsistency, however. Criticism is not the only means of exercising control.

Bases of Power

Participation concerns the exercise of power and the acceptance of authority. Do subordinates in the participative system differ from those in the non-participative in their reasons for accepting authority? French and Raven (1959) suggest five reasons why one person may accede to the influence of another. Referred to as "bases of power," these reasons include the belief that the person exercising control (1) has superior knowledge relevant to the task; (2) can dispense rewards or (3) punishments; (4) is attractive as an individual; or (5) has the *right* to exercise control. French and Raven refer to these respectively as the expert, reward, referent, coercive, and legitimate bases of power. To these we have added a sixth which implies accession to influence out of a sense of commitment to a larger purpose served by the organization. This basis of power has been suggested by Likert and is very much like what Mary Parker Follett calls the "law of the situation" (Metcalf and Urwick, 1940).

Table 12 presents the results in response to the following question designed to measure the above bases of power:

47. When you do what your immediate superior requests you to do on the job, why do you do it?

With respect to each of the six reasons shown in Table 10, responses were made on a scale from 1 (not at all) to 5 (to a very great extent). These reasons represent the above six bases of power respectively.

The pattern of response is remarkably alike among the

plants of the five countries and the rank order correlation of the items is unity or close to unity across all countries for plants both large and small. "Legitimate" and "law of the situation" bases are rated the most important in all countries, followed by expertise, referent, reward, and coercion. This order is similar to the pattern reported by Bachman and others (1968) from earlier studies in a variety of organizations (including a utility, colleges, clerical organizations, and factories), which suggests a broad generality to this pattern.

While all countries rate "law of the situation" high and the reward and coercive bases low, the kibbutz plants are especially high on the first of these bases and outstandingly low on the other two. Differences between countries on these items are highly significant statistically and the uniqueness of the kibbutz plants is consistent with the ideology of the kibbutz and with the associated lack of material incentives and sanctions. The Yugoslav plants are highest among the large plants on "law of the situation," but they are also relatively high on the coercive base among large plants as well as small. This relative standing is not in accord with the presumed formal participativeness of these plants.

These data, which attach little importance to coercion, might seem to contradict the evidence of the previous section, where sanctions were stressed over reward. The earlier data concerning sanctions, however, refer to the behavior of a potential control agent—what a superior does, for example, when his subordinate performs poorly. The present data refer to the reasons for a subordinate's acceding to control. Thus superiors may often behave coercively but subordinates may not respond to the coercion. This at least is what members seem to report, and whether or not they report accurately, they are unanimous as groups, in both small and large plants, in assigning a low score to coercion as an effective basis of control. Earlier research by Bachman and others in which bases of power were correlated with criteria of performance, morale, and total amount of control in organizations also suggests that coercion is indeed a relatively ineffective basis of power in the modern organization (Bachman and others, 1968).

Table 10. Bases of Superior's Power

Basis of Power	Small Plants						Large Plants			
	Italy	Austria	United States	Yugo-slavia	Kibbutz		Italy	Austria	United States	Yugo-slavia
(a) I respect his competence and judgment	3.2	3.6	4.2	3.7	3.5		3.4	3.8	4.1	3.9
(b) He can give special help and benefits	2.2	3.0	3.5	3.1	1.3		2.2	3.1	3.4	2.8
(c) He can penalize or otherwise disadvantage me	2.1	2.4	2.4	2.7	1.1		2.0	2.1	2.7	2.8
(d) He's a nice guy	2.5	3.5	3.4	3.3	2.0		2.5	3.2	3.1	3.2
(e) It is my duty	4.1	4.2	4.2	4.1	4.2		4.3	4.2	4.5	4.4
(f) It is necessary if the organization is to function properly	3.8	4.1	4.5	4.2	4.6		4.1	4.5	4.5	4.6

Summary

The kibbutz and Yugoslav plants included in this study are highly participative according to their formal charters. They appear highly participative also in terms of most of the measures discussed in this chapter. Kibbutz plants in particular stand out. According to our respondents in these plants, members participate substantially in decisions related to the plant as well as their own work. Participativeness appears also to pervade relations between superiors and subordinates. Superiors in kibbutz plants are receptive to the ideas and suggestions of those under them, and they are helpful and supportive in relations with their subordinates. Kibbutz plants are characterized also by a relatively flat, power-equalized distribution of control—although the slope of the control curve is negative, as in the typical industrial organization. Furthermore, the character of control and the bases of power in the kibbutz plants reflect a participative managerial style. Members accede to the influence attempts of superiors largely because of a sense of commitment to the organization ("law of the situation"). Rewards for good work and sanctions for bad are dispensed through social approval and disapproval by co-workers as well as supervisors. Although the kibbutz plant is highly participative, it is not as participative as its formal charter implies nor as participative as members would like it to be. Nonetheless, the discrepancy between the ideal and the reality as members see it is small compared to that in the other organizations.

The Yugoslav plants in this study also correspond to the participative model, although not so closely as do the kibbutz. With respect to measures of participative decision making, the Yugoslav plants as a group rank second only to the kibbutz plants, and the Yugoslav plants show a flatter control curve than any other group of plants. The total amount of control also is high; all hierarchical groups exercise relatively high control. With respect to supervisor-subordinate relations, however, the Yugoslav plants do not appear as participative as some others.

The American, Austrian, and Italian organizations are not as participative as the kibbutz or Yugoslav plants in terms of most criteria—nor are they meant to be. The Italian plants in particular fall closest to the non-participative end of the continuum. In these plants workers have little to say about decisions concerning the plant, or their own work, and superiors are not very prone to invite the ideas and suggestions of subordinates or to provide the helpful, supportive relations that imply participativeness. The distribution of control in Italian plants is sharply hierarchical, as it is in the Austrian and American plants, yet the *total amount* of control is lower than in any of the other groups. Thus, while the Italian plants are the least participative, they are not necessarily the most authoritarian since, after all, the "authorities" do not exercise a very high degree of control in these organizations. Furthermore, these plants as a group show a greater discrepancy than do any others in our sample between the ideal level of participation and the reality as members see it.

The American and Austrian plants resemble the Italian in degree of non-participation, but they are not as extreme as the Italian in most respects. The American organizations diverge somewhat more than the Austrian from the non-participative extreme; they approach in some respects the kibbutz and Yugoslav plants. Especially in the area of superior-subordinate relations do the American plants take on some of the character of the participative organization. Furthermore, although the distribution of control is clearly hierarchical, the total amount of control is greater in the American plants than in the other groups. Thus, while managers are highly influential, workers are not without influence.

Plants in the respective countries were chosen in this study because of the presumed differences between them in ideology and participativeness. The data of this chapter support this choice and serve to verify the design of the study. They also lend some support to the validity of the measures. Nonetheless, there are several findings that do not fit the prevailing pattern of results, and which therefore raise questions about their meaning. One such deviation concerns three items of the Likert index (questions 32, 33, and 38) that define the predicted effects of participation on attitudes and communication. For example, Yugoslav plants that are reported to have a relatively high level of participative decision making are not always described by our respondents as having a correspondingly high level of favorable attitudes and open communication. We see evidence at least that members in these plants, while reporting (accurately we believe) a relatively high degree of participative decision making, are not simply expressing a general, positive feeling in response to our questions. These data, therefore, suggest that formal participation may not have all of the favorable effects on communication and attitude that are predicted for it.

A second question arises with respect to the measure of control (question 26). The results of this question are in important respects consistent with the realities as we understand them in the five groups of plants, but we wonder about several details. It seems meaningful and reasonable, for example, that kibbutz and Yugoslav plants have flatter control distributions than the other groups of plants, as indicated in Figure 4. Is it reasonable, however, that the distribution in Yugoslav plants is flatter than that in kibbutz plants, as implied by the data? The differences in total amount of control between the plants of the five countries suggested by the data aptly describe what we believe to be real and important differences between these plants. The reported high level of control in American plants compared to the Italian and Austrian plants, for example, illustrates how organizations that are basically alike in distribution of control may nonetheless differ in total amount. And it suggests, realistically we believe, that while American managers are more influential than the Austrian and Italian managers, American workers are not less influential than their counterparts. We wonder, however, why kibbutz workers as a group are not more influential than the American workers according to our data.

We conclude that the data of this chapter provide in

their totality a reasonable and realistic description of the plants, but that they may be subject to error in some details. Unfortunately, we cannot always determine which details are accurately described and which are erroneous except by checking their consistency with the total pattern of results and with the results of relevant research conducted by others employing different methods and points of view. We can also evaluate the data against our own experience as members of five societies. Most of the data that we have discussed in this chapter meet one, or another, or all of the above criteria. Given the difficulties of obtaining meaningful comparisons in cross-national research we are encouraged by the results, but we shall be able better to evaluate their validity as the analyses in the following chapters unfold.

IV

EMPHASIS
ON HIERARCHY

Hierarchy in the work organization implies differences between persons in their authority and influence as well as in the rewards, both intrinsic and extrinsic, associated with their work. People at higher organization levels, for example, ordinarily have more varied, interesting, and challenging jobs than people at lower levels, and the former are likely to be paid more than the latter. Costs as well as rewards are associated with high rank, but in a system where hierarchy is stressed, the rewards substantially outweigh the costs—otherwise there would be little incentive for qualified persons to fill the vital positions that hierarchy defines.

All work organizations are structured hierarchically, but some organizations are less hierarchical than others. The participative organization, because of its equalitarian ideology, deemphasizes hierarchy. Formal distinctions based on rank are, in principle, less important. Decision making is broadly

distributed and the system of control and the character of interpersonal relations are different from those in the non-participative organization.

We shall examine in this chapter data that help define
the importance attached to hierarchy and that show how
gradients of authority and reward associated with hierarchy
differ between the plants of the respective countries.

Attitude toward Advancement

The stress placed on hierarchy, and its potential impact
on members, can be gauged in part by the extent to which
members see the hierarchy as a means of achieving personal
success and the consequent desire they have to advance in the
hierarchy. The data of Table 11 describe the mobility aspirations of members. These data are based on a measure taken,
with some modification, from Reed (1962):

48. Imagine you were offered the following possibilities within this plant. Would you accept them or
not? (Circle one number on each line.)

	Yes	No
(a) Move to a higher level position that has considerably more obligations and responsibilties for you	1	2
(b) Move to a higher level position that requires training that entails many sacrifices on your part	1	2
(c) Move to a higher level position where you may be frequently criticized	1	2
(d) Move to a higher level position in which you would have a group of "problem" employees working for you	1	2
(e) Move to a higher level position in which there are more worries than you now have connected with the work	1	2

Respondents in the small Yugoslav and kibbutz plants are remarkably alike in their response to these items, expressing on the average lower mobility aspirations than do respondents in the other groups of plants. Among the large plants, the Yugoslav respondents are lower than any other group, and the American respondents are at the other extreme, as they are among respondents in the small plants, expressing relatively high motivation to advance in the organization. The difference between the small and large plants reflects in part the greater proportion of managerial personnel in the sample within large plants. Managerial personnel, especially in the Austrian, Italian, and U.S. plants, have greater mobility needs than do workers. The greater mobility aspirations in the large plants may also be attributed to the greater chances for advancement in these plants. The average of the correlations in all countries between the mobility aspirations of members and their perceived opportunities to advance is .33.

Hierarchy has different meanings for members in the different systems. High position is attractive and mobility in the hierarchy represents a desired means of achievement in the American plants, and to some extent in the Italian and Austrian ones. Hierarchical advancement is not so desirable in the kibbutz and Yugoslav plants, and this might be explained in a couple of ways. First, it might signify an intended or unintended deemphasis of hierarchy, and the consequent absence of special rewards that accrue to persons of high rank. For many members the benefits of advancement do not justify the costs. Some authors, for example, refer to the "negative balance of rewards" that applies to positions of leadership in kibbutzim (Talmon-Garber, 1956; Rosner, 1965). Kibbutz managers, in contrast to managers in other systems, do not receive greater material advantages than workers. Managers and workers live in similar apartments and share their food in a common dining hall. All members of the kibbutz utilize the services and facilities of the kibbutz according to their needs, not according to rank. At the same time managers in kibbutz plants face unique difficulties. They cannot bring formal sanctions to bear when faced with a difficult worker, and many kibbutz managers suffer

Table 11. Intra-Plant Mobility Aspirations
(Percentage of Respondents Willing to Face Obstacles)

Obstacles	SMALL PLANTS					LARGE PLANTS			
	Italy	Austria	United States	Yugo-slavia	Kibbutz	Italy	Austria	United States	Yugo-slavia
(a) Added obligations and responsibilities	50	39	67	38	38	67	72	85	47
(b) Training that requires sacrifices	45	25	67	33	34	60	43	75	39
(c) Frequent criticism	25	28	50	15	16	36	55	62	18
(d) Problem employees	31	37	34	13	9	38	57	59	12
(e) More worries	47	49	52	34	34	62	77	70	43
Average percent	40	36	54	27	26	53	61	70	32

Note: We do not show the N's in this table and in some of the remaining tables in order to simplify the presentation. Each percentage here (or each mean in subsequent tables) within a country is based on approximately 150–175 cases, except in kibbutzim, where all of the plants are grouped together in which case the N's are somewhere between 300 and 350.

tensions associated with the need to exercise authority over others while adhering to equalitarian values. The managerial role in kibbutz plants implies costs that for many members outweigh the benefits, and members therefore are not anxious to advance in the hierarchy. For a member who does advance, the rewards depend in good measure on his identification with kibbutz ideology and goals and on whatever gratification comes from performing a service in response to public demand. We shall see evidence below for the relatively flat gradients of reward in the kibbutz as well as in the Yugoslav plants.

A second argument concerning the lower mobility aspirations of members in kibbutz and Yugoslav plants is that the chances for advancement are so low that members cannot envision advancement under any conditions. Table 12 reports the results of two questions designed to determine members' perception of their opportunities to advance:

4. Are there real possibilities for people like you to advance in this plant?
   (1) no possibilities at all. . . . (5) very many possibilities

5. Do you think that at some time in the future you will have a position in this plant higher than your present position?
   (1) not at all probable. . . . (5) almost certain

The differences between countries, which are highly significant statistically, show members in the kibbutz plants ranking first in their perception of possibilities of advancement. The rotation principle, which is a unique feature of the participative system in kibbutzim, creates opportunity if not aspiration to move up the hierarchy, and the low mobility aspirations among kibbutz members cannot be explained therefore by a sense of discouragement about chances for advancement. Lack of opportunity may, however, contribute to the lack of desire for advancement in the Yugoslav plants, since the Yugoslav respondents are relatively pessimistic about promotion opportunities.

Table 12.   Opportunity to Advance

Country	Real Possibilities to Advance	Likelihood of Advancement	Overall Average
SMALL PLANTS			
Italy	2.1	2.1	2.1
Austria	2.3	1.8	2.0
U. S. A.	2.7	2.4	2.6
Yugoslavia	2.5	1.8	2.2
Kibbutz	3.2	2.4	2.8
LARGE PLANTS			
Italy	2.6	2.3	2.4
Austria	2.7	2.3	2.5
U. S. A.	3.2	2.8	3.0
Yugoslavia	2.8	1.9	2.4

The difference between small and large organizations suggests that the chances of promotion are greater in the large ones, but this is not because of their higher proportion of managerial personnel or their long hierarchical chains. An analysis within each country shows that persons in long chains do not perceive greater opportunity to advance than those in short and that persons in relatively high positions do not see greater chances of advancement for themselves. Large organizations are said to create problems of morale, but in these organizations lack of opportunity for advancement, as perceived by members at least, is not one of these problems.

Thus members in the American, Austrian, and Italian plants want to move up the hierarchical ladder more than do members in the kibbutz and Yugoslav plants, which is consistent with the predicted emphasis on hierarchy in the former plants. Such advancement is more likely to mean personal success in the first set of plants than in the second—and this difference between groups in mobility aspirations does not simply reflect a cultural difference in achievement motivation. Jews are not less achievement-oriented than Austrians or Italians.*

* Some evidence concerning differences in achievement motivation among cultures can be found in McClelland (1961).

Perceived Benefits of and Requirements
for Advancement

Attitude toward advancement in the hierarchy can be understood more fully by considering the views of members concerning the benefits of and the requirements for advancement. In order to determine members' perceptions of the benefits, we asked:

55. What do you think are the main advantages to moving into a higher position in the plant?

Respondents were asked to rank the first three among the list of advantages shown in Table 13. The figures in this table reflect the average rank of each advantage. (Scores of 5, 4, and 3 were assigned an item that was ranked 1, 2, or 3 respectively. An item not ranked at all was assigned a score of zero and all items were scored zero if a respondent checked a final item in the list of alternatives indicating that "there are no advantages" to advancement.) To facilitate comparisons, a double asterisk is placed next to the number in a cell that ranks first among countries for any one benefit. For example, a double asterisk is placed next to the score for prestige in Italy because Italian respondents rank ahead of the others in viewing prestige as a benefit of high rank. Similarly, a single asterisk is placed next to the lowest-ranking country for each item. Several items in the table do not have asterisks because according to an analysis of variance the countries do not differ statistically.

In the kibbutz plants members perceive variety of work, independence, and chance to enlarge knowledge as relatively prominent rewards of advancement. Wages are irrelevant, and opportunity to make decisions is rated very low as an advantage. By way of contrast, high wages and prestige are prominent in the Italian plants while opportunity to enlarge one's knowledge, which presumably would be important to professionally minded managers, is ranked very low. As in previous data, the Italian and kibbutz plants are more dissimilar than any other pair, representing extremes within which the others fall. This contrast is indicated by a negative correlation (—.23) between the ranking of advantages in these two places. On the other hand, the Italian plants resemble the Austrian more closely than any of the others, the correlations being .78 and .53 for the small and large organizations respectively. In this pair, the correlation for the small plants is greater than that for the large, but the average correlation between the plants in all countries exclusive of the kibbutz favors, if only slightly, the large plants, as in the data of the previous chapters. The averages are .54 and .62 for the small and large plants respectively. Kibbutz plants, however, are relatively deviant, correlating on the average only .11 with the other small plants. The advantages of being a kibbutz manager are not quite like the advantages of being a manager elsewhere, at least in the view of plant members.

Thus all of the plants, excepting those in kibbutzim, resemble one another somewhat in the relative prominence attached to the rewards listed in Table 13. However, all of the plants, including those in kibbutzim, are practically identical in the pattern of *requirements* members perceive for advancement in the hierarchy. In order to determine how members view these requirements, we asked the following question:

> 16. How important are each of the following factors
>   for getting ahead in this company?

Answers were checked on a five-point scale for each of the factors shown in Table 14. In all countries members rank "dependability" and "quality of work" very high, although the kibbutz plants are higher on these requirements than the other small plants and the Italian plants are lower. On the other hand, "having friends in higher management" ranks very low for all small plants, although the kibbutz plants are lower and the Austrian plants are higher than the others on this item. Nonetheless, the correlations between the five countries in pattern of requirements in large and small plants are very high, averaging .82. It would seem that the pattern of requirements for advancement as reported to us by members is rather universal, even among systems that differ radically in ideologi-

Table 13. Perceived Advantages Associated with High Rank

Advantage	Small Plants					Large Plants			
	Italy	Austria	United States	Yugoslavia	Kibbutz	Italy	Austria	United States	Yugoslavia
(a) Prestige or esteem	1.8**	1.1	.4*	.7	.6	2.1**	.9	.6*	.8
(b) Variety of work	1.2	1.4	1.3	.8*	2.0**	1.0	1.1	1.4	.7
(c) Independence	.8	1.0	.6*	.7	1.8**	1.2	1.2	.5	.9
(d) Number of social contacts	.6	.5	.1	.9	.7	.7	.3*	.3*	1.0**
(e) Opportunity to make decisions	1.1	.8	1.4**	1.2	.3*	1.2	1.4	1.3	1.2
(f) Opportunity to enlarge one's skills	1.1*	1.5	2.2	2.4**	1.2	1.2*	2.2**	2.0	2.1
(g) Opportunity to enlarge one's knowledge	.6*	1.1	2.2	2.5**	2.1	1.0*	1.5	2.4**	2.3
(h) Influence with people outside plant	.1	.2	.2	.4	.2	.1	.1	.1	.5
(i) High wages	2.2	2.3**	1.9	1.6	0.0*	1.9	2.8**	2.7	1.3*

* Ranks lowest among countries for this benefit.

** Ranks highest among countries for this benefit.

Table 14. Requirements for Getting Ahead

Requirement	SMALL PLANTS					LARGE PLANTS			
	Italy	Austria	United States	Yugo-slavia	Kibbutz	Italy	Austria	United States	Yugo-slavia
(a) Quality of work done	3.4*	3.9	4.0	4.0	4.2**	3.5*	4.0	4.1**	3.8
(b) Quantity of work done	3.3*	3.5	3.7	4.0**	3.5	3.1*	3.6	3.9**	3.6
(c) His supervisor's opinion of him	3.4	3.6	3.7**	3.5	3.1*	3.6	3.8	3.9**	3.5*
(d) Dependability	3.6*	4.0	4.2	3.7	4.3**	3.6	4.2	4.2	3.7
(e) Creativeness, inventiveness	2.8*	3.0	3.4	3.3	3.8**	3.0	3.3	3.5	3.3
(f) Seniority in the plant	2.8	2.7	2.9	3.2**	2.4*	2.7*	2.8	2.8	3.3**
(g) Having friends in higher management	2.2	2.5**	2.2	2.4	1.7*	2.4	2.7	2.8	2.7
(h) Having good professional knowledge	3.4	3.2*	3.7	3.2*	4.2**	3.5	3.6	3.9	3.8
(i) Taking initiative	3.2	3.0*	3.7	3.2	4.1**	3.3	3.6	3.8	3.4
(j) Having outstanding ability to work with people	3.1*	3.7	3.9	3.4	4.0**	3.2*	3.8	4.0**	3.8
(k) Loyalty to the company	3.3*	3.6	3.8	3.6	4.0**	3.5	3.7	3.9	3.6
(l) Recommendations of political or religious nature	1.8	1.4*	1.7	2.7**	—a	2.1	1.7*	1.7*	2.8**
(m) Elbowing one's way to get head	1.8	1.8	1.6*	2.2**	1.8	2.0	2.1	1.9	2.2

a This item was not included in the questionnaire administered in kibbutz plants.
* Ranks lowest among countries for this requirement.   ** Ranks highest among countries for this requirement.

cal base. Surprisingly, the smallest correlation, .52, occurs between the small Yugoslav and kibbutz plants.

Authority and Influence

Bureaucracy implies a hierarchical distribution of authority and influence, and this hierarchical distribution is one of the bases (suggested in Chapter One) for the gradients in reaction and adjustment that we are investigating. The emphasis placed on hierarchy can be gauged in part by the magnitude of differentials in authority and influence that accompany differences in hierarchical position. Figure 6 shows for all countries combined the mean responses of members at different levels in their organization to two pairs of questions. The first pair is:

    1. In your work, to what extent can you . . . have authority over other people?
  26. How much influence do . . . you personally actually have on what happens in this plant?

The second pair is identical with the first except that it inquires about the amount of authority and influence that the respondents prefer to have. All questions were answered on a five-point scale from "very little" to "a great deal."

The items that make up the index of authority and influence do not intercorrelate equally well in all countries, and the reliability of the index therefore differs among countries. The average reliability within the Yugoslav plants, .16, is especially low and we may want therefore to discount the results from Yugoslavia on this item. (Fortunately, other indices in the Yugoslav data do not suffer the unreliability of the authority-influence index.) In the other countries the range of reliability runs from .63 in Italy to .70 in the United States. Hence the data as a whole are reasonably reliable, and, excluding Yugoslavia, nearly equal in reliability among countries.*

* Reliability is computed with the Spearman-Brown prophecy formula (McNemar, 1957) on the basis of the correlations between the authority item and the influence item computed separately within each

The horizontal axis of Figure 6 defines the position of each respondent in terms of his distance from the top of the hierarchy in his plant, the top person being assigned a score

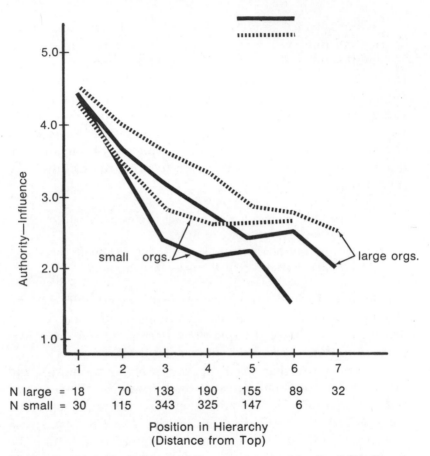

| N large = | 18 | 70 | 138 | 190 | 155 | 89 | 32 |
| N small = | 30 | 115 | 343 | 325 | 147 | 6 | |

Position in Hierarchy
(Distance from Top)

Figure 6. Authority-influence (all countries combined). Solid line is actual; dashed lines are ideal.

of one, his immediate subordinate a score of two, and so on. These scores were obtained from company records. The solid

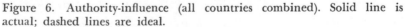

country. We computed but do not present the reliability of all indices employed in this research. In general, these reliabilities are reasonably good in all countries.

lines in the figure represent the results of an average of the
first pair of questions for members of large and small organizations separately. The broken lines represent the results of the
questions concerning preferred or "ideal" authority and influence.

The amount of authority and influence reported by
members conforms in general to the familiar hierarchical pattern. (With the exception of the irregularities near the bottom
of the curves, which are due to the aggregation of data from
chains of different length. For example, levels 2 to 6 in the
large plants and 2 to 5 in the small include some persons at
the bottom of their respective hierarchical chains. Figure 1
illustrates this possibility graphically.) Furthermore, the discrepancy between the ideal and the actual amount of authority
and influence is in general greater near the bottom than near
the top of the hierarchy, very much in the manner found by
Porter and Lawler (1965) and others. The difference between
the small and large organizations in amount of authority reported by members is due partly to the longer hierarchies in
the large organizations. Persons at a given level (defined in
terms of distance from the top) in large organizations have
more levels below them and therefore more authority than do
persons at the same level in small organizations. The slightly
flatter distribution of authority in the large plants may also
be consistent with the contention for which Whisler has found
some evidence, that organizations become less centralized as
they become larger (Whisler, 1964). These arguments reflect
certain features of hierarchy that can be seen more clearly when
chains of different length are examined separately, as in Figure
7. Here we see distinctions that are central to an understanding
of hierarchy and its effects.

First, chains of different length differ systematically in
gradient of authority and influence; longer chains have flatter
gradients. The relative "flatness" of the "tall" chains may seem
paradoxical in view of the prevailing assumption that tall organization means steep gradients. Nor can the flat gradients
in the long chains be explained by the "floor effect" of the
measure, even though the average rank-and-file person is close

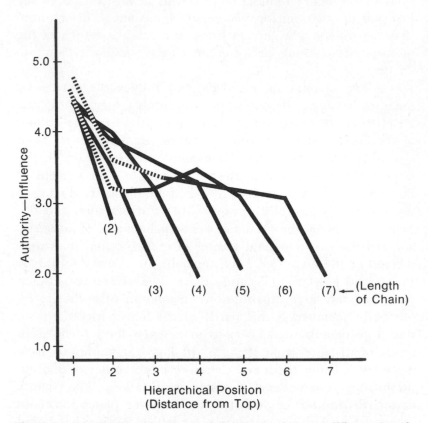

Figure 7. Distribution of authority-influence in chains of different length (all plants, all countries combined). *Note:* Points connected by dotted lines in this figure and subsequent figures are based on less than 15 cases but not less than 5. One organization in the sample contains a chain of eight levels, but the points in this chain, each of which is based on fewer than five cases, are not plotted.

to 2, near the bottom of the authority-influence scale. A floor effect of the scale would suggest a flattening of the curve near the bottom. Quite the opposite occurs in Figure 7. Furthermore, the gradient of authority and influence is flatter in the long chains even when the bottom rank in each set of chains is eliminated, and the gradient from the top down to the first line supervisors is considered. The average first-line supervisor falls near the middle of the scale regardless of length of chain, and the limits of the scale therefore cannot explain why supervisors in long chains are not lower than supervisors in short chains.

Second, the shape of the gradient appears to change with length of chain. The gradient is a straight line, by definition, in a two-level hierarchy. The three- and four-level chains are reasonably good approximations of a straight line, although they need not be by definition. The five-level chains begin to flatten slightly in the middle and this flattening becomes more marked in the six- and seven-level chains. In these longer chains, the gradient is relatively sharp near the top and near the bottom. These data, if they are general, suggest a principle: hierarchical gradients of authority (and of some other variables) are composed of two major differentials. One occurs between the top person and his immediate subordinates; the second occurs at the other end of the hierarchy between the bottom persons and their immediate superior. The two-level hierarchy is the limiting case in which the two components of gradient, that at the bottom and that at the top, merge into one.

Third, we can infer that small organizations differ from large in their average gradients. Small organizations, because they are characterized by short chains, have sharper gradients than large organizations. The six- and seven-level hierarchies, which are relatively flat, are located almost exclusively in the large organizations, and most of the two- and three-level chains, which have quite steep gradients, are located in the small organizations. Smallness apparently does not avoid the problem of hierarchy, if this problem is measured in terms of differentials in authority and influence. In one sense, smallness intensifies the problem since the average differential is greater in small organizations because of their short and sharp hierarchies.

Size of organization appears to have relatively little bearing on the character of the hierarchical gradient, *if chains of equal length are compared.* Graphic representations (not shown here) like that of Figure 7 demonstrate that short chains in the large organizations are very much like short chains in the small organizations. Furthermore, a multiple classification analysis (Andrews and others, 1967) of these data suggests that size of organization does not predict authority and influence very well when length of chain and country are held constant. The predictors in this analysis include: (1) the respondent's position in the hierarchy (defined in terms of distance from the top), (2) the size of plant (small or large) in which the respondent is located, (3) the type of plant in which the respondent works (categorized into each of five industries), (4) the length of chain in which the respondent is located, and (5) the respondent's country.

The multiple correlation based on the five predictors is .66, but the major contribution to this correlation is the respondent's rank. The Beta weight (analogous to a regression coefficient) for rank is .66. For country, the second most important predictor, the weight is .18 and for size and type of plant it is only .03. The relatively strong association between position and authority and influence simply verifies what we already have good reason to believe, and it is encouraging to see our measure validated in this way.

These data say in effect that moving a person from one level in a chain of a given length to another level in a chain of the same length is likely to make a substantial difference in the authority and influence he feels. On the other hand, moving him from a given level in a chain of a given length in a small organization to the same position in a large organization in the same country is likely to make very little difference in his authority and influence. Furthermore, type of industry (considering the five types studied here) does not affect very much a member's response to these questions. Men in given positions defined in terms of distance from the top in a chain of a given length will be substantially alike with respect to the authority and influence they report, whether they are in a large or small plant of any type—furniture, plastics, foundry, metal works, or canning. The picture these data provide is consistent in general with the bureaucratic model. Authority and influence are defined in substantial degree for an incumbent by his position in the hierarchy, regardless of type of industry or size of plant.

But what about differences between countries in gradient of authority? We do not have precise statistical methods for evaluating gradients, and it is therefore necessary to employ several approximations. One important approximation is to define the hierarchical gradient as a straight line. We shall therefore fit straight lines to the data employing the slope of these lines as a measure of gradient. With the exception of six- and seven-level chains, the assumption of linearity is reasonably good and we shall present data along the way to help the reader evaluate how well the regression slopes represent some essential facts of hierarchy. However, because the data in six- and seven level chains do not conform well to the linear model, such chains are eliminated from this analysis. This restriction does not affect comparisons between the small plants because the six- and seven-level chains occur almost exclusively in the large plants. Furthermore, we have only a small number of cases within each country for each of the points in the long chains, and regressions computed from these chains are therefore not as stable as those in the shorter chains, where more substantial data are available. Nonetheless, we shall not ignore the data from the long chains in later analyses. Table 15 presents the regression slopes of authority and influence on hierarchical position. The table shows the slopes separately for chains of different length in small and large organizations in each of the countries. All of the regressions in Table 15 are positive, which means that authority-influence increases with hierarchical ascent.* We have placed parentheses around the Yugoslav data as a reminder of their low reliability. Several of the regressions are computed from fewer than fifteen cases, and they too are placed in parentheses. The column headed "all countries"

---

* We shall follow a convention throughout this and the remaining chapters of assigning a positive sign to regression lines that mean increasing value with hierarchical ascent; negative signs mean decreasing value. A regression slope can be understood as the amount of change in the dependent variable (vertical axis) associated with a unit change in hierarchical position (horizontal axis). For example, in the case of authority-influence, the regression line would be completely flat and the gradient (or slope) would be zero if authority-influence did not change with a change in hierarchical position. A slope of 1.0 means that a change from one rank to the next higher one is associated on the average with an increase of one unit of authority-influence defined in terms of our five-unit scale. A slope of —.5 would mean that persons at succeedingly higher levels have on the average one-half unit *less* authority-influence than persons immediately below them. It is not surprising therefore that all of the regression lines in Table 15 are positive.

Table 15. Gradients of Authority and Influence

Length of Chain	Italy	Austria	United States	Yugoslavia [a]	Kibbutz	All Countries [b]	N [b]
SMALL PLANTS							
2	—	(3.05)	(1.82)	—	1.77 [e]	1.95	58
3	1.64	1.66	1.21	(.72)	1.12	1.30	289
4	1.18	.96	1.04	(.29)	.74	.96	378
5	.88	(.70)	.95	(.08)	.60	.86	139
Average [c]	1.23	1.11	1.07	(.36)	.82		
LARGE PLANTS [f]							
3	—	1.13	.95	—	—	1.05 [d]	57 [d]
4	1.07	1.15	.87	(.25)	—	.99	154
5	.68	.80	.66	(.37)	—	.71	234
Average [c]	.88	.98	.76	(.31)	—		

[a] The Yugoslav data are in parentheses because of their unreliability. The other coefficients in parentheses are computed from fewer than 15 cases.

[b] The Yugoslav data do not enter the computation of these columns.

[c] This average does not include chains with two levels in the small plants and with three levels in the large plants.

[d] Includes 10 cases from Italy and Yugoslavia.

[e] Compared to the other countries, plants in kibbutzim have a relatively large number of persons in two-level chains. One plant has an unusual organizational structure with 12 production workers directly subordinate to the top man. Six of these persons are in the sample. The kibbutz plants also have a number of staff personnel who do not have subordinates. These persons, responsible for finance, marketing, accounting, and design rely for some assistance on general kibbutz administration.

[f] We were able to collect data in an additional foundry of several hundred employees in Austria and the United States. Because of the desirability of enhancing our Ns, we include these additional data in the computation of gradients throughout the research. Plants do not differ in gradient as a function of type of industry (for example, foundry, plastics), and we control statistically for length of chain, which is a major determinant of gradient. Hence the addition of these two plants among the group of large plants in the United States and Austria is not likely to bias our conclusions.

provides an estimate when gradients from all countries are combined. The rows labeled "average" are simple unweighted averages of the gradients within the plants of each country. The two-level chains are excluded from this average in the small plants in order to maintain comparability among countries, since all of them do not have two-level chains. In large plants the three-level chains are eliminated from the average because of insufficient data in Italian and Yugoslav plants. This average is therefore only a very rough guide to the differences between countries.

Table 15 repeats some of the features of hierarchy that we have seen above, and it suggests some additional facts for consideration. First, the relatively participative kibbutz (and Yugoslav) plants have less steep gradients than the other plants, but nonetheless they do have gradients. In fact, gradients of authority and influence in the plants of the four countries (exclusive of Yugoslavia) are not very different. Thus, authority and influence have a clear and sharp hierarchical distribution even under the very special and highly participative conditions of the kibbutz. Second, short chains have steeper gradients than long chains. The column in Table 15 labeled "all countries" shows this general tendency regardless of country. Finally, the similarity between the small and large plants in their pattern of results is striking and an analysis of covariance that compares the slopes of the small and large plants shows these slopes not to differ significantly. For chains of a given length, size of plant appears to have little predictable effect on the magnitude of the gradient. Thus this analysis of covariance is in essential agreement with the multiple classification analysis reported above.

In order to help the reader interpret the scores of Table 15 and those of subsequent tables we have plotted in Figure 8 the regression lines for chains of different length separately for large and small organizations. The slopes of the lines in this figure correspond to the coefficients in the column labeled "all countries" and were drawn through the intercepts computed in a regression analysis. The regression lines for six- and seven-length chains (which occur almost exclusively in large plants) are shown in Figure 8, even though the corresponding coefficients are not presented in Table 15. In fact, the straight line is not a very bad fit for the data concerning authority and influence in long chains. A striking feature of these data is the similarity of the lines for the small and large plants. For chains of length 3, 4, and 5, which are found in both small and large plants, the lines in small plants are almost identical to those in the large.

Table 16.   Gradients of "Ideal" Authority and Influence

Plant Size	Italy	Austria	United States	Yugoslavia	Kibbutz
SMALL					
Average	1.00	.94	.76	.57	.46
LARGE					
Average	.64	.67	.47	.22	—

Note: In order to simplify this table and the following tables of gradients, we do not present information about the number of cases upon which each gradient is computed. The reader can assume that each gradient for the small plants in each country is computed from about 160 cases, except in kibbutzim where the number of cases is about 320. For the large plants the number of cases per country is about 120.

Table 16 shows the regression slopes for the "ideal" amount of authority and influence reported by respondents. We simplify this table as we shall the remaining tables where gradients are presented by showing only the gradients averaged for the three-, four-, and five-level chains in the small plants and the four- and five-level chains in the large. The reader can safely assume that with few exceptions short chains have steeper gradients than long chains, as in the data we have already seen.

The results of Table 16 are essentially like those of Table 15, although, with the possible exception of the Yugoslav plants, the "ideal" slopes are flatter than the "actual." This flattening of the "ideal" distribution occurs because persons at the bottom of the hierarchy desire a greater increase in their authority and influence than do persons at upper levels, which the reader can see hinted in Figure 6. In the kibbutz plants, however, there is an additional reason for a flattening of the

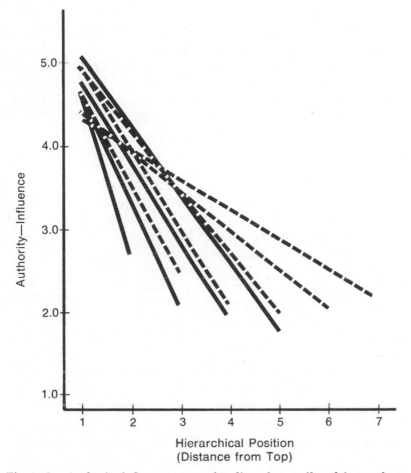

Figure 8.   Authority-influence; regression lines for small and large plants and chains of different length. Solid line is small plants; dashed line is large plants.

ideal curve. Only in these plants do managers want *less* authority than they have. Because of the "negative balance of rewards" and the equalitarian norms, members are reluctant to seek authority.

Opportunities on the Job

Persons at higher more than at lower levels have opportunities to use their own ideas, learn new things, and employ their skills. Such opportunities have been explored in earlier research. They resemble what Blauner defines as non-alienating aspects of work and they have been found by some authors to relate substantially to the satisfaction and involvement of employees (Argyris, 1957; Blauner, 1964; Lawler and Hackman, 1972; Paul and others, 1969; Turner and Lawrence, 1965). These opportunities represent rewards implicit in work and differences in such rewards between persons of different rank help explain the impact of hierarchy on the reactions and adjustments of members. We therefore asked:

1. In your work, to what extent can you:
   (a) Learn new things?
   (b) Use your own ideas?
   (c) Do interesting work?
   (d) Use your skills, knowledge, and abilities?
   (e) Talk with other people during work time?
   (f) Decide your own pace of work? *

A response to each item was checked on a five-point scale from "not at all," to "very much."

A second question parallel to the above asked: "2. In your work, to what extent *would you like to:*" The response categories to this question were precisely the same as to the first.

Data in response to the first question document the general tendency that jobs at upper levels, more than at lower, provide members with opportunities to learn, to use their skills, to do interesting work, and so forth. Furthermore, they demonstrate some of the features of hierarchy that we inferred from Figure 7: the relative steepness of the short chains and the peculiar curvelinearity in the long. The hierarchical distribution of opportunities perceived by organization members, however, shows a less steep gradient than the distribution of authority and influence. Nonetheless the importance of hierarchy as a determinant of these opportunities is demonstrated

---

* A final item included in the question, "Have authority over other people," is not included in this index because it forms part of the authority-influence index discussed in the previous section.

by the results of a multiple classification analysis similar to that discussed in the previous section. Of the factors considered in this analysis, hierarchical position is the single most important determinant of the opportunities provided by a job (Beta = .53). From the point of view of the opportunities measured, a member would in general do better to move up the hierarchy in his own plant than to move to a position at the same level as his own in one of the other plants, whether foreign or domestic, included in this study. However, while this proposition applies to an "average" respondent, it does not apply equally to all respondents. For example, the relationship between hierarchical position and opportunities provided by the job is not the same in all countries, and moving up the hierarchy therefore is not equally advantageous in all countries, as Table 17 indicates. This table suggests differences between

Table 17. Gradients of Opportunities Provided by the Job

Plant Size	Italy	Austria	United States	Yugoslavia	Kibbutz
SMALL Average	.71	.52	.57	.25	.45
LARGE Average	.56	.63	.38	.28	—

countries which correspond, more or less, to the degree of participativeness of the plants in the countries—the steepest gradients occurring in the Italian plants, the flattest in the Yugoslav and kibbutz plants. Rank in the hierarchy appears to have more impact in the former than in the latter organizations.

The multiple classification analysis suggests that country does have some value as a predictor of the opportunities reported by organization members (Beta = .33), although not as great a value as hierarchical position. Figure 9 helps to illustrate the combined effect of country and hierarchical position. The lines in the figure represent approximations based on the linear regression model in which the average of the slopes for three-,

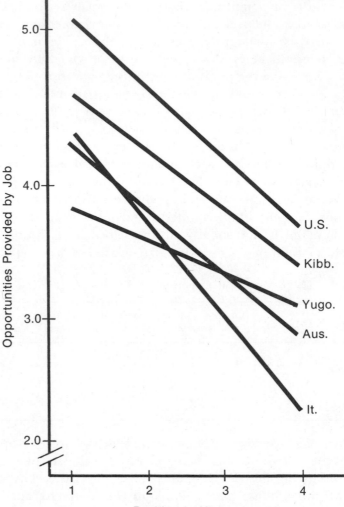

Figure 9. Distribution of opportunities provided by the job (based on a linear approximation for three-, four-, and five-level chains combined in small organizations).

four-, and five-level chains in small plants are drawn through the average intercepts for these chains in the respective countries. The reader might interpret these lines as representing the gradients in an average chain of about length 4. This figure shows how advancement in the hierarchy of the Italian plants yields the greatest rate of increase in opportunities provided by the job. Despite this rate of increasing opportunities that accompany advancement, however, an advancing Italian member is not likely to catch up to his counterparts in the Yugoslav and Austrian plants until he approaches the very top of his organization. Furthermore, he may never catch up to his counterparts in the kibbutz and American organizations. The Italian worker starts out too far behind, in addition to which the likelihood of advancement is not very great for members in the Italian plants, as we have seen in Table 12. The situation of the Austrian member is not very different from that of the Italian. The Yugoslav rank-and-file worker, on the other hand, does moderately well compared to the worker in Italian and Austrian plants but advancement in the hierarchy does not pay off as well, so that the advancing member's advantage relative to his counterparts in the other countries declines, until as a manager he falls behind. These data point to what is widely recognized among students of organization in Yugoslavia as a problem for managers in Yugoslav plants.

With the exception of the small plants in Yugoslavia, data concerning the opportunities members would like in their jobs yield gradients that are flatter than those in Figure 9, which implies that, except in Yugoslavia, the discrepancy between the opportunities members have and what they would like to have is greater at the bottom than at the top of the hierarchy. In Yugoslavia, the managers apparently experience the greater discrepancy. In any event, differences between countries in gradient of "ideal" opportunities do not appear great although among the small plants the kibbutz rank last in magnitude of gradient (.27) and the Italian rank first (.48). Among the large plants the Yugoslav and American plants have equally low gradients (.26), and the Austrian plants have the highest gradient (.40).

Physical Qualities of the Job

Each respondent was asked to respond to the following:

3. Mark with a check along the following lines more or less near to the end that most closely describes your work.

Nine scales were defined in terms of the following end points:

(a)	tiring . . .	not tiring
(b)	unhealthful . . .	not unhealthful
(c)	physical . . .	mental
(d)	dirty . . .	clean
(e)	heavy . . .	light
(f)	same tasks during the day . . .	different tasks during the day
(g)	dangerous . . .	safe
(h)	alone . . .	together with others
(i)	dependent on others . . .	independent of others

In general the left end of each scale implies an undesirable quality and the right end a relatively desirable one; all of the items were coded in terms of a seven-point scale except in Austria, where a five-point scale was used. Hence the Austrian data are excluded from Table 18. The responses to these items intercorrelated well exclusive of the last two, and an index was therefore formed without these two.

The data from the small plants conform reasonably well to the expectation that gradients in the formally participative kibbutz and Yugoslav plants will be flatter than those in the less participative Italian and American plants, but the results among the large organizations distinctly do not conform to our expectation. We considered in the previous chapter the argument that technology plays a more important role in determining reactions of members in large plants than in small. We wonder, therefore, whether the failure of our hypothesis among the large plants may be attributable to the lesser importance of ideology among the large plants, especially with respect to these data concerning physical conditions of work.

Salary

High salary is an important reward of rank in most work organizations. Kibbutzim are a notable exception; members in kibbutz plants do not receive salaries beyond a small allowance provided all members. The hierarchical gradients of salary, however, are not uniformly steep in all organizations where salary is a reward of rank, as Table 19 indicates. This table presents the gradients as a ratio of the regression slope relative to the average salary at the bottom of the hierarchy. (Different currencies in the four countries render a direct comparison of regression slopes less meaningful.) For example, in small Italian plants, the average increment in salary (slope) that accompanies a unit increase in rank is 2.85 times the average salary of persons at the bottom of the Italian plants. In small

Table 18.   Gradients of Job Qualities

Plant Size	Italy	Austria	United States	Yugoslavia	Kibbutz
SMALL	.65	—	.80	.58	.39
LARGE	.36	—	.55	.68	—

Table 19.   Gradients of Salary
(Ratio of Slope to Salary at Lowest Rank)

Plant Size	Italy	Austria	United States	Yugoslavia	Kibbutz
SMALL	2.85	.95	1.41	.49	.00
LARGE	2.18	.80	.61	.53	—

Yugoslav plants, the corresponding increment is only .49 times the average salary of the bottom persons. It is apparent from these data that hierarchical gradients of salary are rather steep in Italian plants and flat in the Yugoslav. American and Austrian plants are intermediate, and of course the kibbutz plants have a completely flat gradient. We thus see further evidence for the relative importance of hierarchy in the Italian, Austrian, and American plants compared to the Yugoslav and kibbutz.

The difference between the large and small American organizations is striking. It occurs primarily because top managers in the small plants earn a good deal more than their counterparts in the large. For example, the average top man in the small plants has a monthly salary close to $2,500. In large plants the figure is close to $1,900. This difference is probably explained by the fact that the manager in four of the five small plants is the owner, and family members are included among the top management. On the other hand, the manager is owner in only two of the large plants. Furthermore, these salaries do not include special bonuses or stock options which are part of the monetary rewards of the top personnel in the large plants (as well as in the small).

The contrast between the relatively steep gradients in the small American plants and the flat gradients in the Yugoslav can be seen in the simple comparison of the top to the bottom salaries in the two countries. For example, in the small American five-level chains the average monthly salary at the top is $2,400, and at the bottom it is $390. Thus the top men make 6.2 times as much as those at the bottom. In the three- and two-level chains the ratios of top to bottom salaries are 5.4 and 4.4 respectively. In the small Yugoslav plants, which are almost identical to the large, the top salaries are 2,130, 1,750, and 1,600 dinars in the five-, four-, and three-level chains respectively and the bottom salaries in these chains are 600, 750, and 720 dinars, making ratios of 3.1, 2.3, and 2.2. The American ratios of top to bottom salaries in small plants are therefore about two times the ratios in Yugoslavia. In Italy these ratios are about four to five times those in Yugoslavia. A rough comparison of these data to those in China, where an effort is being made to minimize hierarchical inequality can be seen in computations by Whyte (1973) based on data collected by Richman (1969). The ratio of maximum to minimum salary is generally less than 2 in Chinese plants in the size range of the *large* plants of this study. This ratio implies gradients in Chinese plants lower than those in the plants of this study— excepting those in kibbutzim. With respect to financial reward, at least, Chinese industrial plants are close to the equalitarian end of the continuum, although they clearly fall within the limits defined by the plants of this study.

Demographic Characteristics and Hierarchy

Persons at different positions in a hierarchy can be expected to differ in characteristics such as age, education, sex, and seniority—especially where hierarchy is stressed. Gradients in these characteristics may reflect implicit (if not explicit) criteria for advancement. Steep gradients imply restriction or discrimination in the promotion (or election) of members. Flat gradients, insofar as the characteristics in question are concerned, imply that anyone can advance in the hierarchy.

Age. Table 20 shows the average age of respondents in the small and large plants respectively. The age of members in kibbutz plants is high compared with that in the other plants since kibbutz industry was created partly as a means of employing older persons who find difficult the rigors of agricultural work. In the other countries, respondents from the large plants are slightly older than those from the small plants because of the larger proportion of managerial personnel in the sample of the large plants.

The lines of Figure 10 represent approximations based on the linear regression model. Among the plants represented in this figure the size of gradient conforms well to the ranking of the plants on participativeness and to the emphasis placed on hierarchy that we have inferred from the data presented so far. The Italian and Austrian plants show the steepest gradients and look a good deal more like gerontocracies than the kibbutz plants, which appear rather equalitarian with respect to age. But again we find little support in the large plants for expected differences among countries. The range of gradients for the large plants runs from .26 in Austria and Italy to .36 in Yugoslavia, by way of contrast with the small plants, where the range runs from .19 in the kibbutz plants to .80 in the Italian.*

* Small discrepancies may be apparent between average scores such as those in Table 20, and averages inferred from best fit lines such as those shown in Figure 10. These discrepancies, which occur between several tables and figures in this book, have several explanations: (1) the best-fit lines are approximations; (2) only persons in chains of lengths 3, 4, and 5 enter into the calculations of the best-fit lines shown in the figures, while data from all respondents enter into the averages of the tables; (3) the scores of the table refer to an "average" person near but not at the bottom of the hierarchy; (4) the lines in the figure are arbitrarily cut at point 4 on the horizontal axis on the assumption that each line (based on three-, four- and five-level chains) illustrates a chain of 4 levels.

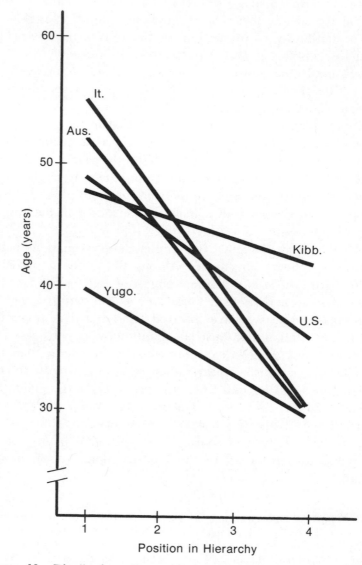

Figure 10. Distribution of age of organization members (based on a linear approximation for three-, four-, and five-level chains combined in small organizations).

Education. Responses to the following question were employed to compute the best-fit lines of Figure 11:

Table 20. Age of Members

Plant Size	Italy	Austria	United States	Yugoslavia	Kibbutz
SMALL	35	35	39	33	43
LARGE	38	38	40	37	—

Table 21. Level of Education of Members *

Plant Size	Italy	Austria	United States	Yugoslavia	Kibbutz
SMALL	2.8	3.9	4.9	3.3	4.7
LARGE	3.4	4.4	5.0	3.8	—

Note: * See text for scale.

Table 22. Plant Seniority of Members (years)

Plant Size	Italy	Austria	United States	Yugoslavia	Kibbutz
SMALL	5.8	4.4	4.2	5.0	5.2
LARGE	6.1	6.3	5.5	6.0	—

57. How many years of school did you finish?
   1. Less than four years
   2. Four to six years
   3. Six to eight years
   4. Eight to ten years
   5. Ten to twelve years
   6. More than twelve years

This figure is an idealized representation, based on the linear model, of data that are not in all cases linear, yet it portrays well in summary form some of the essential facts concerning the hierarchical distribution of education. The contrast between countries is striking. The Italian and kibbutz plants represent extremes, the gradients being small in kibbutzim and veering in the negative direction (−13). The Yugoslav plants, however, show relatively steep gradients (.92), and these plants rank second only to the Italian (1.08) in magnitude of gradient. Thus, with respect to education, the Yugoslav plants (large as

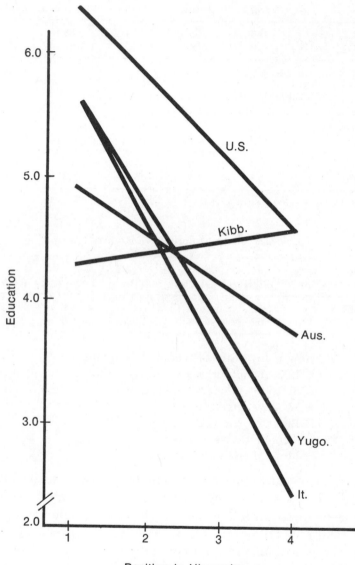

Figure 11. Distribution of education of members (based on a linear approximation for three-, four-, and five-level chains in small organizations).

well as small) are out of step with their general tendency to show flat gradients. (In fact Yugoslav plants rank first in gradient among the large plants, with a score of 1.00.) Yugoslav plants are also similar to the Italian in average level of education of members, as can be seen in Table 21.

Figure 11 shows the average regression lines drawn through the average intercepts for chains of length 3, 4, and 5 in small plants of the respective countries. This figure is an idealized representation based on the linear model of data that are not in all cases linear, yet it portrays well in summary form some of the essential facts concerning the hierarchical distribution of education. Kibbutz workers at the bottom of the hierarchy rank first among workers of the five countries in education, followed by the American. Italian workers rank last. The relative level of education near the top of the five groups of organizations is quite different, the Yugoslav and Italian managers appearing to be an educated elite in their plants.

Seniority in the Plant. Respondents were asked in an interview, "How long have you worked in this plant?" Responses were coded on an eight-point scale from less than six months to over twenty years. Table 22 shows the average level of seniority in the plants of the five countries, and Figure 12 shows the idealized best-fit straight lines for the data in the small plants. Seniority is a noteworthy variable since it is the only one for which the gradient in kibbutz plants is on the average as high as or higher than that in the other plants. This fact may seem to contradict the results of Table 14, which shows kibbutz members ranking behind all others in citing seniority as a requirement for advancement. It need not be a contradiction, however. Managers in kibbutz plants are elected, and experience is probably an important consideration in these elections. While seniority per se is not a requirement for advancement, knowledge acquired through experience may be a requirement. Thus, although kibbutz plants show flat gradients on the variables we have considered so far, they are relatively steep in the gradient of seniority that accompanies hierarchy. By way of contrast, members in small Yugoslav plants, where the gradient of seniority is flat, are more likely than

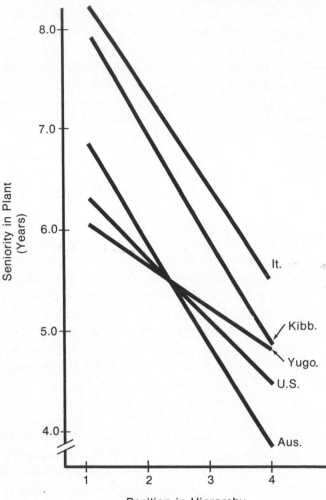

Figure 12.   Distribution of seniority of members (based on linear approximation for three-, four-, and five-level chains in small plants).

kibbutz members to see seniority as an important requirement for getting ahead. But compared to other requirements listed in Table 14, seniority does not rank high for the Yugoslavs.

Thus the gradients of seniority in the small plants do not fit the hypothesis of flat gradients in the formally participative systems. Nor do the data from the large plants fit the hypothesis. The largest gradient (.69) occurs in the Austrian plants, but the smallest (.27) occurs in the American plants.

Sex. The hierarchical distribution of sex departs radically from linearity, and the regression line therefore is a very poor representation of gradient. Virtually no women are found in top positions in any of the countries, and we therefore present the data in terms of two hierarchical categories, managerial and non-managerial. The former includes persons who have one or more subordinates; the latter do not have subordinates. Plants grouped by country differ in their proportion of women, but almost all of the women in these plants, regardless of country, are at the bottom of the hierarchy, as Table 23 indicates. For example, 5 percent of the kibbutz managers compared to 27 percent of the non-managers are women (but none of the top personnel are women). The Austrian small plants stand out in the percent of managerial (as well as non-managerial) women, and one small Austrian plant as well as one American is headed by a woman. Ironically, private ownership, which may be less equalitarian than collective ownership according to many criteria, has an "equalitarian" effect in the case of these female directors, who happen to be tied by family to the ownership. But none of the plants are equalitarian in the sense of equal proportions of managerial and non-managerial women, and the kibbutz and Yugoslav plants do not except themselves from this generalization. Nonetheless, the difference between the proportion of women who are managers (or supervisors) and those who are not managers—which is a very rough measure of gradient— appears from Table 23 a little lower in the formally participative compared to the non-participative systems.

Summary and Conclusions

The kibbutz and Yugoslav plants are formally more participative than the American, Austrian, and Italian. The data of this chapter suggest also that hierarchy is in a number of respects less salient in the former than in the latter, at least among the small plants. Table 24 summarizes the data that illustrate the relative saliency of hierarchy in the plants of the

Table 23. Percent of Managerial and Non-Managerial Persons Who Are Women

Hierarchical Position	Italy	Austria	United States	Yugoslavia	Kibbutz	(N) All Members
SMALL PLANTS						
(a) Managers	2	17	8	4	5	240
(b) Non-managers	34	59	40	29	27	741
Total % Women	24	42	30	22	23	981
(b)-(a)	32	42	32	25	22	—
LARGE PLANTS						
(a) Managers	0	4	2	7	—	417
(b) Non-managers	39	36	35	34	—	359
Total % Women	18	18	16	26	—	776
(b)-(a)	39	32	33	27	—	—

respective countries. Among the small plants, the Italian and kibbutz provide the most consistent contrast, the highly participative kibbutz plants being clearly less hierarchic than the non-participative Italian. The small Yugoslav plants, like the kibbutz, show a relatively low saliency of hierarchy. The picture among the large plants, however, is less clear, and the Yugoslav plants are not the least hierarchic according to the summary measure of Table 24.

One indication of emphasis on hierarchy is the interest on the part of members to advance in the hierarchy. Such interest is relatively low in the formally participative plants. Desire to move up is quite strong in the American plants and moderately so in the Italian and Austrian. Furthermore, although the desire of kibbutz members to advance in their plant hierarchies is relatively low, the actual chances of moving up are greater in these plants than elsewhere and the kibbutz plants are therefore highly equalitarian in this respect. Lack of opportunities for mobility defines the extent to which hierarchy takes on the character of a rigid status or class system, and gradients of authority and reward are likely to mean something different to members in a system where they are placed permanently in positions of fixed status than where persons at lower levels can expect to move into higher positions.

Rotation, which is part of the participative system in kibbutzim, probably explains the high likelihood of advancement in kibbutz plants. Rotation implies also the probability of moving down, laterally, or out, but movement downward does not have the implications for kibbutz members that it has for members in other systems. Kibbutzniks may suffer some loss of reward associated with high rank, but this loss may be outweighed by reduction in the burdens related to managerial responsibility. Similarly, Yugoslav members may not lose or gain as much as their counterparts in the American, Italian, and Austrian plants by mobility in the hierarchy. Gradients of pay, and of other attractive qualities of the job, are in general relatively flat in the Yugoslav plants, as in the kibbutz. But the physical qualities of work show a relatively sharp gradient in the large Yugoslav plants. These physical characteristics, deter-

Table 24. Rank Order of Plants in the Five Countries on Measures of the Emphasis Placed on Hierarchy

	Small Plants					Large Plants			
	Italy	Austria	United States	Yugo-slavia	Kibbutz	Italy	Austria	United States	Yugo-slavia
Mobility Aspirations	2	3	1	4	5	3	2	1	4
Unlikelihood of Advancement	2	1	4	3	5	1.5	3	4	1.5
Gradient of									
Authority-influence	1	2	3	(5)	4	1	2	3	(4)
Job opportunities	1	3	2	5	4	2	1	3	4
Job qualities	2	—	1	3	4	3	—	2	1
Salary	1	3	2	4	5	1	2	3	4
Age	1	2	3	4	5	2	3.5	3.5	1
Education	1	4	3	2	5	2	3	4	1
Plant seniority	3	2	4	5	1	3	1	4	2
Sex	(2.5)	(1)	(2.5)	(4)	(5)	(1)	(3)	(2)	(4)
Average Rank	1.6	2.3	2.6	3.9	4.3	2.0	2.3	3.0	2.6

mined largely by technological considerations, may not be very amenable in the large Yugoslav plants to modification that would mitigate inequalities along the hierarchy.

The relative deemphasis of hierarchy in the kibbutz and small Yugoslav plants is reflected in the flatness of gradients defining the distribution of several demographic characteristics as well as of reward. There are notable exceptions, however. The distribution of sex is clearly hierarchical in all of the countries. With minor exceptions, women are located at the bottom of the hierarchy. Kibbutz and Yugoslav small plants are not much less hierarchic in this respect than the other plants.

Furthermore, Yugoslav plants, like the Italian, are characterized by very steep gradients of education, with rank-and-file workers in both these groups of plants being quite low in level of education, and managers looking like an educated elite. Lack of education appears to set sharp limitations on advancement in the Italian and Yugoslav plants. This limitation may in time be mitigated in the case of Yugoslavia by workers' universities through which members might increase their education, but the level of education of workers is nonetheless low and the possibility of advancement is therefore limited for many.

On the other hand, kibbutz plants provide a remarkable contradiction to the tenet that superiors be more highly educated than subordinates. In kibbutz plants all members have a reasonably high level of education, and subordinates are as highly educated as their superiors—if not more so. The generally high level of education combined with the flat gradient define one of the conditions under which rotation functions in kibbutz plants. Each member is reasonably well educated in the rudimentary intellectual skills that a supervisor or manager needs. He then acquires through experience the practical skills that may qualify him and that lead to his election as a supervisor or manager. Thus kibbutz plants stand out in the steepness of their hierarchical gradient of seniority, which is really a gradient of experience. Seniority is the only variable considered in this chapter for which the gradient is steeper in the kibbutz plants than in the others.

Authority and influence are basic correlates of hierarchy and an index which combines a measure of these variables shows sharp hierarchical gradients in the plants of all countries, with the possible exception of the Yugoslav, where the data on this index are unreliable. Excepting Yugoslavia then, the Italian plants show the steepest and the kibbutz plants the least steep gradient, but the most striking feature of these data is the extent to which authority and influence increase with hierarchical ascent regardless of country. It is difficult to escape the implication, even in the highly participative kibbutz plants, that authority and influence increase substantially with rank.

This conclusion may not surprise students of organization, but the data of this chapter suggest several additional features of hierarchy that we could not anticipate on the basis of the existing literature on organizations, although we think these features may be general to organizations. We were surprised to learn, for example, that short chains have sharper gradients than long, and that as a consequence small organizations have steeper gradients than large. Large organizations are not predictably different from small in the steepness of their hierarchical gradients, however, when chains of equal length are compared. This contradicts our intuitive expectation that large organizations and tall hierarchies imply steep gradients. Furthermore, size of organization and type of industry (within the range of the five types included in this study) have relatively little value as predictors of most of the variables with which we are concerned in this chapter. The single best way for the "average" member in this study to increase his authority and influence or the quality of his job (exclusive of salary) is to move up his own hierarchy, rather than to take a comparable position in another plant, domestic or foreign. There are exceptions to this general rule, however, depending upon where the aspiring member is located. Some hierarchies, like the Italian, are "better" to move up than others because reward increases at a greater rate in the Italian plants. But the chances of moving up are not very good in the Italian plants. Aspiring members in the middle of long chains may also be exceptions to the generalization suggested above because of the flatness in the middle range of the long hierarchies. In these long chains, movement in the middle range is not likely to make as much difference to a member in terms of his authority and influence or the other opportunities measured as does movement near the bottom or near the top of his chain.

The data of this chapter have implications for traditional arguments about control and stratification in social systems. According to some sociologists, special rewards are needed to induce able persons to undertake training for crucial roles in the system and to assume the responsibilities of high rank. (For a discussion, see Davis and Moore, 1945; Tumin, 1953, 1969; Davis, 1953; Wesolowoski, 1966; Parsons, 1954.) Nonetheless, kibbutz plants function effectively without a stratified system of monetary rewards. Furthermore, prestige is of relatively little significance as a reward of the managerial role in the kibbutz plants (Table 13) even though approval is important (Table 6). Davis and Moore (1945) distinguish between prestige and approval. Prestige is assigned to a role, but approval or esteem is tendered only to those who perform a role well. Leaders in kibbutz plants, being highly visible, derive rewards associated with such approval. They also derive rewards from their sense of commitment to the success of the plant (Table 10) and from certain intrinsic qualities of high position such as variety in the work and independence (Table 13), which Tumin argues are important inducements for persons to take leadership roles. These rewards of leadership do not outweigh the costs for many kibbutz members, however, and members of kibbutz plants (as well as of the Yugoslav) are not as anxious to advance in the hierarchy as are members in the plants of the other systems (Table 11). This is the problem suggested by those who argue for a stratified system of material rewards. Despite this problem, however, kibbutz plants compare favorably in efficiency and profitability to plants of similar size and technology in Israel (Melman, 1970–1971).

The model of stratification that maintains the necessity of sharp inequality of economic reward and prestige does not apply well to kibbutz plants. The model may be more appropriate in describing the plants of the other systems, but even these systems differ in their conformance to the model. The Yugoslav plants and even the American show flatter gradients of monetary reward than do the Italian, and members in the Yugoslav and American plants compared to those in the Italian attach relatively little importance to prestige as a reward of high rank. The American plants function as effectively as the Italian in terms of most criteria but with less inequality than the Italian. A normative model that advocates stratification of reward might therefore consider the problem of too much inequality as well as not enough.

But whether inequality of material reward is functionally necessary or not, such inequality is inevitable according to Michels (1959) because of the inclination of leaders to take a disproportionate share of the material rewards available in the organization. The organization leaders acquire privileges which they try to protect by restricting entry of others into leadership roles. (For a discussion, see Lipset and others, 1956; Tumin, 1969.) As a consequence, opportunities for advancement are limited, an elite develops, and the organization divides into the leaders and the led. An exploitative oligarchy is the inevitable result. This is the "iron law of oligarchy" proposed as a universal truth by Michels and others. The evidence of this chapter suggests, however, that some plants fit this elite, oligarchic model better than others do, and that the goodness of fit is inversely proportional to the formal participativeness of the plants. The kibbutz plants with their rotation principle, relatively high mobility opportunities, high level and flat gradients of education do not fit the model well. The equalitarian reward system helps make rotation work. Because sharp differences in material rewards do not exist, members do not compete for office; on the contrary, some have to be persuaded to assume the burdens of leadership. "Monopolization" of leadership by a few is therefore not so likely to occur as in other systems. The Yugoslav small plants differ in degree from the kibbutz. Gradients of monetary reward exist, but they are not as steep as in the Italian, Austrian, and United States plants. The steep gradients of education and the low level of opportunity for advancement, however, represent serious, if temporary obstacles to the realization of a more equalitarian organization.

The Italian plants fit better than the others the elite, oligarchic model—and it is interesting to see that the classical proponents of this model—Pareto, Mosca, Dorso, and Michels—all lived and wrote in Italy. These plants have steep gradients of monetary reward and of education along with restricted opportunities for advancement and high value placed on prestige associated with rank. These plants, more than the others, operate under conditions that imply conflict between the leaders and the led, especially since many members have mobility aspirations that are not likely to be realized. The conflict and frustration implicit in this system are manifest in the dissatisfaction and alienation and in the relatively sharp hierarchical gradients of reaction and adjustment that we shall explore in the next chapter.

Thus Michel's iron law of oligarchy and other elite models cannot be said to define absolute and universal laws. They no doubt apply well to many organizations, but their appropriateness is a matter of degree. They describe the Italian plants better than the American, and the American better than the kibbutz. These models assume an inherent conflict of interest between members. Organizational forms based on this assumption may in fact create conditions that justify the assumption. On the other hand, the participative model more than the oligarchic assumes a prevailing common interest, and organizations based on this model may create conditions that justify the assumption. Some models of organization are in this sense self-fulfilling prophecies. But organizations exist in a larger social context where assumptions of common interest or of conflict of interest prevail, or where the appropriateness of one assumption or another may be justified. The kibbutz plant exists in a society where members share a common way of life and all have a more or less equal stake in the success and survival of that society. Common interest is explicitly assumed by most members. Italian plants, on the other hand, function in a society which has significant elitist bases and where status,

prestige, and power traditionally have been restricted to a privi-
leged few. Italian society is changing, but many long-standing
traditions still apply in some degree.

Students of organization have argued that differences in
power and in the rewards associated with rank contribute to
conflict and to dysfunctional reactions on the part of organization members. Formal systems of participation, like those in
Yugoslav and kibbutz plants, are designed to mitigate these
dysfunctional effects by reducing some of the inequalities that
ordinarily accompany hierarchy. We shall explore some of these
hypothesized effects in the next chapter. The data of this
chapter and of the previous one lead us to suggest several
additional hypotheses and to pose some questions about the
conditions that may mitigate (or accentuate) the effects of
hierarchy.

First, the plants of the five countries differ not only in
the gradients of reward that accompany hierarchy, but in the
average level of reward, and we suspect that the effect of a
hierarchical gradient of reward will be different under conditions where the base is high compared to where it is low.

Second, we suspect that the effects of inequalities in
reward that accompany hierarchy may depend on the degree
of upward mobility of members. A member at the bottom of
a hierarchy will react differently to the deprivations of his
position where he anticipates the possibility of changing that
position compared to where he sees little possibility of change.
The plants in the five countries suggest different combinations
of distribution of reward and opportunities for mobility. The
kibbutz plants are equalitarian in distribution of reward and
members perceive great opportunities for upward mobility.
The Yugoslav plants are also relatively equalitarian in reward,
but members see little opportunity for advancement. The
American, Austrian, and Italian plants, on the other hand, are
characterized by inequality in distribution of reward. However,
opportunities for advancement, as perceived by members at
least, are relatively good in the American plants and poor in
the Austrian and Italian.

Third, participativeness within a plant may be defined

in terms of formal structures and procedures, such as workers' councils and election of managers, or it may be defined informally, in terms of interpersonal relations between superiors and subordinates, as we have seen in Chapter Three. We propose that informal participativeness may mitigate the effects of hierarchy, especially where the organization is not formally participative.

Fourth, differences between the large plants in the gradients examined in this chapter and in degree of participativeness examined in Chapter Three are not as simple and clear as among the small. The highly participative kibbutz plants contribute to the range of differences among the small plants, but not the large, and the absence of the kibbutz plants may explain the less sharp differentiation among the latter. But even when kibbutz plants are removed from the analysis, the small plants appear to differ between themselves more than do the large. Two further explanations, therefore, deserve consideration. The first is statistical. Because of the sampling procedure a greater proportion of managerial personnel are sampled in the large than in the small organizations. This means a greater proportion of persons at middle levels where the hierarchy tends to flatten out. The relatively heavy weighting of middle-level persons working in the large plants has the effect of reducing the slope of the regression line in the former compared to the latter, and therefore of reducing the differences between the large plants of the respective countries. But another explanation for the lack of clear difference among the large plants is suggested by the intriguing thesis of Kerr and others (1964) concerning the coming together of industrial societies. Large organizations more than small, like organizations of the future compared to those of the past, may be affected by technological and administrative considerations that supercede ideological. Large organizations that are alike in technology may conform, more than technologically alike small organizations, to a universal, standardized format. We therefore wonder whether the small size of kibbutz plants is not an important condition for maintaining the highly participative system of these plants. Is it possible that large organizations more than small, whether in kibbutzim, Italy, or Siberia, follow a universal "logic of industrialization"? The proponents of such logic argue that because large organizations are more complex administratively and more sophisticated technologically they are also likely to be more professional managerially—and the professional manager follows a rationality very much like that of other professional managers regardless of culture. In the small organization where technology may be less important than in the large, managers will manage according to whatever "theory" of organization happens to prevail—and this varies among cultures and political systems and, indeed, even among managers within a culture. But where technology is costly and where *it* rather than human energy determines the efficiency of the productive process, the argument will seem more compelling that organizations be set up to maximize the machine's contribution rather than to satisfy an ideological principle or a social norm. And the logic of the machine does not vary from place to place. Principles of ownership may continue to differ among systems reflecting ideological differences, but such principles will survive only insofar as they do not contradict the implacable "logic of industrialization." Furthermore, ownership is only one among a number of potential determinants of organizational effectiveness and it may not, after all, be the most important determinant. If in time it proves to be of major importance then *it* will become part of a universal rationality. Thus, common principles will grow up in organizations even in cultures and political systems that differ. This does not mean necessarily more hierarchy or less in future industrial organizations compared to past, only a more common rationality among these future organizations, whatever the consequences for hierarchy.

V

GRADIENTS
OF REACTION
AND ADJUSTMENT

W_e have seen evidence of differences in participativeness and of corresponding differences in emphasis placed on hierarchy in the plants of the five countries. The Italian, Austrian, and American plants are in a number of respects less participative and more hierarchical than the corresponding kibbutz and Yugoslav plants.

Participation has been justified on moral as well as pragmatic grounds. Morally, participation is associated with democratic and equalitarian values; participation is therefore valued where democracy and equality are valued. Pragmatically, participativeness is believed (by some) to be a highly effective system of organization. Among other things, participation reduces conflict and it mitigates, as we have proposed, many of the unintended and dysfunctional results of hierarchy. Several arguments have been offered in the literature for this effect.* Participative decisions are more likely than hierarchical to take into account the needs and interests of all parties. Through participation workers can influence decisions and perhaps even affect policy in ways that are consistent with their own self-interest, and these decisions and policies are less likely to seem arbitrary and disadvantageous. Participation therefore increases the identification of members with the organization and their motivation to contribute to the organizational effort. Individuals who participate in decisions feel some responsibility for carrying out these decisions.

Participation can also be satisfying as well as ego-enhancing for persons of low rank. For example, participation may involve group meetings where interesting topics are discussed. These meetings may include challenging activities that draw upon the intellectual, technological, and human relations skill of workers. Workers in the participative organization who contribute to decisions will therefore feel a sense of self-esteem as well as satisfaction that workers in the non-participative organization will not feel. Furthermore, interpersonal relations and communication in the participative system differ from those in the traditional bureaucracy. Where supervisors are supportive of their subordinates and receptive to their ideas and suggestions, they contribute to a sense of personal worth on the part of their subordinates. Supervisors do not transmit communiques and orders unilaterally from above, as in the traditional organization; the supervisor is someone to work with rather than against. Participation also encourages the exchange of feelings and ideas, thus reducing discrepancies in perceptions, ideals, and loyalties—discrepancies which exist characteristically between persons at different ranks and which may contribute to conflict.

Participation mitigates some of the effects of hierarchy by adding qualities of the managerial role to non-managerial jobs. Participation, to some degree, brings workers into management. Hierarchical gradients with respect to satisfaction, self-esteem, alienation, identification with and responsibility

* The following arguments are from Tannenbaum (1966).

for the enterprise should therefore be less steep in the participative organization than in the non-participative. Similarly, the participative organization will manifest fewer symptoms of disaffection and conflict between persons of different rank.

The above effects of participation, however, may not always be realized in organizations that are formally chartered according to participative principles. For one thing, an organization that is participative in formal plan may not be participative in actual operation. Furthermore, different systems of participation differ in their effects. For example, systems of *indirect* participation, in which workers elect representatives who participate in decision making, differ in their effects from systems in which participation is direct and more pervasively distributed in the organization (Kavčič and others, 1971; Lammers, 1967). Strauss (1963) has suggested a number of reasons why participation may not have the favorable effects that are predicted for it: "(1) individuals whose opinions have been rejected by the group may become alienated from it; (2) participation may lead to greater cohesion, but it may be cohesion against management; (3) participation may set up expectations of continued participation which management may not be able to satisfy; and (4) participation often takes a great deal of time, can be frustrating to those involved, and frequently results in watered-down solutions" (p. 70). Strauss' critique was developed primarily in the context of "Human Relations" approaches to participation, but it might apply to other approaches as well. We shall try to learn here whether in fact different forms of participativeness mitigate the effects of hierarchy, and if so, how.

We shall examine in this chapter differences in gradients of reaction and adjustment within the five countries in order to explore the hypothesis that these gradients will be less steep in the participative compared to the non-participative systems; and we shall explore how the correlates of hierarchy, including authority and reward, along with the demographic characteristics discussed in the previous chapter, help explain the impact of hierarchy on members. The reactions and adjustments we shall investigate include the member's (a) satisfactions with and attitudes toward the enterprise, (b) motivation in the plant, (c) psychological adjustment including feelings of alienation, and (d) perceptions and ideals regarding aspects of the enterprise and his role in it.

Satisfaction and Attitudes

Persons at higher levels are relatively advantaged when judged in terms of the values most members share; these persons have more authority and influence, greater opportunities provided by their job, higher salaries and other rewards. It follows that they should be more satisfied and have more favorable attitudes toward the enterprise than persons at lower levels. In fact a good deal of research in the United States and abroad, some of which is reviewed by Inkeles, supports this contention (Inkeles, 1960). The gradients of satisfaction and attitude, however, should be less steep in the participative systems, according to the theory we are exploring.

Job Satisfaction. Row 1 of Table 25 (p. 136) shows the average scores in the five countries computed from the responses to an index based on the following questions:

> 8. How much satisfaction do you get from your job in the plant compared to what you can do after leaving the plant?
>
> 9. Do you like working for this company?
>
> 10. Do you like the work you are doing in this plant?

Each question was answered on a five-point scale and high scores in Table 25 imply high satisfaction. Although the differences between countries appear small, they are significant statistically at the .05 level or better. The kibbutz and Yugoslav plants, contrary to our expectation based on the participativeness of these plants, do not rank high on these items. Yugoslavia does stand out, however, on one item (question 8) within the index, ranking first in the satisfaction members report they derive from their job *compared to* the satisfaction they derive from activities outside the plant. Work is *relatively* satisfying compared to other aspects of the total life situation of the Yugoslav respondent—which implies perhaps some dissatisfaction in the out-plant life of the Yugoslav.

We do not have data concerning the relevant circumstances, but some facts about the situation in Yugoslavia support the interpretation that Yugoslavs are passing through a difficult period. Yugoslav society is in flux, not only because of rapid industrialization but also because of the many formal changes in the legal structure of the economy. Some of these changes have resulted in improved living conditions but the rate of inflation is nonetheless very high, contributing to some confusion and insecurity, and to a degree of general dissatisfaction. In this context, while job satisfaction may not be high, it is higher than other, out-of-plant satisfactions. Nonetheless, the hierarchical gradient of job satisfaction is relatively flat in the Yugoslav plants, as we shall see, and consequently it is primarily Yugoslav managerial and supervisory personnel, not workers, who show a disadvantage in job satisfaction compared to personnel in the other countries. Yugoslav workers report about as much job satisfaction as workers elsewhere. The Italian workers, not the Yugoslav, show the lowest job satisfaction of all.

All countries show the predicted hierarchical tendency; members near the top feel more satisfied with their jobs than those near the bottom, as the first row of Table 26 and as Figure 13 suggest. The Italian small plants stand out in the sharpness of these differences and the Yugoslav plants are the least hierarchical. Gradients of satisfaction may be universal, but the magnitude of these gradients obviously can vary. Position makes more of a difference in some systems than in others. The relatively low level of job satisfaction expressed by members in the Yugoslav and kibbutz plants is explained by the relatively low satisfaction of managerial groups in these plants compared to plants in the other places.

The distributions of job satisfaction shown in Figure 13 resemble the distributions of opportunities provided by the job, shown in Figure 9. The gradients are less steep, however,

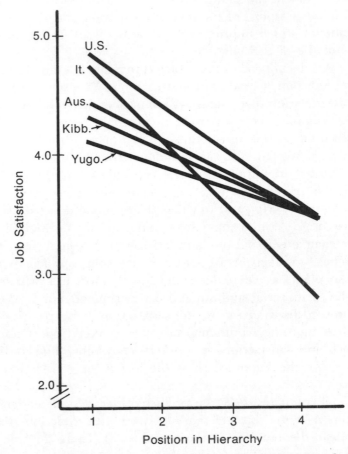

Figure 13. Distribution of job satisfaction (based on average slopes and intercepts for three-, four-, and five-level chains in small organizations).

and the differences between countries are smaller in the present figure compared to the earlier one. A member's position determines in large measure important features of his work situation including opportunities that the job provides for self actualization. These features of the job in turn affect his sense of satisfaction. Hierarchy, in other words, affects satisfaction through its effect in determining the opportunities and other characteristics of the job. Thus we find no relationship in any country between hierarchical position and job satisfaction when important characteristics of the job, such as the opportunities it provides (p. 101), its physical qualities (p. 105), the amount of authority (p. 91), and salary associated with it are held constant through regression procedures. Table 27 summarizes the results of such an analysis in which members' job satisfaction is predicted from their position in the hierarchy and the other variables associated with position. This table lists the variables in the order of their average importance, measured in terms of standardized Beta weights, in all countries combined, and the numbers in the table indicate the rank order of importance within each country. An asterisk indicates that the Beta weight is statistically significant at the .05 level; numbers in boldface mean that the relationship is negative; the values in parentheses are the multiple correlations within each country. Thus, an index that measures the opportunities a job provides is the single most important correlate of job satisfaction in all countries except Austria. The components of this index, which include the opportunity to use one's ideas and skills, to learn new things and to set the pace of one's work, come very close to defining what most people mean by a satisfying job—and as we have seen in the previous chapter, these characteristics are found more at the top than at the bottom of the hierarchy.

With the possible exception of Austria, then, job satisfaction is related in very much the same way in all countries to the index of opportunities we have defined. In Austria, a member's authority and influence is the single most important correlate of his satisfaction on the job. Authority is important in the other countries, too, but the kibbutz plants prove an exception to this trend. Members here do not value authority as much as do members in the other countries, and only in kibbutz plants have we found substantial numbers of respondents saying that they have more authority than they want. Authority here implies responsibilities and difficulties for which sufficient additional reward is not always provided.

It is ironic that authority and influence do not have more substantial implications for job satisfaction in kibbutzim, since kibbutz plants compare very favorably to the others in the amount of authority and influence members feel. Job satisfaction in kibbutz plants might be higher if the exercise of authority had the positive implications in kibbutzim that it apparently has in the other plants. The absence of a relationship between authority and satisfaction under the controlled conditions defined by Table 27 does not mean, however, that persons in higher positions who have more authority than those at lower levels are not more satisfied. On the contrary, job satisfaction in kibbutz plants is clearly greater for persons at higher levels and therefore for persons who have relatively great authority. Table 27 simply suggests that in the kibbutz plants the greater satisfaction of persons at higher levels is not likely due to their greater authority. In the plants of the other countries, however, the greater job satisfaction of upper-level persons is probably attributable in part to the greater authority they have. The simple, zero-order correlation between authority and job satisfaction in the kibbutz plants is .34.

A second irony is that education, which is a positive value in most societies, has negative implications for job satisfaction. Educated persons who are equal to less educated persons in the opportunities provided them on the job or in some of the other characteristics shown in Table 27 are likely to be *less* satisfied than are less educated organization members. This finding, which is in accord with the results of other research (Mann, 1953; Morse, 1953; Lawler, 1971) may be fairly universal, although Mann suggests that it applies more to persons in unskilled than in skilled occupations.

The order of variables listed in Table 27 fits the thesis that intrinsic aspects of the job are more important than extrinsic ones as determinants of job satisfaction (Dunnette, 1967; Wernimont, 1966; Barnowe and others, 1972). The first two variables in the table, "authority and influence" and "opportunities the job provides" (for example, to learn new things and to use one's skills) come closer to defining intrinsic aspects of work than do "physical job qualities," (including a variety of working conditions) and salary, each of which illustrate extrinsic aspects of work. The hypothesis that intrinsic factors are more important is supported consistently within each country by the direct, zero order correlations between each of the factors and job satisfaction; the correlations involving the intrinsic factors are higher than the correlations involving the extrinsic factors in each country. The average correlations, when data are combined for all countries, are "authority-influence," .40; "job opportunities," .42; "job qualities," .26; and salary, .23. Table 27, which summarizes the results of a regression analysis suggests, however, some difference between countries in the relative importance of these factors when a number of variables are taken into account simultaneously. In kibbutz plants, for example, working conditions, an extrinsic factor, may be more important than authority and influence, an intrinsic factor *when job opportunities are held constant.* In the Austrian plants working conditions may be more important than job opportunities *when authority and influence are held constant.* These data therefore suggest a qualification of the hypothesis that intrinsic qualities are more important than extrinsic: If some important intrinsic qualities are manifest in a job, additional intrinsic qualities may not contribute to job satisfaction as much as some extrinsic qualities may contribute. Furthermore, qualities that are important in one social system (for example, authority and influence in Austria) may be relatively unimportant in another (for example, authority and influence in kibbutzim).

Satisfaction with Knowledge. Workers at the bottom of a bureaucracy presumably know less than a manager at the top about how their respective jobs relate to the functioning of the plant as a whole. And in fact, managers in all of the plants report substantially more knowledge than do workers in response to this question: "53. Do you know how your present job fits into the functioning of this plant?" Managers should also be more satisfied than workers with their knowledge. Question 53 was therefore followed by another: "53a. Are you satisfied with your level of knowledge?"

The systems differ significantly in the amount of knowledge reported and in satisfaction with that knowledge. The data, however, do not entirely fit our predictions. American and kibbutz respondents are higher than respondents in the

Table 25. Members' Satisfaction and Attitudes

Satisfaction and Attitude	SMALL PLANTS					LARGE PLANTS			
	Italy	Austria	United States	Yugo-slavia	Kibbutz	Italy	Austria	United States	Yugo-slavia
1. Satisfaction with Job	3.3	3.7	3.9	3.6	3.6	3.6	3.7	4.0	3.8
2. Satisfaction with Knowledge	3.2	3.7	2.6	3.0	2.9	3.3	3.6	2.5	3.2
3. Attitude toward Company Leadership [a]	3.0	3.3	3.9	3.3	3.7	3.2	3.5	3.7	3.3

[a] High scores mean favorable attitude.

Table 26. Gradients of Satisfaction and Attitude

Gradient	SMALL PLANTS					LARGE PLANTS			
	Italy	Austria	United States	Yugo-slavia	Kibbutz	Italy	Austria	United States	Yugo-slavia
1. Job Satisfaction	.58	.32	.42	.21	.29	.26	.36	.22	.04
2. Satisfaction with Knowledge	.47	.35	−.05	−.02	.31	.34	.20	−.19	−.06
3. Attitude toward Company Leadership	.33	.44	.28	.07	.26	.26	.20	.26	.13

Table 27. Rank Order of Importance of Determinants
of Job Satisfaction

Determinant	Italy (.57) [a]	Austria (.46)	United States (.59)	Yugo- slavia (.45)	Kibbutz (.54)
Opportunities on job	1 *	5	1 *	1 *	1 *
Authority influence	2 *	1 *	4 *	2 *	7
Physical job qualities	4 *	3 *	3 *	5	2 *
Education	3 *	4	6 *	4 *	3 *
Age	5	2 *	2 *	8	8
Seniority in plant	7	7	8	6	4
Length of chain	8	9	7	3 *	5
Level in hierarchy	9	8	5	7	6
Salary	6	6	9	9	—

Note: Importance is measured in terms of standardized Beta weights. An asterisk indicates that Beta is significantly different from zero at the .05 level. Boldface indicates that Beta is negative.

[a] Numbers in parentheses are the multiple correlations predicting the dependent variable from all of the independent variables. In general, the first several independent variables account for this correlation, the remaining variables contributing little if anything.

other countries in amount of knowledge they report (data not shown), but American and kibbutz respondents are relatively low in satisfaction with that knowledge, as the second row of Table 25 indicates. The gradients of satisfaction however are quite flat in the American and Yugoslav plants, despite substantial gradients in amount of knowledge reported in both places. Satisfaction with knowledge apparently does not run parallel to amount of knowledge. The second row of Table 26 and Figure 14 present some of these data.

The American manager stands out in dissatisfaction with his knowledge despite the high level of knowledge he reports. This is an unusual result, since American managers ordinarily rank high on satisfaction and attitude. Regression analyses suggest a unique constellation of conditions in the American plants that helps to describe this peculiarity. Education relates importantly to amount of knowledge about how one's job fits in the American plants, as in the plants of other countries. Furthermore, the level of education in the American plants is

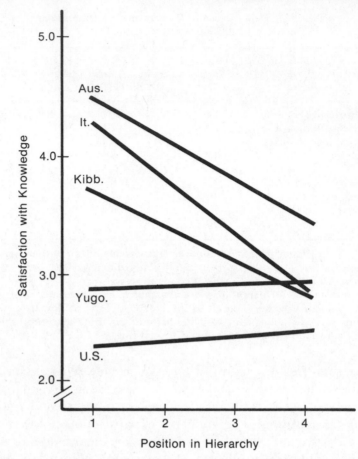

Figure 14. Distribution of satisfaction with knowledge (based on average slopes and intercepts for three-, four-, and five-level chains in small organizations).

high, as we have seen; hence the high level of knowledge reported in these plants. But only in the American plants does education show a significant negative implication for satisfaction with knowledge, according to a regression analysis.

Moreover, in the American plants, members who report high knowledge are not more likely to be satisfied than those who report little knowledge. The correlation between the amount of knowledge reported and satisfaction with knowledge in these plants is —.08. In the plants of each of the other countries, however, the correlation is significantly positive ($r = .31$). In these plants members who report having much knowledge are likely to be relatively satisfied. Why the American case proves exceptional we cannot say, except to speculate that education instills a desire for knowledge. American education, however, may be more pragmatically oriented than European. In the system of higher education through which managers pass in Western Europe, "theory rather than applied practice is given predominant emphasis. . . . For example, in the engineering universities, there is a great emphasis on higher mathematics and engineering design and relatively little on industrial engineering or on the application of engineering principles to factory operations. . . . In Italy, France, and Belgium the successful management of an enterprise is not an end in itself. The European businessman may strive for and even enjoy leisure! His interests are apt to be broader than those of our modern tycoons. The captains of industry in Europe are certainly as brilliant as, and, if anything, more broadly cultured than, the American" (Harbison and Burgess, 1954). Hence the European manager, educated as a "generalist," seeks knowledge about many questions but not necessarily about the mundane questions concerning plant operations. The American manager, however, trained pragmatically, and with a more specialized interest than his European counterpart, wants knowledge about the practicalities of running the plant—and he is dissatisfied because he does not have as much knowledge as he would like.

Attitude Toward Company Leadership. Several questions were asked to measure the attitude of respondents toward leadership in the company:

24. Do you think the responsible people here have a real interest in the welfare of those who work here?
25. Do the responsible people in this plant improve working conditions only when forced to?
28. When a worker in this plant makes a complaint about something is it taken care of?

Each question was answered on a five-point scale, and the third row of Table 25 shows the scores of the questions averaged for respondents who, according to an analysis of variance, differ statistically among the five countries. The results are not entirely in accord with our expectations based on the formal participativeness of the plants.

The third row of Table 26 presents the gradients in the five countries. The Yugoslav plants predictably have a flat gradient of attitude; workers do not differ very much from managers in their attitude toward the company leadership. This desired outcome, however, is accompanied by some unintended consequences. Yugoslav top managers are last among managers of the five countries in favorableness of attitude.

These data concerning attitude are in a number of respects like the data concerning job satisfaction, and a regression analysis (Table 28) indicates that attitude toward leadership

Table 28. Rank Order of Importance of Determinants
of Attitude Toward Company Leadership

Determinant	Italy (.48)	Austria (.46)	United States (.51)	Yugo-slavia (.40)	Kibbutz (.42)
Authority-influence	5	1 *	1 *	2 *	3 *
Opportunities on job	1 *	3 *	7	1 *	1 *
Age	4 *	2 *	3 *	3 *	6 *
Seniority	6 *	5	4 *	6	2 *
Physical job qualities	3 *	9	2 *	4	7
Level in hierarchy	7	4	5 *	5	5 *
Education	2 *	8	9	9	8
Salary	8	7	6	7	—
Length of chain	9	6	8	8	4 *

Note: See notes to Table 27 for key to symbols.

is related in much the same way as job satisfaction to some of the other, hierarchy-connected variables. The positive implication of age for attitude, however, deserves additional consideration. The favor with which older persons view plant leadership in all countries is consistent with the notion that older persons are more conservative than younger persons, even if older persons earn the same salary and are at the same level as their younger associates. Older persons also feel greater satisfaction with their job and their pay, in some countries at least (Tables 27 and 29). This relatively "favorable adjustment" of older workers has been noted in earlier research and occurs despite the less happy adjustment of older persons compared to younger persons in certain aspects of non-work life (Gurin and others, 1960; also Morse, 1953). Crozier (1971), Marenco (1959), and others (Herzberg and others, 1957) explain in terms of a "classic pattern" the general tendency for older workers to be more favorably disposed than younger: a younger worker enters a job with high hopes and a positive attitude but he is soon disillusioned and his attitude declines sharply. In time, however, he accommodates to the realities of organizational life, learns how to cope with some of the difficulties on the job, and develops a tolerance for the frustrating aspects of organization that a younger man would find disturbing. Hence there is a steady growth of positive attitude with age and seniority following an initial decline.

Whether the relationship between age and attitude is in fact curvilinear as this explanation suggests, data from earlier research supports the hypothesis that favorable attitude toward the company increases on the average with age. We add evidence here to the generality of this proposition under a variety of social and economic conditions. Furthermore, these data suggest that the generally increasing satisfaction (or decreasing dissatisfaction) that accompanies age is not attributable to seniority per se. The more senior man is likely to have a *less* favorable attitude than his junior counterpart—unless, of course, the senior man is also older and has more authority or greater opportunities on the job.

Satisfaction with Pay. A single question (number 59) was asked to measure a member's satisfaction with his pay: "Are you satisfied with your wages?" The average responses to this question are virtually identical in the four countries where this question was posed (kibbutz members, of course, were not asked this question). The uniformity among countries occurs despite large manifest differences in the salary members receive. A member's satisfaction depends not so much on his absolute salary as on his salary relative to that of persons to whom he compares himself (Patchen, 1961b). A worker in one country does not compare himself primarily to workers in another but rather to his own peers, superiors, subordinates, friends, or relatives. Hence the average member in one country, comparing himself to others in his own milieu, feels as satisfied (or dissatisfied) as the average member in another country. But persons at upper levels have a salary advantage relative to those below, and this advantage is greater in some places than in others. Consequently, the *gradients* of satisfaction differ between countries, as Figure 15 indicates. Furthermore, the gradients correspond reasonably well in their rank order to the ranking of gradients of salary shown in Table 19. This correspondence suggests that, within each country where similar standards apply to most members, salary is an important determinant of satisfaction, and Table 29 bears out this expectation in all countries but the United States.

The lack of relationship in the American plants in contrast to that in the other countries is difficult to explain,* although it is tempting to cite Maslow's thesis (1943), which might argue that the relatively high pay scale of the American worker means that his economic-security need is satisfied and other needs therefore become prepotent. For example, a survey by Form (1973) shows that 46 percent of Italian Fiat workers compared to only 7 percent of American Oldsmobile workers rate securing higher wages as the most important function for their union. On the other hand 75 percent of the American workers compared to 31 percent of the Italian consider obtaining better working conditions as the most important function

---

* In the American plants a correlation of .19 indicates a small significant positive relation between salary and satisfaction when the other variables of Table 29 are not held constant. Lawler and Porter (1966) find a correlation of .27 between pay and satisfaction with pay. A regression analysis by Lawler and Porter in which a number of demographic factors are held constant demonstrates that salary is the single most important determinant of satisfaction with pay. The Lawler-Porter study and the present one involve different controls, however, and the results are not directly comparable.

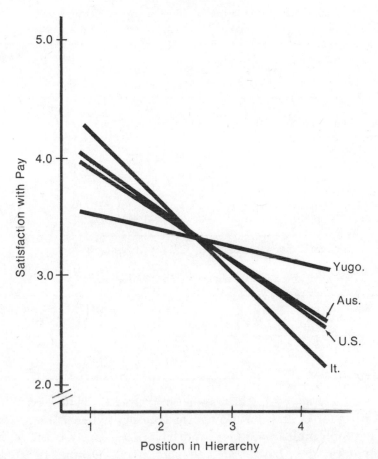

Figure 15. Distribution of satisfaction with pay (based on average slopes and intercepts for three-, four-, and five-level chains in small organizations).

of their union. Under these circumstances satisfaction in American plants depends less on salary than on other considerations. Yet it is apparent that the American worker is not indifferent to money. Americans, for example, are more prone to strike than their European counterparts, and wages are manifestly the single most important issue in these strikes (Tannenbaum, 1965). A recent national survey shows that American workers rate adequate financial reward second in importance among five aspects of their job. Having sufficient resources (like receiving enough help and equipment to get the job done, and

Table 29.   Rank Order of Importance of Determinants
of Satisfaction with Pay

Determinant	Italy (.48)	Austria (.34)	United States (.38)	Yugo-slavia (.33)
Salary	1 *	1 *	6	1 *
Education	2 *	6	2 *	3 *
Job qualities	3 *	3	1 *	7
Seniority	7	5	3 *	2 *
Age	9	2 *	4 *	5
Opportunities on job	6	4	8	4 *
Authority-influence	5	7	5	6
Level in hierarchy	4	9	9	9
Length of chain	8	8	7	8

Note: See notes to Table 27 for key to symbols.

Table 30.   Gradients of Satisfaction with Pay

Plant Size	Italy	Austria	United States	Yugoslavia
SMALL	.61	.37	.40	.14
LARGE	.24	.35	.24	—.06

having a competent supervisor, and clearly defined responsibilities) ranks first; but doing challenging, self-enriching work, having pleasant co-workers, and having an easy job prove less important than having an adequate salary (Quinn, 1972). Indeed, the data of the present study show that the American respondents are no more satisfied with their salaries than are the respondents in the other countries, although the hierarchical distributions of satisfaction may differ between the countries. Other considerations appear to be more important than money per se as a determinant of satisfaction with pay—among them, education and physical qualities of the job. These factors are important in some of the other countries, too, and in much the same way among the countries. Education has a negative effect, as Andrews and Henry have proposed on the basis of earlier research. (Andrews and Henry 1963; see also Patchen, 1961. Lawler and Porter, 1966, do not find this negative relationship.) A member will be dissatisfied if he is more educated than others who earn the same pay as he. On the other hand, the positive implications of job qualities for satisfaction in at least two countries suggest that a member is likely to be relatively satisfied with his pay if his working conditions are better than the conditions of those who earn the same as he. A man's satisfaction with his pay, as Patchen and others have suggested, is not simply a reaction to the absolute level of his wage, but rather to his standing relative to others on a number of dimensions relevant to pay (Patchen, 1961; Lawler, 1971).

The importance of physical qualities of the job (in the United States and Italy) or of opportunities provided by the job (in Yugoslavia) for satisfaction with pay suggests a curious relationship between satisfaction with job and with pay in some countries at least. Money per se does not make a job satisfying in any country, as we have seen in Table 27, even though it may contribute to satisfaction with pay. Nonetheless, many persons, if given the opportunity, choose jobs and careers on the basis of the money offered. They may regret the choice, however, because they are not likely to be satisfied with their job simply because it pays well. But if they choose a job where conditions are congenial or opportunities for self actualization are available, then they are likely to be satisfied with their pay *as well as* with the job itself. The moral is that one who seeks high satisfaction with pay might further this objective by choosing a job on the basis of pay, but he risks being dissatisfied with his job. On the other hand, he might very well achieve satisfaction with pay as well as satisfaction with job by choosing work that is congenial or that provides opportunities for self-actualization. Babe Ruth is said to have expressed amazement that he could actually be *paid* for playing baseball.*

The economic man model assumes that man is entirely rational and that he not only anticipates accurately the material consequences of his choices but that he anticipates the utilities of these consequences. In fact, utilities may be different under future circumstances, and we may sometimes find after acquir-

* Thanks to Lloyd Ulman for this example.

ing something we wanted that we do not really want it (Simon, 1965; Taylor, 1965). The above determinants of satisfaction with pay and job illustrate some of the limitations of the economic man model. While it would seem rational for an individual who wants to maximize *economic* utility to make a choice of jobs on the basis of purely economic considerations, in fact, the economic utility of a job is determined in part by noneconomic considerations. The implications of these noneconomic considerations for job satisfaction may be obvious, but their implications for satisfaction with pay—the function to be maximized—may not be anticipated. Thus it is not entirely rational to choose a job simply on the basis of economic considerations *even when trying only to maximize economic utility*. Money as the sole criterion of choice becomes, of course, even less rational when one wants to maximize more than just economic utility.

Motivation

An organization, if it is to be effective, requires three kinds of behavior of its members, according to Katz and Kahn (1966). First, members must join and stay in the system; second, they must behave dependably, meeting fully the requirements of their role; third, they must contribute in spontaneous and innovative ways beyond formal requirements. Favorable attitude of members and satisfaction with aspects of the job, which we considered in the previous sections are conducive to the first requirement. Persons who like the company and who are satisfied with the wages offered will join and stay. Members who derive satisfaction from their work are less likely than dissatisfied members to be absent. The second and third requirements, including high standards of performance and innovativeness are not likely to be met, however, simply because members are satisfied with their jobs or like the company (Brayfield and Crockett, 1955). Appropriate behavior here depends on the motivation of members including a sense of responsibility for the success of their immediate task group if not for the plant as a whole. Prior research suggests, however, that such motivation is not widely felt in the traditional industrial organization.

Persons at upper levels may be highly motivated but persons at lower levels are not. The participative organization, on the other hand, is designed to instill motivation and responsibility on the part of all members.

Sense of Responsibility. Table 31 shows the average scores of respondents in the plants of the five countries in answer to the following question (number 11): "To what extent do you feel really responsible for the success of: your own work group; your department; the whole plant?" Answers were checked on a five-point scale from "not at all" to "very much," in relation to each of the three areas of responsibility. In appraising the amount of responsibility indicated in Table 31 the reader should remember that the sample includes a substantial number of supervisory and managerial personnel, especially in the large plants.

Two facts are suggested by this table. First, members understandably feel more responsible for their own work group and department than for the plant as a whole, although the difference between responsibility felt for the work group and for the plant may be greater in some plants like the Italian and Austrian than in others like the kibbutz and Yugoslav. Second, an analysis of variance reveals highly significant differences between countries in sense of responsibility reported by the average respondent. The data are in some respects unexpected, however, on the basis of the hypothesis that members in the formally participative systems will feel more responsible than members in the nonparticipative. Although members in the Italian plants predictably rank last, members in the U.S. plants (not the kibbutz) rank first. The kibbutz members are by no means low on this measure, but is it possible that it is with respect to the community rather than with respect to the plant that kibbutzniks feel more responsible than do persons in all the other places? Or is it possible that the procedure of electing supervisors and managers in kibbutz plants explains why members are not higher? Elections provide a means through which members delegate to elected persons formal responsibility for their work area. Members may thus feel somewhat absolved and not fully responsible, having participated in a procedure through which they formally delegate responsibility to others.

A further explanation for the moderate level of responsibility shown in Table 31 for members in the kibbutz plants compared to the American might be the substantial proportion of managerial personnel in the sample. Perhaps the effects of participation on responsibility are felt primarily by rank-and-file members. Table 32 helps to define how this sense of responsibility (averaged for work group, department and plant) is distributed in the plants of the five countries, but it does not support the expectation that the gradients in the kibbutz plants are flatter than in the American. The Italian plants, however, show as expected the sharpest gradient and the Yugoslav plants show a relatively flat gradient.

A regression analysis (Table 33) indicates a remarkable consistency among the five countries in the importance of authority and influence as a predictor of responsibility. This factor is first in importance in all countries but Yugoslavia, and there it ranks second. The index of authority and influence apparently has implications for sense of responsibility even in kibbutz plants, where as we have seen, the index does not relate to job satisfaction. Authority and influence may not make the kibbutznik happy, but they make him responsible. We thus see some support under a broad variety of conditions for theories that attach primary importance to influence of members as the basis for enhancing their sense of responsibility in the organization (Likert, 1961; Tannenbaum, 1968a).

Moviation and Initiative. Our interpretations concerning responsibility should be qualified by data in response to two questions designed to measure the motivation and initiative of members in their work:

6. In your kind of job, is it usually better to let your superiors worry about introducing better or faster ways of doing the work?

7. How often do you try out on your own a better or faster way of doing the work?

The responses to these questions do not intercorrelate well, for reasons we shall consider below, and Table 34 shows the mean scores for each based on the responses of all respondents in each country. All of the differences between countries are highly significant statistically, with the exception of the differences between the large plants on the second question.

Kibbutz members rank high on these items, as expected, but Yugoslav members are prone to let their superiors worry about introducing better and faster ways of doing work—which does not conform to the expected effects of the system of workers' self management. Furthermore, and contrary to our prediction, the gradient of response on this item is quite steep in the small Yugoslav plants as Figure 16 indicates, and among the large plants Yugoslavia ranks second only to Italy in the magnitude of the gradient. The results of a regression analysis summarized in Tables 35 and 36 help explain these unusual results. The key appears to be education. The less educated members think it better to let their superiors worry about introducing better or faster ways of doing the work. This dependency on superiors by the less educated applies in all countries with the possible exception of kibbutzim, where members do not differ from one another very much in formal education. Hence the low level and steep gradient of education that prevail in the Yugoslav plants (Figure 11) help explain the unusually low score and sharp gradient on this measure of initiative.

Much the same logic applies to the Italian data. The Italian plants are distinctly lower than the Yugoslav, however, in the feeling of responsibility reported by members, as we have seen (Table 31) and the gradient of responsibility felt by members is steeper in the Italian plants (Table 32), even though education does not have much if any bearing on sense of responsibility, as we have seen (Table 33). The low level of initiative and responsibility and the steep gradients in Italy therefore cannot be explained easily in terms of education alone.

The education level of a member apparently is relevant to the initiative he will take vis-à-vis his superior. The less educated he is the more hesitant he will be to behave in ways that imply he understands more about the work than his superior does. Having less education than his superior he may feel that

Table 31. Scores of Sense of Responsibility

Responsibility for	Italy	Austria	United States	Yugo-slavia	Kibbutz
SMALL PLANTS					
Work Group	3.0	3.5	4.0	3.9	3.6
Department	2.9	3.3	4.0	3.9	3.7
Whole Plant	2.5	2.9	3.7	3.6	3.4
Average	2.8	3.2	3.9	3.8	3.6
LARGE PLANTS					
Work Group	3.4	4.1	4.4	4.2	—
Department	3.2	3.9	4.4	4.0	—
Whole Plant	2.7	3.5	3.9	3.7	—
Average	3.1	3.8	4.2	4.0	—

Table 32. Gradients of Sense of Responsibility

Plant Size	Italy	Austria	United States	Yugoslavia	Kibbutz
SMALL	.74	.70	.42	.40	.55
LARGE	.58	.54	.13	.16	—

Table 33.   Rank Order of Importance of Determinants
of Sense of Responsibility

Determinant	Italy (.68)	Austria (.68)	United States (.58)	Yugo-slavia (.51)	Kibbutz (.52)
Authority-influence	1 *	1 *	1 *	2 *	1 *
Opportunities on job	2 *	4	2 *	1 *	2 *
Age	3 *	2 *	3 *	9	5
Salary	8	3	4	5 *	—
Level in hierarchy	9	5	6	4	3
Job qualities	7	7	5	3 *	8
Length of chain	6	8	7	8	4
Seniority	4	9	8	6	6
Education	5	6	9	7	7

Note: See notes to Table 27 for key to symbols.

Table 34.   Average Responses on Measures of Motivation
and Initiative in Work

Response [a]	Italy	Austria	United States	Yugo-slavia	Kibbutz
SMALL PLANTS					
Let superior worry	2.5	2.8	3.3	2.4	3.4
Try out better way	3.0	3.4	3.8	3.9	3.9
LARGE PLANTS					
Let superior worry	2.9	3.4	3.8	2.7	—
Try out better way	3.4	3.7	3.9	3.8	—

[a] High scores in this table imply high motivation and initiative.

Table 35. Rank Order of Importance of Determinants of Initiative
(Measured in terms of disagreement that superior alone
should worry about introducing new methods)

Determinant	Italy (.48)	Austria (.56)	United States (.61)	Yugo-slavia (.52)	Kibbutz (.32)
Education	2 *	1 *	3 *	3 *	6
Opportunities on job	1 *	4 *	2 *	6	2 *
Level in hierarchy	8	2 *	6	1 *	4
Authority-influence	4	7	1 *	7	3
Salary	3	3 *	7	9	—
Age	6	8	5	8	1 *
Seniority	5	5 *	9	4	7
Length of chain	9	6	8	2 *	5
Physical job qualities	7	9	4 *	5	8

Note: See notes to Table 27 for key to symbols.

Table 36. Rank Order of Importance of Determinants of Motivation
(Measured in terms of how often respondent tries better methods)

Determinant	Italy (.59)	Austria (.42)	United States (.41)	Yugo-slavia (.37)	Kibbutz (.42)
Authority-influence	2 *	1 *	1 *	2	2 *
Opportunities on job	1 *	2 *	3 *	1 *	1 *
Seniority	4 *	6	6	4	3
Salary	3 *	9	2 *	8	—
Level in hierarchy	6	3 *	4	9	6
Physical job qualities	5	7	9	5	4
Length of chain	7	4	5	7	7
Age	8	5	4	6	8
Education	9	8	8	3	5

Note: See notes to Table 27 for key to symbols.

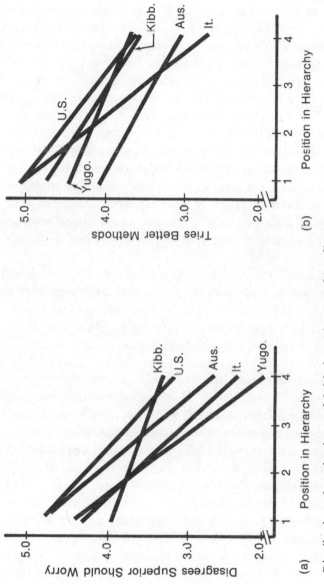

Figure 16. Distribution of motivation and initiative: (a) respondent disagrees that superior should worry about introducing new methods; (b) respondent tries better methods.

he does not know enough to introduce improvements that his superior has not already thought of—and in fact he may be realistic in his feeling. But the less educated member does not feel less responsible than his more educated co-worker, as we have seen in Table 33, and he is not less motivated to try better and faster ways, when this does not imply any direct challenge to his superior, as Table 36 indicates. Education makes little difference here, ranking last in importance in the regression analysis. This contrasts markedly with the measure of initiative that implies something about the respondent's relationship to his superior, and this contrast may explain why these measures of initiative and motivation do not intercorrelate well. Furthermore, these data are consistent with the data concerning responsibility in their support of theories that attach primary importance to authority and influence as an important basis for enhancing a member's sense of responsibility and his motivation to do a better job.

Table 36 is unique in several ways. We see for the first time a statistically significant relationship in one country having a direction opposite to that of a significant relationship in another. Higher-paid members are more likely than lower-paid members to try out new and better ways of improving the work in the American plants, but in the Italian plants higher-paid members are less likely to show such motivation. The American result conforms well to a model that assumes members are rewarded for initiative. Does the Italian result imply that members are being rewarded on bases other than, and perhaps conflicting with initiative? In considering this question it is important to remember that the effects of salary are being observed under special statistical conditions. We are comparing persons who differ in salary but who are at the same hierarchical level, and who have (or see themselves as having) the same authority and influence as well as opportunities on the job. The Italian data do not imply therefore that persons who earn high salaries (and who are at higher ranks) show less initiative than less well paid members. They imply that earning a higher salary is associated with exerting less initiative only for those who are at the same hierarchical level and who have comparable authority. In fact, a simple correlation between initiative and salary is $+.28$ in Italy indicating at least some degree of positive relationship between these factors when the conditions considered in Table 36 are not held constant.

The negative relationship between hierarchical level and motivation in the Austrian plants is unusual. Because we hold authority constant in this analysis, we are looking in effect at persons who differ in rank but not in authority and influence. High-ranking persons with little authority may experience a form of status inconsistency, and consequent disaffection (Jackson, 1962; Lenski, 1964). Having the rank but not the authority of their cohorts they feel less motivated than their colleagues. Negative feelings associated with rank-without-authority in Austria are also hinted in Tables 28 and 33 concerning attitude toward company leadership and sense of responsibility. On the other hand, the Austrian plants show a distinct positive effect of rank on initiative described in Table 35.

Adjustment

Superiors are more satisfied with their jobs than are subordinates, as we have seen. The psychological and physical qualities of work that vary systematically with rank help explain this difference in satisfaction. Prior research, however, suggests that the psychological impact of work may go beyond the satisfaction or dissatisfaction members feel. Deeper implications include despair, depression, alienation, and lack of self-esteem that members, particularly at lower levels, may feel as a result of their work. These reactions are a natural consequence of jobs that imply failure and that frustrate members' need to express their individuality and to control their own fate. (Allport, 1933; Argyris, 1964; French, 1963; Gurin and others, 1960; Kasl and French, 1962; Marx, 1964; Kornhauser, 1954; for some conflicting evidence concerning the effect of job qualities on self-esteem, see Lefkowitz, 1967.) General reactions of this type are affected by many conditions external to the plant, as well as by some within. Nonetheless, conditions of work that apply differentially to persons in different positions suggest that the mental adjustment of lower-level members is likely to be poorer than that of upper level persons—except in participative organizations, where according to the theory we are exploring the adjustment of all members should be relatively favorable and differences between persons of different rank should be minimized.

     Psychological Adjustment. Hunt and others (1967) drawing upon a large body of prior research have developed a measure of aspects of adjustment that include measures of depression, resentment, and self-esteem. We employed their question, which is phrased as follows:

> 49. How true are the following statements?
>   (a) I feel depressed
>   (b) Other people are always more lucky than I
>   (c) I usually do a good job
>   (d) I often feel bored
>   (e) I seem not to get what is coming to me
>   (f) Usually everything I try seems to fail
>   (g) Things seem hopeless
>   (h) I feel resentful
>   (i) Almost every week I see someone I dislike
>   (j) I sometimes feel that my life is not very useful
>   (k) It seems to me that I am a failure
>   (l) When I do a job, I do it well

The question was answered by checks on a scale from 1, for very true to 5, for very untrue, and an analysis within each country shows that the items intercorrelate reasonably well excepting (c), (e), and (l), which were therefore eliminated. The remaining items comprise a highly reliable general index, which we refer to as psychological adjustment.

     Table 37 (p. 163) shows average responses to items in the index as well as the index as a whole for each country. The scores indicate on the average some disagreement by members with statements that imply poor mental health; adjustment in terms of this measure therefore appears generally to be good. An analysis of variance, however, demonstrates highly significant differences among the countries on all items. The relatively poor adjustment of the Italian members and the positive adjustment of the kibbutz workers fit well the hypothesis that adjustment is likely to be better in participative than non-participative organizations. But the Yugoslav data do not conform to this prediction. Yugoslav members on the average indicate levels of depression, resentment, and lack of self-esteem as great if not greater than that of Italian members.

The low adjustment scores in the Italian and Yugoslav plants suggest a commonality among these groups despite radically different formal systems. Educational level of workers is one commonality which would seem in principle to offer an explanation, but education per se has little if any effect on responses to this measure of psychological adjustment, according to a regression analysis. Hence the low level of formal education does not help explain the poor adjustment of these workers.

We thus have at best only mixed support for the hypothesis that members in the formally participative systems will have a better psychological adjustment than those in the non-participative. Furthermore, there is little support for the hypothesis that the gradients will be less steep in the former plants than the latter. The small plants conform in some degree to the hypothesis, as Figure 17 indicates, but the large plants do not, the gradient scores in Italy and Yugoslavia, for example, being .17 and .36, respectively.

Psychological adjustment, more than satisfaction with job or pay, is affected by circumstances external to the plant. We have already considered, for example, the confusion and insecurity associated with industrialization in Yugoslavia. Such circumstances might very well create problems of adjustment that we are measuring here. In the following chapter we shall control statistically some of the circumstances common to a nation that may affect these results. In the meanwhile we can explore other indices of adjustment, including alienation and peptic ulcer, that are known from prior research to be related to hierarchical position.

Alienation. The concept of alienation has philosophic roots in the writings of Hegel and Marx. Alienation implies

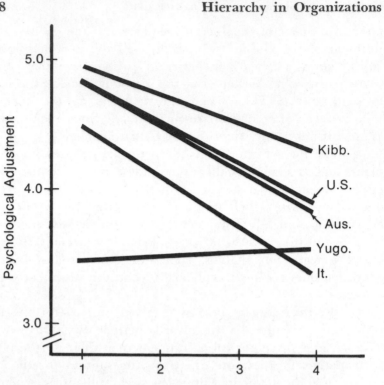

Figure 17. Distribution of psychological adjustment (based on average slopes and intercepts for three-, four-, and five-level chains in small organizations).

maladjustment, a "fragmentation in man's existence and consciousness which impedes the wholeness of experience and activity" (Blauner, 1964). Unlike traditional psychological conceptions of maladjustment, however, the onus is on the social system, not the individual. If the worker is alienated, it is not he but the system that is maladjusted. For Marx, the source of alienation resides in capitalist property arrangements, including industrial technology and the sharp division of labor inherent in these arrangements. The worker in a capitalist society is "separated" from the means of production and from the product of his labor which he neither owns nor controls. "The object produced by labour, its product, now stands opposed to it as an alien being, as a power independent of the producer" (Marx, 1964).

Marx defined alienation in terms of the objective relation of man to ownership and control of the means of production. Alienation for Marx nontheless has psychological implications. "Alienation is apparent not only in the fact that my means of life belong to someone else, that my desires are the unattainable possession of someone else, but that everything is something different from itself, that my activity is something else, and finally (and this is also the case for the capitalist) that an inhuman power rules over everything." [Marx, 1971, p. 83.]

Alienation has been interpreted in many ways since Marx's early treatment, and it has been considered from both objective and subjective standpoints. Work, for example, has objectively defined features that are alienating. We have already considered some of these through our measure of opportunities provided by the job. Work is alienating if it is routine or overly simple in relation to the skills of the worker or if it does not permit him to determine his own pace (Blauner, 1967; Seeman, 1967). On the other hand, alienation has a subjective aspect—the feeling that one is "alienated." Seeman (1959) has defined five meanings of alienation that provide an excellent operational basis for understanding alienation subjectively defined, and Dean (1961) has developed an instrument to measure several of Seeman's concepts. We have adapted some of Dean's items and added some of our own as a result of a pretest in the five countries.

The first of Seeman's concepts of alienation is powerlessness, the belief that one cannot determine the outcomes one seeks. We measured this concept by asking respondents to indicate on a five-point scale how true or untrue are the following statements:

    (c) Men like me cannot influence the course of events; only men in high positions can have such influence

    (d) I have never had the influence over others that I would have liked

The second concept is meaninglessness, a person's sense of confusion or lack of clarity about what he ought to believe. The two statements respondents were asked to judge are:

(e) Public affairs are so complicated that it is im-
    possible to orient oneself in them
(f) Despite the many advantages science has made, life
    today is too complicated

The third component is normlessness which is related
to Durkheim's notion of "anomie." Here the alienated person
sees his world in disarray, without effective norms or rules to
regulate individual conduct. The statements designed to measure this concept are:

(i) Life seems to be moving on without rules or order
(j) Nowadays it is hard to know right from wrong

The fourth component is social isolation, which implies
a sense of apartness or detachment from others or from group
norms.* The two statements are:

(a) It is not possible to rely on others
(b) Today it is practically impossible to find real
    friends because everyone thinks only of himself

Finally, there is self estrangement, which implies that
a person's behavior is a means toward some end with which the
person does not identify. It is as if he were separated from himself, behaving on behalf of some external force. The following
statements are designed to measure this conception:

(g) I can never do what I really like because circum-
    stances require that I do otherwise
(h) Life is so routinized that I do not have a chance
    to use my true abilities

Conditions at lower levels of the hierarchy—lack of
ownership (in some systems), routineness of work, lack of control over pace, absence of opportunity to use fully one's skills—

---

* This is a modification of Seeman's notion which refers to socially
isolated persons as "those who, like the intellectual, assign low reward
value to goals or beliefs that are typically highly valued in the given society" (Seeman, 1959, pp. 788–789).

are alienating. Persons at lower levels should therefore *feel* more alienated than those above. The nature of the system, however, should make a difference. In the formally participative systems included here, workers directly or indirectly own the means of production and control their enterprise. They should therefore feel less alienated and the gradient of alienation should be flatter in these systems than in the non-participative.

Table 38 presents the average score for each of the mean-ings of alienation as well as a general average within each country. The Italian and kibbutz plants define the two ex-tremes: Italian members feel quite alienated, kibbutz members do not. American respondents, however, are not very different from the kibbutz, and Yugoslav respondents are close to the Italian and Austrian.

These results are not entirely encouraging for the hy-pothesis concerning differences between systems. But these averages include the responses of managers as well as workers. How do workers in the respective systems compare to one another, and how do workers compare to managers within each system? Figure 18 helps answer these questions. The gradients presented here are based on an index in which the responses to all of the items dealing with alienation are combined.*

Persons near the bottom of these 52 organizations feel more alienated than those near the top, with the possible excep-tion of persons in the small Yugoslav plants. This exception is not unexpected on the basis of our major hypothesis; but contrary to our expectation, kibbutz plants show the usual hierarchical gradient, and among large plants the Yugoslav have gradients about equal to those in the other places (for example, .22 compared to an average of .28 in the other plants). The nature of the system as we have defined it appears to be only a very partial explanation of these findings. Alienation among workers is the rule rather than the exception, although some workers, like the Italian and Austrian (and the Yugoslav in large plants), satisfy this rule more than do others.

---

* Although the sub-items measuring each of the five conceptions of alienation inter-correlated better than do the other items with each other, the inter-correlations between all items are nonetheless good in all countries, and we thus have a single, highly reliable index of alienation.

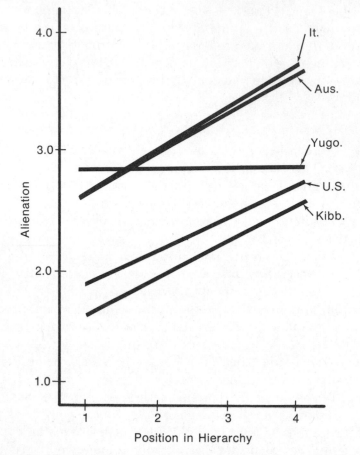

Figure 18. Distribution of alienation (based on average slopes and inter-cepts for three-, four-, and five-level chains in small organizations).

Alienation as we have measured it describes a general adjustment to life of which work is only a part. Factors external to the plant as well as those within no doubt have an important bearing on this adjustment. Education is one such factor. We have seen in an earlier section that educated persons tend to be less satisfied with their jobs than less educated associates at the same level. We now see (Table 39) that the more educated respondents are also less likely to be alienated than their associates in comparable positions. Thus, while education con-tributes to dissatisfaction it also has the effect of reducing aliena-tion.

Table 37. Psychological Adjustment

(Degree of Disagreement with Statements that Imply Poor Psychological Adjustment)

	Small Plants					Large Plants			
	Italy	Austria	United States	Yugo-slavia	Kibbutz	Italy	Austria	United States	Yugo-slavia
(a) I feel depressed	3.1	3.6	3.7	3.1	4.5	3.5	3.8	3.8	3.2
(b) Others more lucky	3.0	3.3	3.9	3.2	4.5	3.6	3.6	3.9	3.2
(d) Often feel bored	2.9	4.1	3.6	3.8	4.0	3.5	4.3	3.9	3.6
(f) Everything I try fails	3.9	4.1	4.3	3.5	4.6	4.2	4.3	4.4	3.5
(g) Things seem hopeless	3.6	4.1	4.4	3.4	4.6	3.9	4.5	4.4	3.7
(h) I feel resentful	3.6	4.1	4.4	2.9	4.6	4.0	4.2	4.3	3.0
(j) My life not useful	4.0	4.1	4.3	3.6	4.5	4.2	4.4	4.5	3.5
(k) I am a failure	4.3	4.1	4.4	3.3	4.7	4.4	4.6	4.6	3.7
Index	3.5	3.9	4.1	3.3	4.5	3.9	4.2	4.2	3.4

Note: High scores mean disagreement with the statements in the left-hand column; high scores therefore imply a positive adjustment.

Table 38.   Alienation *

Components of Alienation	Italy	Austria	United States	Yugo-slavia	Kibbutz
SMALL PLANTS					
Isolation	3.7	3.4	2.3	3.5	2.1
Powerlessness	3.2	3.3	2.5	3.1	2.4
Meaninglessness	3.7	3.2	2.9	3.5	2.3
Self-alienation	3.4	3.0	2.4	3.1	2.4
Normlessness	3.0	2.9	2.3	3.0	2.1
Index (Average)	3.4	3.2	2.5	3.2	2.3
LARGE PLANTS					
Isolation	3.4	3.1	2.2	3.4	—
Powerlessness	3.0	3.0	2.3	3.2	—
Meaninglessness	3.5	2.9	2.7	3.4	—
Self-alienation	3.1	2.6	2.4	3.0	—
Normlessness	2.8	2.6	2.1	2.6	—
Index (Average)	3.2	2.8	2.3	3.1	—

* High scores imply a high degree of alienation.

Table 39.   Rank Order of Importance of Determinants
of Alienation *

Determinant	Italy (.45)	Austria (.54)	United States (.48)	Yugo-slavia (.41)	Kibbutz (.48)
Education	2 *	4	1 *	2 *	3 *
Opportunities on job	1 *	3 *	5	4	2 *
Physical job qualities	6	1 *	2 *	3 *	4
Length of chain	4	8	4 *	1 *	5
Salary	3	2 *	7	6	—
Authority-influence	5	7	3	8	1 *
Seniority	7	6	8	7	7
Age	8	5	6	9	8
Level in hierarchy	9	9	9	5	6

Note: See notes to Table 27 for key to symbols.

The world is probably less confusing to educated persons than to the less educated, and educated persons may understand better their role in the larger scheme of things. They are therefore less alienated in this sense, although they may not like what they see or understand any more than do less educated persons. Furthermore, a worker may have acquired skills through education that help him cope with problems outside the plant, if not within it, thus reducing the sense of powerlessness that he might otherwise feel. But he may also have developed aspirations that are the basis for dissatisfaction. Thus, all other things being equal, an educated person is likely to feel relatively dissatisfied but not alienated, while a less educated person is likely to feel alienated but not dissatisfied. Education is in this sense a mixed blessing.

The data of this study show small negative (zero-order) correlations between alienation and job satisfaction in all plants except the kibbutz, where the correlation is positive (.27). In the kibbutz plant the satisfied member, not the dissatisfied, is the more likely to feel some alienation. We have seen, in fact (Table 25), that the kibbutz member compared to members in other plants is relatively dissatisfied with his job, contrary to our initial expectation. We explained the low satisfaction partly in terms of the high education level of members. Similarly, high education is consistent with the low level of alienation that we find among members of the kibbutz plants.

The distinction between alienation and job satisfaction in kibbutz plants is further elaborated by noting the effect of authority and influence. Kibbutz plants are the only plants in which authority and influence show no relation to job satisfaction (Table 27). On the other hand, *only* in the kibbutz plant do we find a relationship between authority and alienation, under the controlled condition of the regression analysis of Table 39. Kibbutz members feel some reservation about having authority, as we have noted, and hence authority contributes little to sense of satisfaction with the job. Alienation, however, is not simply dissatisfaction with work, it refers to a general sense of powerlessness, meaninglessness, and normlessness. Authority and influence in the kibbutz plants may contribute to a reduction of such feelings (just as it contributes to the sense of responsibility in the kibbutz member) without making the job any more enjoyable. Why authority does not have the same effect on alienation in the plants of the other countries is difficult to understand, although the zero-order correlations do show a predictable negative correlation between authority and alienation in all countries ($\bar{r} = -.32$), and the relationship between authority and alienation in Table 39, though not significant statistically in each country, is consistently negative, a result that would occur by chance fewer than five times out of a hundred. Apparently some of the other factors in Table 39 that are correlated with authority are sufficiently important so that when they are held constant the effect of authority is reduced to insignificance. These other factors concern characteristics of work, either its physical qualities (such as working conditions) or the opportunities it provides (to set one's own pace, to learn new things, to use one's skills). In all countries one or another of these general features of work ranks high as a correlate of alienation, which is in accord with Marx's argument that the nature of work in mechanized industry is a source of alienation. Daniel Bell (1958) stresses this point to the exclusion of Marx's hypothesis concerning the importance of property relations: "Marx once said that the machine 'multilates the worker into a fragment of a human being, degrades him to become a mere appendage of the machine, makes his work such a torment that its essential meaning is destroyed, estranges him from the intellectual potentialities of the labor process in very proportion to the extent to which science is incorporated into it as an independent power' [Marx, *Capital*, I, p. 713].

"Here for Marx was one of the sources of alienation in modern life. But the source of this alienation is *not* in property relations, but in the technological process" (Bell, 1958).

Property relations per se may not hold the answer to alienation, as Bell suggests, yet there is a rough correspondence among plants between ownership and the alienation of workers (if not managers). The chances are reasonably good of finding alienated workers in the privately owned Italian and Austrian plants. Alienation among workers in the kibbutz plants, however, is rare.

Peptic Ulcer. A member's rank is a basis for the respect or esteem accorded him in an organization. Persons who are esteemed by others are likely to esteem themselves and members at upper levels will therefore feel more self-esteem than do those below. Self-esteem in turn has significant implications for physical and mental health (French, 1963; Kasl and French, 1962).

French has found evidence that low self-esteem, particularly with respect to popularity, is associated with a high level of pepsinogen in the blood which is related in turn to peptic ulcer. Low organizational status which implies low self-esteem might therefore help explain the high incidence of peptic ulcer that Vertin found among lower-status compared to higher-status blue collar workers (Vertin, 1954). Earlier research has also suggested that the first-line supervisor, not the rank-and-file worker, is especially prone to peptic ulcer. The first-line supervisor is said to be a "man in the middle," caught in the cross-fire between management and the worker. Although his formal status is above that of the worker he does not have the status of management, and he must frequently behave in ways that are unpopular. Often, he is no more than a messenger transmitting orders from above. "On the one hand, he must bear the brunt of resistance and expressed grievances from below and, on the other, must suffer criticism from above for the failure of his subordinates to conform to expectations. The seriousness of the situation is compounded by the fact that orders coming from above are often formed without the advantage of adequate knowledge of conditions at lower levels. . . . The orders which he is responsible for relaying, then, are often the least likely to gain full acceptance, thus making his position all the more untenable and that of his subordinates all the more difficult" (Tannenbaum, 1962b). Ulcer may thus result from the tension and lack of self-esteem, especially with respect to popularity connected with the foreman role. (See, for example, the reaction of one worker toward another who was promoted to foreman, mentioned in Chapter One.)

These arguments along with the results of prior research led us to expect a connection between hierarchical status and peptic ulcer. We shall therefore examine two hypotheses: that the incidence of peptic ulcer is more likely at lower than at upper levels; and that the incidence is particularly acute for the first-line supervisor. Such effects of hierarchy, however, should be less manifest in the formally participative compared to the non-participative organization, since status differences and the conflicts associated with status are not as great in the former as in the latter, according to the general theory we are exploring.

We can examine the relationship of hierarchy to ulcer through a questionnaire measure of ulcer developed by Dunn and Cobb (1962) and validated against medical records. Their question, which applies only to males, involves several parts:

50. During the last thirty days, did you have any pain in your stomach?
    1. Yes
    2. No (If *No,* go to question 53)
If yes:
    (a) Did these pains come on before eating, while eating, right after eating, a couple of hours after eating, or when?
        1. Before eating
        2. While eating
        3. Right after eating
        4. Two or three hours after eating
        5. Not associated with eating
    (b) Was this pain relieved by eating, drinking milk, bicarbonate of soda or other antacid, or by anything else?
        1. Eating
        2. Drinking milk
        3. Bicarbonate of soda or other antacid
        4. Anything else
        5. Nothing
    (c) Did the stomach pain wake you up or keep you up at night?
        1. Yes
        2. No
    (d) Thinking still about this past four weeks, on how many days would you think you had this pain for at least part of the day?
        _____ Days

The question is coded as follows:

(a) If the respondent answers question 50, "yes" and question 50a "before eating" or "after eating," or 50b "eating" or "drinking milk" then he is scored the number of days in response to question 50d.

(b) Or if he answers question 50, "yes" and 50c, "yes," then he is scored the number of days in response to question 50d.

(c) Other responses are scored 00.

The final score thus represents the number of days the respondent suffered stomach pain due to peptic ulcer.

We present the data concerning ulcer in a different manner than the data of earlier sections because the hierarchical distribution of ulcer departs sharply from linearity, and linear regressions therefore provide a very poor approximation. Furthermore, we are interested in the hypothesis that the first-line supervisor is more prone to peptic ulcer than are other members and we shall want to see how first-line supervisors compare to others. Because females are not included in these data (the question concerning stomach pains not being an appropriate measure of ulcer for women), the number of cases at several points in the hierarchy within countries is small and we therefore combine the data for groups of countries and for different lengths of chain.

Table 40 presents the results for all countries combined. The first column defines the number of hierarchical levels *below* a respondent, regardless of the length of chain in which he is located. Thus, zero defines members at the bottom of the hierarchy; these persons have no subordinates. One refers to first-line supervisors; they have one level below them. Two refers to persons immediately above the first-line supervisor, and so on. All chains are included in this table excepting two-level chains, since these do not have first-line supervisors.

This is a gross representation of the data combining all chains in all plants, but it suggests that in general peptic ulcer is slightly more prevalent at lower levels than at higher. The "average" first-line supervisor suffers 1.1 days of stomach pain

Table 40.   Hierarchical Distribution of Peptic Ulcer
(Number of days per month stomach pain)
All Countries Combined

	Number of Levels Below Respondent	Days/Mo. Stomach Pain	N [a]
	0	1.3	596
First-Line Supervisor	1	1.1	337
	2	1.0	175
	3	1.1	91
	4	.4	42
	5–6	.0	19

[a] The N's in this table are slightly inflated since a manager may enter more than once. See explanation under discussion in Chapter One defining hierarchical position.

per month, but his subordinates and immediate supervisors are not less likely to have this psychosomatic symptom. It is persons at or near the top of the organization who appear to be relatively free of ulcer.

Figure 19 combines for the small plants the Italian, Austrian, and American data on the one hand and the kibbutz and Yugoslav data on the other. The contrast between these two groups is striking; one distribution is almost the mirror image of the other. Furthermore, the first-line supervisor appears especially prone to ulcer in the formally non-participative systems but not in the participative, very much as predicted. In the latter systems ulcer is as likely for upper levels as for lower— if not more so.

Regression lines provide only very crude indications of the trends represented by these data, because of their sharp departure from linearity. Regressions were nonetheless computed as in previous analyses for each length of chain within each country, and they are consistent as far as they go, with the results shown in Figure 19. The average slope of regression line for the small Italian, Austrian, and United States plants is .76, and for the Yugoslav and kibbutz plants —.08. There are differences within these two groups of plants, however. The formally non-participative group ranges from 1.12 in the Ameri-

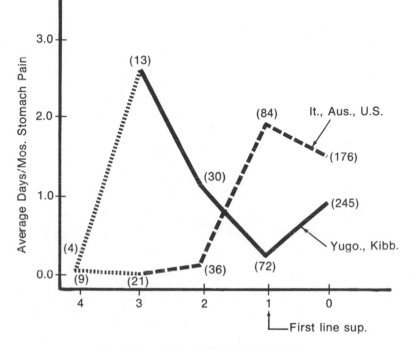

Figure 19. Distribution of peptic ulcer (formally participative vs. non-participative systems, small plants). Numbers in parentheses are respondents at each point. Dotted lines call attention to the small number of cases at point 4.

can plants to .28 in the Austrian. On the other hand, the kibbutz plants have an average slope of —.37 and the Yugoslav .22.

Figure 20 shows the data for the large plants. The differences between the formally participative and non-participative plants, however, do not fit our predictions. The Yugoslav plants, but not the others, show a peak at the level of the first-line supervisor and both groups of plants show a slight tendency for ulcer to be more prevalent at lower levels. Regression slopes, computed as in previous analyses, provide a very rough indication of this tendency. The Italian, Austrian, and American plants average .19 and the Yugoslav .18. The range within the first group, however, goes from .50 in the Italian to —.08 in the Austrian plants. An examination of the data from different

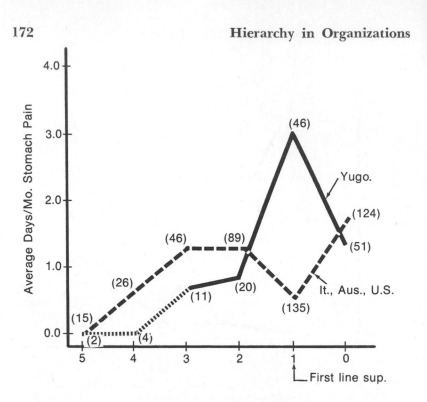

Number of Level Below Respondent

Figure 20. Distribution of peptic ulcer (participative vs. non-participative systems, large plants). Numbers in parentheses are respondents at each point. Dotted lines connect points that have small numbers of cases.

chain length (not shown here) suggests that supervisors who have ulcer are likely to be in relatively long chains rather than in short ones. They are found, for example, in the five-level chains of the small organizations and the six-level chains of the large (Yugoslav) organizations. These are the chains in which supervisors confront production workers rather than clerical workers and conditions that exacerbate ulcer may be prevalent here. But first-line supervisors in the long chains of the large Italian, Austrian, and American plants do not conform to this pattern.

Instances where the data peak at the foreman level are tantalizing in the context of the hypothesis that the foreman is especially susceptible to this psychosomatic effect, but we do not understand why the data peak for the supervisor in some chains and not in others. Supervisors may be especially prone to ulcer under certain conditions, but what these conditions are we do not know. Nonetheless, the data suggest that ulcer is less likely among persons at upper levels than it is at lower levels in most of these organizations. The kibbutz plants are a predictable exception.

Perceptions and Ideals

Studies of hierarchy suggest that persons in different positions often perceive differently the same facts of organizational life. Indeed, persons encounter the organization quite differently, depending on their position, and some perceive the organization through one set of experiences while others perceive the organization through another. Persons at different levels thus develop their own stereotypes. They also acquire stakes in the organization and position comes to define the self-interest of a member. What a manager deems good for the organization or for himself will therefore differ in some degree from what the worker deems good. Furthermore, because of their superior authority, upper-level personnel can affect the organization more substantially and in ways consistent with their self-interest than can persons at lower levels. The discrepancy between the realities of organizational life and the preferences that members have therefore declines with hierarchical ascent except in the participative organization, where according to theory power differentials are not as great as in the non-participative and members share a common interest. Persons of different rank should therefore share common perceptions and ideals in such organizations more than in the non-participative.

Four topics relevant to organizational functioning were selected: (a) decision making; (b) influence-control; (c) bases for advancement in the hierarchy; and (d) rewards and sanctions received by workers for good work and bad. Each topic has significant value connotations and should therefore be subject to distortions of perception. For each topic a question designed to measure members' preference was asked, along with a question designed to measure his perception. Data showing the average responses to these measures in each group of plants are presented in Chapter Three. We shall now see how these perceptions may be subject to bias due to rank of the respondent.

Perceptions. The first measure of perception is an index concerning the extent to which workers participate in decisions. It is constructed by averaging the responses to three questions (34, 36, and 39), which were discussed in Chapter Three (see Figure 2). The hierarchical gradients on this index are not very steep in any country, but the largest gradient occurs in the Italian plants as usual. In these plants upper-level persons are more likely than lower to see their plants being participative.

Figure 21 shows the best-fit lines averaged for three-, four-, and five-level chains in the small plants. The striking features of this graph is not the difference in slopes among plants, but rather the difference in height of the lines. Kibbutz and Yugoslav plant members especially, regardless of position, are more likely than their counterparts in the other countries to see their plants as formally participative.*

The next several measures concern the perception of influence exercised by workers, managers, and management board, respectively, as described in Chapter Three, Figure 4. Perception of the influence exercised by workers is more subject to bias due to rank than is perception of the influence exercised by managers and by the management board, according to the data. Especially in the Italian plants persons differ in perception as a function of rank. The gradients in the Italian small and large plants are .40 and .58, respectively; the American plants rank second to the Italian with gradients of .32 and .21; and Yugoslav plants have the flattest gradients, —.03 and —.02. The gradients are also rather small, .11, in the kibbutz plants. But in some organizations at least, like the Italian and perhaps the American, information provided by members about the influence of workers depends on where the informants are located

---

* Figure 21 implies that members in American small plants report slightly more participativeness than do members in the corresponding Austrian plants. Figure 2, however, shows the American and Austrian plants more nearly equal on an average of the items in this index. The footnote on p. 109 explains the slight apparent discrepancy between the two figures.

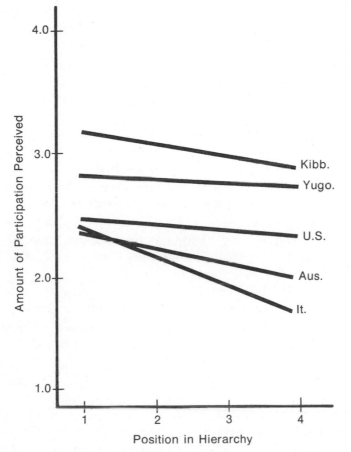

Figure 21. Perception of participative decision making (small plants; three-, four-, and five-level chains averaged).

in the hierarchy; managers attribute more influence to workers than do the workers themselves.

Three perceptions concerning bases of advancement were measured through the question "How important are each of the following factors for getting ahead in this company?" (See Table 14.) Three indices were formed on the basis of a correlational analysis. The first averages the scores for the factors of "quality of work," "quantity of work," "creativity," and "ability with people." Positive gradients imply that upper-level personnel more than lower-level employees see these qualities as important requirements for advancement in the company, and in fact the gradients are positive everywhere except the Yugoslav large plants. But these gradients are typically small, the largest, .30, occurring in the Italian large and small plants.

The second index concerning bases of advancement combines the following qualities: "supervisor's opinion," "dependability," "good professional knowledge," "initiative," and "loyalty to the company." Upper-level persons more than lower-level workers are likely to cite these qualities as important, although the gradients are small. The largest, .32, occurs in the Austrian small plants, and the smallest gradient, .13, occurs in the kibbutz plants. Among the large plants Italy has the largest gradient, .22, and Yugoslavia the smallest, −.05, but the gradient in the American large plants is also small, .08.

The third index concerning bases for advancement is composed of the following qualities: "having friends in higher management," "recommendations of a political or religious nature," and "elbowing one's way to get ahead." These are likely to be viewed as negative qualities, and in fact all but the Yugoslav small plants indicate predictably that lower-level persons more than upper-level employees perceive these unfavorable qualities to be important bases for advancement in their plants. The largest gradient (−.38) again occurs in the Italian small plants, but among the large plants the differences among countries are unpredicted; they are all small, the Italian plants ranking last.

The final set of perceptions concerns the rewards that are provided to members when they do a good job and the sanctions suffered by members for poor work. The questions on which these perceptions are based are described in Chapter Three, Tables 6 and 8, and the gradients of these items follow the pattern we have described: in general the gradients are steepest in the Italian and relatively flat in the Yugoslav and kibbutz plants, although the data for each item in the indexes of reward and sanction do not always conform to this pattern.

All in all, the gradients of perceptions considered in this section are not large, contrary to our expectation, and the differences between countries are therefore not very great. The largest gradients occur in Italy, averaging .32 among small plants. By way of contrast the smallest gradients are found in kibbutzim and in Yugoslavia, where the averages are .14 and .17, respectively.* Among the large plants Italy again ranks first with an average of .35, and Yugoslavia is last with an average of .16.

Ideals and Discrepancies. Each of the questions designed to measure the perceptions described above was accompanied by a question to ascertain the members' preferences. For example, in the area of decision making, members were asked two questions:

* Systematic biases in the perceptions of members have obvious methodological significance for research (including the present study) in which attempts are made to obtain from members facts about their organization. It is fortunate, from the methodological standpoint, that bias due to rank is relatively small, at least with respect to most of the perceptions reported here. Nonetheless, studies that are designed to compare organizations with respect to facts about the organization as reported by members should employ large numbers of informants who differ in position, so that the extent of bias due to position can at least be appraised. If the biases due to rank are similar in each of the organizations, then the relative standing of the organizations is not very much affected by the position of the informants, providing they occupy comparable positions in the respective organizations. There is probably an advantage in any event to samples that include informants from all ranks if we assume that the biases of upper-level personnel cancel those of lower-ranking persons when these biases are averaged. Obviously, the organizations themselves must differ substantially in the facts concerning which they are being compared if such facts are to be measured through the perception of members. For example, if biases affect the perception of size of organization, a comparison of organizations on size measured through the perceptions of members is not likely to be very reliable or valid if the organizations are very similar in size. Small differences will be obliterated by the biases, systematic as well as random, of the informants. Comparisons can be reasonably valid, however, if one organization has only 50 members and another 500. The biases and errors of judgment are not likely to be so large as to mask the basic difference in size between these two organizations. In the present study we assume that the differences between plants of the respective countries are in fact substantial with respect to many of the characteristics, such as participativeness and influence of workers, on which the organizations are being compared. We also assume that the biases due to rank, which are partly cancelled out through averaging, as well as other systematic biases due to "culture," are relatively small compared to the real differences between groups. We shall consider in the next chapter the effect of cultural bias when we compare organizations within each of the countries separately.

34. Do workers participate in making important decisions related to their work?
35. *Should* workers participate in making important decisions related to their work?

The second of these questions is designed to measure the respondents' ideal.

The results show surprisingly flat gradients on most items. For example, lower-level personnel do not profess a more participative decision-making ideal than do upper-level personnel in any of the countries. A negative gradient, −.10 in Italy, is the only one where the sign of the relationship between rank and ideal conforms to the expectation that lower-level personnel will prefer a more participative organization than upper-level personnel. But the magnitude of this gradient is very small. Likewise the hierarchical gradients concerning the amount of influence that workers should exercise is quite flat in the plants of most countries.

Although the data are weak, the Italian plants, as usual, show the steepest gradients and the kibbutz plants show relatively flat ones. However, the gradients in the Austrian plants are also quite flat on these items, and the Yugoslav gradients rank second to the Italian.

The respondent's score on each question designed to measure his perception was subtracted from his "ideal" score and the absolute value of this difference is taken as a measure of the discrepancy between ideal and actual. This discrepancy tends in general to decrease with hierarchical ascent, as predicted in the plants of the five countries, but the gradients of the discrepancy are quite small and the differences between countries in these gradients are therefore small. For example, a relatively large difference in gradients occurs in the small plants with respect to the items concerning decision making. The range in gradients runs from .31 in Italy to −.03 in Yugoslavia. Thus in the Italian plants, but not in the Yugoslav, the discrepancy between the amount of participativeness that members would like and the amount they perceive in their plants decreases somewhat with hierarchical ascent. A ranking of the average of the gradients for all items in the small plants orders the plants from high to low as follows: Austrian, American, Italian, kibbutz, Yugoslav. In the large plants the order is American, Austrian, Italian, Yugoslav.

Summary and Conclusions

The data of this chapter demonstrate gradients of reaction and adjustment associated with hierarchy. Persons at upper levels, compared to those below, are predictably more satisfied with their jobs and their salaries; they are more favorably disposed toward the company and feel more responsible and motivated in their work; they are in a number of respects "better adjusted"; and they see the organization in ways that conform in some degree to a more positive stereotype. These tendencies help define a widely recognized principle of organization: "positive" reaction to and support for the system increase with hierarchical ascent.

But there are exceptions, or at least qualifications, to this principle. Countries differ in magnitude of gradient; hierarchy has less impact on the reactions and adjustments of members in some systems than in others. This differential effect is predictable in part from differences in formal participativeness and in underlying ideology that separate the five countries. Ideology defines the general rules and rationalizations concerning how an organization is to be governed. Ideology may be legally established, as in the kibbutz and Yugoslav systems, or it may be expressed as an implicit philosophy of management based on tradition or the contemporary realities of power in a society. But ideology manifests itself concretely in the nature of the organization hierarchy—in the gradients of authority and reward and in the consequent reactions and adjustments of members.

Kibbutz and Yugoslav organizations are designed on an equalitarian ideological basis. They are formally more participative than the conventional industrial bureaucracy and they deemphasize hierarchy through a relatively equalitarian distribution of authority, reward, and other conditions, as we have seen in the previous chapter. Consequently the reactions and adjustments of members are also less sharply graded in these organziations. American organizations are not formally participative, but a tradition of equalitarianism explains some informal participativeness at least greater than that in the Italian and Austrian plants. The gradients are therefore in general less sharp in the American plants than in the other non-participative plants.

Table 41 summarizes some of the data of this chapter by presenting the rank order of gradients on each measure of reaction and adjustment for the respective countries. In general, the Italian plants demonstrate the sharpest gradients. Position in the hierarchy makes a substantial difference to members in these plants; persons near the top clearly differ in reaction and adjustment from those near the bottom. Position makes less difference to members in the kibbutz and Yugoslav plants—although it does make a difference. These formally participative systems may reduce but they do not entirely eliminate the effects of hierarchy.

The impact of hierarchy measured in terms of magnitude of gradient is more apparent with respect to some reactions and adjustments than others. Gradients are relatively steep with respect to satisfaction with job and salary, sense of responsibility, motivation and initiative. Gradients are less steep with respect to psychological adjustment, alienation, and some measures of the perceptions and ideals of members. Conditions associated with position are more clearly relevant to the former reactions and adjustment than to the latter. For example, the opportunities that a job provides, which are closely tied to role in the hierarchy, have clear relevance to the satisfaction a member will derive from his job. The relevance of such opportunities to the *general* adjustment of members is less apparent. Furthermore, many circumstances external to the plant are likely to have a bearing on criteria of general adjustment more than on satisfaction with job. Similarly, the effects of hierarchical conditions on the perceptions and ideals of members are indirect and perceptions are determined by many conditions beyond hierarchy itself. While perception is subject to autistic distor-

Table 41. Rank Order of Plants in the Five Countries on Gradients of Reaction and Adjustment

Gradients	Small Plants					Large Plants			
	Italy	Austria	United States	Yugo-slavia	Kibbutz	Italy	Austria	United States	Yugo-slavia
Satisfaction with job	1	3	2	5	4	2	1	3	4
Satisfaction with knowledge	1	2	5	4	3	1	2	4	3
Attitude toward leadership	2	1	3	5	4	1.5	3	1.5	4
Satisfaction with pay	1	3	2	4	—	2.5	1	2.5	4
Sense of responsibility	1	2	4	5	3	1	2	4	3
Initiative	3	2	4	1	5	1	3	4	2
Motivation	1	4	2	5	3	1	3	4	2
Psychological adjustment	1	2	3	5	4	4	2	3	1
Alienation	1	2	4	5	3	3	1.5	1.5	4
Peptic ulcer	2	3	1	4	5	1	4	3	2
Perceptions	1	3	2	4	5	1	4	3	2
Ideals	1	4.5	3	2	4.5	1	4	3	2
Ideals-Actual	3	1	2	5	4	3	2	1	4
Average Rank	1.5	2.5	2.8	4.0	4.0	1.8	2.4	2.8	3.0

tion, perception is also affected very substantially by the realities being perceived and a member's perception is therefore constrained by those realities. Furthermore, some of the realities do not have the strong value connotations for members that lead them to distort their perception in a way to conform to or rationalize a value position. Nonetheless, our questions do refer to realities that are often ambiguous and that are sometimes relevant to the values of the perceiver. Systematic bias therefore enters and persons at upper levels, in some systems at least, are more likely than those below to report, for example, that their plant conforms to a positively valued, participative decision-making pattern.

The gradients of reaction and adjustment considered in this chapter are not as steep as the gradients of authority, reward, and other conditions considered earlier. These conditions, studied in the previous chapter, are *assigned* to position explicitly or implicitly and they become part of the meaning of hierarchy itself. The reactions and adjustments considered here are not so much a part of hierarchy as they are a consequence in part of the authority, reward, and other conditions that help to define hierarchy. Hierarchy, abstracted from these conditions, has relatively little psychological impact on members. Persons at upper levels are not more satisfied with their pay than those below simply because they have high rank but rather because they receive high pay. Upper-level persons are not more satisfied with their jobs than lower-level person simply because they are high in the hierarchy but rather because their jobs afford greater opportunity for self-actualization. When these conditions are defined out of the hierarchy statistically through regression procedures, little difference in reaction and adjustment between persons of different rank remains. And when these conditions are in some measure defined out of the hierarchy in actuality, as in the formally participative system, the effects of hierarchy are at least reduced.

Kibbutz plants go all the way in defining a gradient-free organization on financial reward, and they formally limit the gradient of authority. Superiors do not have the right to promote or fire a subordinate, to award benefits or impose penalties that are the underpinnings of authority in other systems (see Table 10). And kibbutz plants have procedures for all members formally to influence important decisions. Hence differences in authority between ranks are formally limited. It may be easier, however, to limit the authority and rewards assigned to leaders than it is to limit the problems faced by leaders. Thus while some rewards are equalized, some of the responsibilities that leaders face are not. In fact, the gradient of "responsibility felt by members" is, in terms of our original expectation, surprisingly steep in kibbutz plants. Such a gradient implies commitment and concern on the part of leaders greater than that of workers. Hence, some leaders may feel the "negative balance of rewards" to which we referred in the previous chapter. The suggestive tendency, unique to kibbutz plants, that upper-level personnel suffer more peptic ulcer than lower-level persons may indicate this negative balance. The Yugoslav manager also appears, in terms of a number of reactions and adjustments, to fare poorly when compared to the managers of other plants, although the Yugoslav worker does not do badly compared to his counterparts elsewhere. The cost-benefit balance of high rank, calculated in terms of some of the adjustments considered in this chapter, is less favorable in the Yugoslav and kibbutz plants than in the others. Despite this disadvantage, however, leaders in the kibbutz plants and in the Yugoslav are "better off" than their rank and file on many of the indicators studied here. There is a limit on how far organizations can go in mitigating the inevitable consequences of hierarchy.

Thus, all systems show some degree of hierarchical effect which, considering the diversity of ideology and formal structure among them, suggests a universality to the principle of hierarchy we are investigating. In fact, the similarities between countries are as important as the differences and the systems are impressively alike even with respect to some of the relationships underlying the effects of hierarchy. For example, the opportunities and authority that a job provides, along with certain physical qualities of the job, help explain a member's satisfaction with his job in all countries. Education also affects job satisfaction but the impact of education is, in all countries, negative. The kibbutz worker does not differ in this respect from the Italian, or from the worker in other systems. The more educated he is the less likely he is to be satisfied with his job, holding rank and other hierarchical conditions constant. Such consistency between systems is not easily explained by chance, and we can be reasonably confident that we are dealing with a rather general feature of organizational life. Furthermore, factors that are important in explaining one effect, like job satisfaction, may be unimportant in explaining another effect, and some *patterns* of relationship vary in similar ways among the countries. For example, salary has no bearing on job satisfaction in any country although it does quite reasonably affect satisfaction with pay in at least three of the four countries where members are paid. (The result in the fourth country is in the same direction as the other three, although it is not significant statistically.) Authority and influence are clearly associated with a sense of responsibility in all countries, but education is not associated with sense of responsibility in any country (under the controlled conditions of the regression analysis). On the other hand, education is relevant to the initiative a member will take vis-à-vis his superior in all countries, but authority and influence are not, except in the American plants. The impact of education is intriguing because of its conflicting implications in all countries in terms of commonly held values. Educated members feel less alienated than their co-workers of the same rank, but they are more dissatisfied with their jobs than are their co-workers. Education in this sense is a mixed blessing in all of the countries studied. These data show some differences and even some uniqueness in the five countries, but they also show impressive similarities that testify to basic commonalities among them. Some principles of organization transcend culture and ideology.

Plants of the five countries differ not only in gradient but also in average level of reaction and adjustment. Members in the relatively hierarchical and non-participative Italian plants, for example, when compared to members in other plants, are dissatisfied with their jobs and their pay; they are distrustful of plant leadership and feel little sense of responsibility, motivation, or initiative. Members' psychological adjustment, relatively speaking, is poor and members in the Italian plants rank ahead of members in the other plants in sense of alienation and frequency of peptic ulcer. Such differences between plants apply to the average member in our sample who, given the nature of the sample, is located near but not at the bottom of the hierarchy. The situation of the rank-and-file worker in the Italian plants is certainly not better in terms of the above reactions and adjustments.

The relatively "poor" adjustment of members in the Italian plants fits well the hypothesis that conflict and frustration will be greater in the non-participative system than in the formally participative system. The highly participative kibbutz plants, too, conform to the hypothesis; members here generally respond positively to questions concerning the above reactions and adjustments. But members in the less participative American plants also rank high on these items, while members in the Yugoslav plants do less well, as do those in the Austrian plants. Formal participativeness seems to be a better predictor of the *distribution* than of the *average level* of adjustment in a system.

But it is the combination of distribution *and* level of adjustment that best describes the fate of members. A steep gradient of adjustment obviously means something different for members when the average level of adjustment is high rather than low, and the plants in the five countries can be roughly categorized in terms of the combination of these characteristics, as in Table 42. This rough classification of the five countries is based on our sample, which includes a larger number of persons near the bottom of the hierarchy than near the top. It therefore reflects the adjustment of members located close to but not at the bottom. A classification in which the adjustment only of top managers were to be considered would certainly make a difference in the placement of countries in the table. The Italian and Austrian plants would move to the right while the Yugoslav and kibbutz plants would slip, relatively speaking, to the left. The advantage a member enjoys in one system com-

pared to that of his counterpart in another depends on whether
he is a manager being compared to other managers or a worker
being compared to other workers.

Table 42. Plants in the Five Countries Categorized According
to Gradient and Quality of Adjustment

Gradient of Adjustment	Quality of Adjustment		
	Low	Medium	High
Flat	X	Yugoslavia	Kibbutz
Medium	X	Austria	United States
Steep	Italy	X	X

Hierarchy has both intended and unintended consequences, some of which we have observed and tried to understand in this chapter. Other variables unconnected to hierarchy
may provide a more substantial basis for explaining the reactions and adjustments we are investigating, but hierarchy has
special importance because it is consciously designed and formally established in an organization. We have, in other words,
some choice in principle concerning the character of hierarchy.
Furthermore, the fact that hierarchy is a structural feature of
organization adds to the significance of its consequences. Compare two organizations with an equal number of disaffected
members, but one in which these persons are dispersed ran-
domly in the organization and another in which they are placed
together. Hierarchy implies such clustering of persons who
share a common adjustment—although hierarchy is not the only
basis for such clustering. Intentionally, hierarchy organizes the
behavior of members so that the behavior is appropriate to
the organization's purposes. Intentionally or not, hierarchy also
arranges and systemmatizes members' satisfaction and dissatisfaction, motivation, and adjustment. Hierarchy organizes the
feelings of members as well as their behavior, and it organizes
these feelings more substantially in some systems than in others.

VI

THE HIERARCHICAL
ORGANIZATION

I t is reasonable to think that some organizations are more hierarchical than others in the sense that hierachy expresses itself more clearly in some than in others, and that there is a consistency within an organization in the extent to which gradients characterize hierarchy.* We have seen intimations of some consistency in the data of the previous chapters, where countries distinguish themselves with some regularity in hierarchical gradients. This consistency can be seen more plainly when we look at the plants themselves. For example, a plant that has a steep gradient of one rewarding social function such as authority and influence is also likely to have steep gradients of other rewards, such as salary and opportunities provided by the job. "Degree of hierarchy," in other words, is an organizational characteristic that can be measured with some reliability,

* This chapter was written by D. Nightingale and A. Tannenbaum.

and we shall examine in this chapter whether plants differ from one another *within* a country in their degree of hierarchy as they do *between* countries, and, if they do differ, whether differences in the participativeness of plants help to explain differences in hierarchy.

Participativeness is one apparent explanation suggested in previous chapters for differences in gradient *between* countries, but the differences documented in earlier chapters leave open questions about variables associated with a country that we have not taken into account and that may be the real source of the difference in gradient. Perhaps the "culture" of a country or the way persons are inclined to respond to a questionnaire explains why the gradients in one country are steeper than those in another according to our measure. Hence the attempt in this chapter to reduce if not eliminate the effect of some of these extraneous, country-related characteristics by comparing plants within each country. We try in this way to hold "culture" constant.

One might expect that partictipativeness, which seems to explain differences in gradient between countries, explains variation within countries too. But important differences in the formal structure of control of plants that distinguish countries from one another and that presumably are a basis for differences in gradient do not exist within one country. Ownership of the plant, for example, which has implications for formal control, is virtually constant for the plants of this study within each country. *All* of the plants in kibbutzim are owned by the kibbutz of which the workers are members, and the right of members to make policy decisions follows from that ownership. *None* of the plants in Italy are owned by the workers, and the formal right to decide policy is reserved for the top management in all of these plants. Thus variation in participativeness within each country is limited by prescriptions of the larger system. Are such limits broad enough to allow significant variation in participation and in degree of hierarchy, and, if so, does the principle that participation mitigates the effects of hierarchy apply to variation within a country, as it apparently does between countries? Or are the large differences in the formal structure of control that occur between countries necessary to demonstrate the mitigating effect of hierarchy? We can not assert causality, of course, in response to such questions, because our correlations demonstrate only an association among variables. But we can at least know whether participative plants show flatter gradients than non-participative within a single country, as they seem to show when plants of the different countries are compared.

To demonstrate such an association assumes not only some variation in participativeness among plants, but also some validity in the measure of this variation. There is little doubt that real and substantial variation occurs *between* countries, where the differences are clearly documented independently of our research instruments. We do not have independent documentation for differences in participation within a country, however, and intranational comparison must rely exclusively on data derived from the questionnaire. We might nonetheless feel some confidence in the questionnaire data concerning decision making, because they prove reasonably consistent with the objective evidence of differences between countries, and we therefore employ these data in our search for a tentative answer to the questions posed above. The unit of analysis will be the plant itself. We shall construct indices that define how hierarchical each plant is and how participative it is, and we shall examine covariation between these variables within countries and between them.

Degree of Hierarchy in a Plant

Table 43 shows correlations between several indices of gradient that define how hierarchical each plant is. Since each index characterizes a plant, the unit of analysis in this table is the plant itself, of which there are 52.* The table presents

---

* Regression procedures were employed to compute the slope of a best-fit-line that defines the relationship between a dependent variable (for example, authority-influence) and hierarchical position separately within each plant. Each plant, therefore, has a score that defines its gradient with respect to a particular variable in question. These analyses within each

partial correlations in which the effect of size of plant and its average length of chain are removed because small plants and short chains generally have steeper gradients than large plants and long chains—as we have noted in previous chapters. The correlations therefore do not simply reflect the tendency that the gradients in some organizations will be flatter than those in other organizations, because some organizations are larger and have longer chains than others.†

Two sets of correlations are shown in this and in the following tables. The first is based on a computation in which all of the plants, regardless of country, are analyzed together. Data from plants in Italy, for example, are correlated along with data from plants in kibbutzim and in the other places. These correlations therefore reflect the covariation that occurs between, as well as within, countries. Correlations in the second set, enclosed in parentheses, are an average of correlations computed separately within each country. These correlations eliminate the effect of covariation between countries and a high correlation means that the variables in question relate strongly to one another *within* each country regardless of how they may covary between countries.‡ Political, economic, and cultural differences that distinguish countries from one another and that

---

plant were done controlling for length of chain because the meaning of hierarchical position defined in terms of distance from the top (or bottom) depends on the length of the chain. See the discussion on pp. 19–21. Technically, this control seemed an appropriate correction, but in fact it has only a very minor effect on the magnitude of the gradients computed.

† We shall continue throughout this chapter to control for size of plant and length of chain, and the reader may assume that this control has been applied even though it is not mentioned explicitly in the text. In some instances additional controls are introduced, in which case they will be described, but size of plant and length of chain will be controlled unless otherwise indicated. The transformation Log_{10} size was employed rather than size itself because the relationship between size and the other variables tends to be more logarithmic than linear. See also Tannenbaum (1962c, pp. 113–114).

‡ The score of each plant within a country was subtracted from the mean score for that country for each variable, and these intranational deviations for all 52 plants were employed in a single matrix to obtain the above parenthetical correlations. These correlations come very close to describing an average of the correlations within the countries.

may affect the non-parenthesized correlations have no bearing on these intranational scores.

Table 43. Correlations between Gradients of Authority and Reward, Reactions and Adjustments, and Perceptions and Ideals
(N = 52)

	Reactions and Adjustments	Perceptions and Ideals	Overall Degree of Hierarchy
Authority and Reward	.63 * (.56) *	.42 * (.30) *	.80 * (.65) *
Reaction and Adjustment		.49 * (.45) *	.80 * (.80) *
Perceptions and Ideals			.53 * (.49) *

Note: Asterisks denote correlations that we estimate to be significant at the .05 level of confidence. We employ the 5 percent level of confidence in defining statistical significance although our statistical calculations are only very approximate. The sample of plants does not conform to the simple model of random selection upon which the usual statistical tests have been formulated, and we employ these tests only as a rough guide to our statistical appraisal of the results. In calculating confidence levels we assume that in the intranational analysis we have the equivalent of N-5 degrees of freedom, where N is the total number of plants and 5 is the number of countries. We assume that in the analysis where country is not controlled the number of degrees of freedom is probably greater than 10, the number of plants in each country, but less than 52, the total number of plants. We have arbitrarily accepted 30, which is close to an average of the two limits. When partial correlations are computed, we assume that one additional degree of freedom is lost for every variable held constant, and when directional predictions are made we employ the one-tailed test.

The first gradient of Table 43, authority and reward, was constructed by averaging within each plant the gradients considered in Chapter Four that describe the distribution of economic and social rewards in a plant, including members' salary, the amount of authority and influence members perceive themselves to have, and their opportunities—for example, to use their skills, learn new things, and do interesting work. The average correlation between the gradients that comprise this index is .53 when all plants are considered together, and analyses done within each country yield an average correlation of .36. The intranational correlations are lower than those in which the effect of country is not controlled partly because gradients do not vary as much within countries as between them. There is absolutely no variation in gradient of salary in kibbutzim, for example, and the correlation between this gradient and the others is therefore zero among kibbutz plants.

Working conditions, which are among the rewarding aspects of position considered in Chapter Four, do not have a gradient that correlates with the other items of this index, contrary to our expectation, and it is therefore not combined into the index. This lack of correlation does not mean an absence of gradient with respect to working conditions. On the contrary, such gradients are substantial in all plants. Jobs at the bottom of a hierarchy are generally dirtier, heavier, more physical and hazardous than those at the top, but gradients of these conditions do not vary between the plants in a way that corresponds to the items of the above index, perhaps because such working conditions are determined by technological and other circumstances that are not affected.as much (if at all) by ideology as are salary, authority, and other rewarding functions of position.

The second index of Table 43, gradient of reaction and adjustment, is based on the gradients considered·in Chapter Five (job satisfaction, sense of responsibility, alienation, and the others), exclusive of the gradients of perceptions and ideals. The average correlation between these gradients is .25 but some interrelate better than others, and the seven "best" items (out of a total of eleven) were selected to compose the above index, yielding an average correlation of .35.*

The third index, gradient of perceptions and ideals (concerning decision making, control, bases of advancement in the company, and so on, see Chapter Five), is based on a selection

---

* The seven "best" items are gradients with regard to: (a) initiative on the job; (b) knowledge of how job fits into plant; (c) satisfaction with knowledge; (d) job satisfaction; (e) feeling of responsibility; (f) attitude toward company leadership; (g) alienation. All these items are described in Chapter Five.

of the eight most highly correlating gradients among the 27 gradients of perceptions and ideals considered in Chapter Five. The total group of gradients from which this index is a selection does not, in fact, form a very coherent set, although differences are apparent in the perceptions and ideals of members as a function of their rank. Persons at lower levels see their organization differently and express different preferences for the organization compared to those at upper levels. Furthermore, the discrepancies between what members perceive and what they prefer for their organization are predictably greater for persons at lower levels than at upper. These facts of organizational life are apparent in the data of all countries. Yet gradients of perceptions and ideals in general are not as large as gradients of authority and reward or of the reactions and adjustments considered above. Nor do the items of perception and ideal that we have measured make up a simple, unitary set of gradients. Some gradients of perception correlate highly with others, but some show very poor and even negative correlations, the average being only .13. The magnitude of gradient with respect to perceptions and ideals—at least those that we have measured—therefore does not provide as stable an index as do the other gradients. A selection of the eight "best" items yields an average correlation of .37 and provides the basis for the index of Table 43. Because this is such a select group of the total set, however, it does not make a very adequate general index of gradient with respect to perceptions and ideals, and we find in subsequent analyses that correlations involving this index are usually close to zero and rarely significant statistically. We therefore eliminate this index from the following tables in order to simplify the presentation. Apparently the perceptions that members were asked to report are subject only weakly to biases associated with rank and our hypothesis about the effect of hierarchy on these perceptions is supported only very weakly. There is some consolation in this failure since it suggests that hierarchy is not a strong source of bias with respect to the reporting of some social facts about the organization—whatever other sources of bias may affect the report of these facts by respondents. We may, of course, have selected the "wrong" facts-to-be-perceived; other, more sensitive facts may be more subject to the biasing effect of hierarchical position. A large body of data suggests that this is indeed likely to be the case.

To the three indices described above we add a fourth, which we refer to as "overall degree of hierarchy." This index consists of *all* of the gradients of Chapters Four and Five, including the gradients of demographic characteristics and the other gradients eliminated from the preceding, more selective indices.* Since this index includes all of the gradients considered in this research, it overlaps with the preceding ones and provides a general index of degree of hierarchy. Table 43 shows how this index correlates with the others.

Plants with steep gradients of authority and reward are likely to have steep gradients of reaction and adjustment and of some perceptions and ideals indicating consistency with respect to degree of hierarchy in an organization (Columns 1 and 2 of Table 43). Furthermore, it seems reasonable to think that the gradients of authority and reward "explain" the other gradients. The former are defined in an organization through policy, and are very much subject to norms that prevail in a society. The magnitude of these gradients are therefore set within fairly narrow margins, and these gradients in turn affect the distribution of satisfaction and other reactions of members.

The Participative Organization

Indices concerning decision making and control that have implications for participativeness have been computed for each plant. The first index, which we refer to as "decision making," defines the extent to which workers participate in decisions concerning their work as well as the plant itself, as reported by all of the sampled members of the plant (questions 34, 36, 39, see Chapter Four). The second index, which we

---

* This index was formed from three major components. The first consists of all of the gradients of Chapter Four; the second consists of all of the gradients of reaction and adjustment of Chapter Five; the third consists of all of the gradients of perception and ideals of Chapter Five. Each of these components is given equal weight.

refer to as "slope," defines the difference between the control or influence exercised by top echelons and that exercised by the rank and file in a plant, as estimated by members (see Chapter Four). Slope is derived from the "control graph," and a low score means a small difference in control between lower and upper ranks (Tannenbaum, 1968a).* While participation implies that lower-ranking members exercise substantial influence, it does not mean that leaders are uninfluential. The effective, participative organization is likely to be characterized by influential leaders *and* members, by a high *total amount* of control, contrary to stereotypes that assume participation to be a vaguely permissive or laissez-faire system (Tannenbaum, 1968a). A third index, therefore, is the sum of the control exercised by all echelons in the organization. Derived from the "control graph," it defines how much control the hierarchical groups exercise en toto. Finally, "interpersonal participativeness" defines the approachability of superiors and their receptivity to the ideas and opinions of subordinates (questions 41, 42, 43, and 46, Chapter Four). Interpersonal participativeness is an indication of informal, day-to-day participation in the interactions of superior and subordinate. The first three columns of Table 44 show the correlation between these indices, and the final column presents the correlation of each index with an overall index that is an average of them all.

Participation and Gradients

The participative organization should have flatter gradients than the non-participative one according to the theory

---

* Note that the measure of slope differs from that of gradient as we have operationalized these terms. A gradient is obtained by fitting a line to the responses in which members at various points in the hierarchy provide information about themselves. A steep gradient occurs, for example, when the top man reports that he personally has a great deal of influence and the bottom persons report that they have little or no influence. Slope of the control curve, on the other hand is obtained by asking all members to report about the influence exercised by persons at the top and also by persons at the bottom. Slope is derived by subtracting the control attributed to the persons at the bottom from that attributed to those at the top.

Table 44. Correlations Between Plant Characteristics
Relevant to Participativeness
(N = 52)

Aspects of Participativeness	Slope	Total Control	Inter-personal Partici-pativeness	Partici-pativeness Index
Decision Making	−.57 * (−.60) *	.56 * (.68) *	.61 * (.51) *	.72 * (.87) *
Slope [a]		−.26 (−.28) *	−.20 (−.30) *	−.69 * (−.78) *
Total Control			.61 * (.44) *	.72 * (.69) *
Interpersonal Participativeness				.80 * (.73) *

Note: Asterisks denote correlations that we estimate to be significant at the .05 level of confidence.

[a] A positive score for slope means that the top leadership exercises more control than does the rank and file. Slope therefore correlates negatively with the other items that measure participativeness, and the negative of slope was therefore entered into the Participativeness Index.

Table 45. Correlations between Aspects of Participativeness
and Gradients, All Plants (N = 52)

	CORRELATION WITH GRADIENT OF		
Aspects of Participativeness	Authority and Reward	Reaction and Adjustment	Overall Degree of Hierarchy
Decision Making	−.72 * (−.21)	−.43 * (−.23)	−.62 * (−.24)
Slope of Control Curve	.42 * (.24)	.17 (.08)	.21 (.08)
Total Amount of Control	−.32 * (−.01)	−.47 * (−.25) *	−.36 * (−.14)
Interpersonal Participativeness	−.46 * (.03)	−.38 * (−.11)	−.60 * (−.30) *
Overall Participativeness	−.62 * (−.15)	−.44 * (−.19)	−.58 * (−.24)

Note: Asterisks denote correlations that we estimate to be significant at the .05 level of confidence.

we are testing, and Table 45 provides correlations that shed some light on this expectation. The four components of the participativeness index, along with the index itself, are listed on the left. The remaining columns refer to the indices of gradient that we have constructed (exclusive of the index of perceptions and ideals). But relationships occur more clearly in the small organizations than in the large ones, as in previous chapters, and Table 46 shows the correlations between the small plants only. These correlations are probably a more realistic description of relationships since comparability between the small plants is better than it is for the total group. It is difficult to control the many extraneous considerations that enter when plants with as few as 50 members are analyzed along with plants having as many as 1,500.

Figure 22 illustrates graphically the relationship between participativeness and emphasis on hierarchy among the small plants. Best-fit-lines are drawn for each country to help identify the relationship within each country, although each line, based on only a very small number of plants, is subject to a good deal of error. The total pattern is nonetheless consistent with the correlations of Table 46, the participative plants in general showing a lesser degree of hierarchy than the nonparticipative plants, even in the case where both plants are within the same country.

The countries differ from one another in average level of participativeness and corresponding degree of hierarchy, but the differences do not define clear dichotomies. Plants from one country overlap with those from others, partly because of errors of measurement but probably also because of real continuity between the plants. Even the *relationship* between participativeness and degree of hierarchy within countries appears reasonably consistent among them—the apparent exception of Yugoslavia notwithstanding, being based as it is on so small a sample.*

---

* The exceptional slope of the Yugoslav line is attributable to one plant in the lower left-hand corner of the Yugoslav set. If this plant is removed, the remaining plants fit very well a line that conforms in slope to that of the other countries.

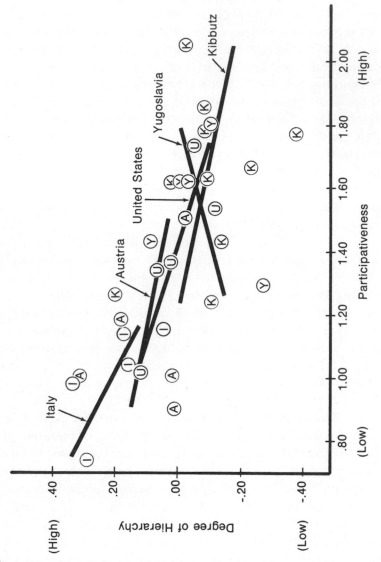

Figure 22. Overall degree of hierarchy plotted against participativeness of plant (small plants). Degree of hierarchy is measured as an index of all gradients. The scores on the vertical axis represent deviations from the regression line of "degree of hierarchy" on average length of chain and $\log_{10}$, size of plant thus controlling for the effects of these characteristics of the plant. A = Austria; I = Italy; K = Kibbutz; U = United States; Y = Yugoslavia.

Table 46. Correlations between Aspects of Participativeness
and Gradients, Small Plants (N = 30)

	CORRELATION WITH GRADIENT OF		
Aspects of Participativeness	Authority and Reward	Reaction and Adjustment	Overall Degree of Hierarchy
Decision Making	−.75 * (−.25)	−.57 * (−.43) *	−.70 * (−.38) *
Slope of Control Curve	.51 * (.13)	.32 (.31)	.37 (.20)
Total Amount of Control	−.31 (.01)	−.52 * (−.35) *	−.40 * (−.19)
Interpersonal Participativeness	−.48 * (−.10)	−.52 * (−.27)	−.67 * (−.48) *
Overall Participativeness	−.66 * (−.13)	−.60 * (−.40) *	−.69 * (−.41) *

Note: Asterisks denote correlations that we estimate to be significant at the .05 level of confidence.

Table 47. Demographic Characteristics and Gradients
(N = 52)

	CORRELATION WITH GRADIENT OF		
Demographic Characteristics	Authority and Reward	Reaction and Adjustment	Overall Degree of Hierarchy
Average Seniority in Plant	−.02 (.01)	−.06 (−.27)	−.11 (−.17)
Percentage of Females	.30 (.38) *	.30 (.32) *	.46 * (.50) *
Average Education	−.45 * (−.33) *	−.36 * (−.05)	−.48 * (−.14)
Average Age	−.20 (.28)	−.11 (.10)	−.24 (.25)

Note: Asterisks denote correlations that we estimate to be significant at the .05 level of confidence.

Demographic Characteristics and Gradient

Table 47 presents correlations between the hierarchical gradients and each of the demographic characteristics considered in earlier chapters. Gradients are likely to be steep where the proportion of women in the work force is great or where the level of education is low. There are obvious exceptions to this rule, but the relationship between these characteristics of the work force and gradient seems nonetheless to prevail on the average.

Sex and education help to "explain" some gradients within countries as well as between them. These characteristics of members are, of course, related to each other; women in general have less formal education than men. It is therefore of interest to consider the relationship of participativeness and each of the demographic factors to hierarchical gradients while holding the others constant, and Table 48 presents the results of a regression analysis designed to achieve this result.* This table shows partial correlations between each of the predictor variables and the measures of gradient, controlling for all of the other predictors. The correlations computed from the small plants (which are not shown here) are slightly larger than those indicated in the table. Nonetheless these tables suggest that holding constant the demographic features of a plant reduces the effect of variation in participativeness. For example, the sex composition of a plant appears to be the single most important correlate of gradient among the plants within the countries. These data therefore point to characteristics of the work force that may be as important as participation, if not more so, in affecting the nature of hierarchical gradients in a plant.

The Participative Superior

The superior who invites the ideas of his subordinates and who is supportive, psychologically, to those below him

---

* The dependent variables in this analysis are deviations from a regression line in which size of plant and average length of chain are the independent variables. Size of plant and length of chain are controlled in this way in the analysis of Table 48.

Table 48. Relative Importance of Demographic Characteristics
and Participativeness for Degree of Hierarchy
(N = 52)

	CORRELATION WITH GRADIENT OF		
Predictors of Gradient	Authority and Reward	Reaction and Adjustment	Overall Degree of Hierarchy
Multiple Correlation	—.68 * (—.50) *	—.56 * (—.45) *	—.71 * (—.57) *
Overall Participativeness	—.55 * (—.07)	—.36 * (—.15)	—.46 * (—.16)
Percentage of Females	.03 (.24)	.10 (.21)	.25 (.38) *
Education	—.34 * (—.24)	—.29 (.12)	—.35 * (.07)
Age	.20 (.21)	.19 (.15)	.12 (.24)
Seniority	—.15 (—.01)	—.19 (—.28)	—.19 (—.21)

Note: Asterisks denote correlations that we estimate to be significant at the .05 level of confidence.

should, according to our hypothesis, create a smaller difference between himself and his subordinates in their reactions and adjustments. This notion, which refers specifically to the differential between the superior and his immediate subordinates, is consistent with the data we have seen concerning participativeness and gradients at the plant level, and it is consistent with several other facts suggested by this research.* For example, a superior who is judged participative by his subordinates appears to elicit a more positive reaction from subordinates than does the non-participative superior. Persons under the

* The material in this section is drawn from the thesis of Donald Nightingale, and the construction of indexes is slightly different from that employed elsewhere in this book. Measures of superior's participativeness and of supportiveness, which in earlier sections of this chapter are combined into a single index called interpersonal participativeness, are treated separately in this section.

former feel less alienated and are more satisfied with their work situation compared to persons under the latter, and such positive reactions are likely to approximate the reactions of the superior himself. Furthermore, persons under a superior they judge to be participative report that they communicate more often with their superior and that they rely on their superior, rather than on peers, formal meetings, or written communiques for information about what is going on in the plant. Compared to other subordinates they have more trust in and favorable attitude toward their superior, and the participative-supportive superior therefore is likely to be a credible as well as a substantial source of information. Hence, subordinates will come to share some of the superior's perceptions of organizational life.

We have taken the differences between each superior and his immediate subordinates in their response to 47 questions as a basis for investigating this issue, and we correlated the superior's degree of participativeness and supportiveness (as judged by his subordinates) with each of the 47 discrepancies. The correlations are small in each country, many being close to zero, but excepting Yugoslavia they are predominantly in the direction predicted. In Yugoslavia only slightly over half of the correlations are "correct," compared to about 90 percent in each of the other places; the more participative or supportive the superior, the smaller the differences between his responses on the 47 measures and those of his subordinates.

We are able to explore, through regression procedures, the effect of each variable, participativeness and supportiveness, while holding the effect of the other constant; and we can also control for characteristics of the superior such as his age, education, and seniority, as well as his position in the hierarchy and the length of chain in which he is located. According to such an analysis these demographic characteristics do not, in general, predict the discrepancy between superior and subordinates when the superior's participativeness and supportiveness are held constant. Participativeness or supportiveness, however, does show some relationship to the discrepancies, although not all of the results are consistent with expectation. Of a possible

470 correlations (47 in each country for each of the two predictors, participativeness and supportiveness) 92 prove significant statistically, but 27 of these are in a contrary direction, and with respect to the supportiveness of superiors in kibbutz plants, six out of seven significant correlations are contrary to expectation.

We find this result in the kibbutz plants puzzling, but several features of kibbutz plants may provide a clue to its explanation. Participative superiors are likely also to be supportive, the correlation between these characteristics being .54 in kibbutz plants (and .40 to .59 in the other places). Some superiors who are supportive, however, may not be participative. This rarity, when it occurs, may be especially problematic in kibbutzim, where support is conveyed more implicitly than explicitly (see Chapter Three) and where an important indication of support may be the receptivity of the superior to the ideas and suggestions of his subordinates—that is, the extent to which the superior is in fact participative. A superior who is verbally "supportive" but non-participative may therefore be conveying inconsistent messages and, especially in kibbutz plants, where participation is expected, the inconsistency of "support" without participation may increase rather than decrease the gap between superior and subordinate.

Whether we are correct in our reasoning and its possible relevance to the kibbutz data, the peculiarity is not duplicated in any other country, and in Yugoslavia the regression analysis suggests a result that in some degree reverses the pattern in kibbutzim. In Yugoslav plants, the participativeness of a superior does not show the expected relationship to the discrepancy between superior and subordinate, but supportiveness does.

Thus the principle connecting participativeness and supportiveness, or one of them, to degree of hierarchy seems to apply to the superior-subordinate relationship as it does to the plant as a whole, although the data analyzed at the level of the superior and his immediate subordinates are less clear than those at the level of the plant. The difference between superior and subordinate is relatively small and unstable compared, for example, to the differential represented by a plant gradient, since the latter is the cumulative result of many superior-subordinate differentials. Correlations that involve interpersonal gradients are therefore typically very small. But they are persistently in the expected direction, and we therefore take the data as providing at least marginal support for the notion that participative or supportive superiors will be closer to their subordinates in reaction and adjustment than are non-participative ones.

Summary and Conclusions

The above analyses illustrate several questions of methodology that we would like to discuss before considering the substantive implications of this chapter.

We have employed in this study two general sources of data: the questionnaire, and sources independent of the questionnaire. The questionnaire is intended to provide information about each respondent as well as information reported by the respondent about facts outside of himself, such as the character of control or of participation in a plant. Data independent of the questionnaire come from records, charters, and reports of various kinds. Such data include information described in Chapter Two that documents gross differences in formal decision making between the plants of kibbutzim and Yugoslavia, on the one hand, and Italy, Austria, and the United States on the other. Information about the hierarchical position of each respondent also comes from a source independent of the questionnaire. Thus when we compute a gradient we correlate data from company records about the hierarchical position of each respondent with data from the questionnaire concerning the respondent's authority and rewards or his reactions and adjustments.

This research has been concerned in large measure with relationships between data obtained from these independent sources, and because these data provide a reasonably consistent and meaningful pattern, we have been encouraged to think that they have some validity. In this chapter, however, we rely exclusively on data from the questionnaire for the measure of participativeness since we do not have independent documentation concerning differences in participation between plants within a country. The measures of our variables therefore are not entirely independent of one another. But while these analyses suffer such limitations, they have the advantage of holding "culture" constant, and they can therefore be helpful in supplementing the data of previous chapters.

The principle that asserts a mitigating effect of participation on hierarchy seems, according to the data of this chapter, to apply to variation within a country as well as to variation among countries—except that the measurable effect of participation is smaller within a country, perhaps because variation in participation is smaller. The measurable effect of participation is further reduced at the level of the superior and his immediate subordinates, where a superior's participativeness shows only a very weak association with the differentials between himself and those under him. We wonder whether this reduced predictability is attributable to purely methodological considerations, including the statistical rule that large, aggregated sets of data (such as those describing plants) will yield larger correlations than small sets (such as those describing the relationship between a superior and his immediate subordinates). The indices of gradient and of participativeness at the plant level are more reliable than the measures at the level of the superior and his immediate subordinates. Or, do we see an implication that the important differences and the major effects represented in these data are better understood in terms of large social structures rather than in terms of interpersonal relations?

The data of this chapter seem consonant, on the face of it, with the argument that social structure rather than interpersonal relations is the more substantial basis for understanding outcomes such as the distribution of reactions and adjustments within a system (Perrow, 1970, 1972; Katz and Kahn, 1966). The small correlations at the interpersonal level however, do not mean that what goes on interpersonally has no bearing on the system as a whole. Although the predictability of differentials between a superior and his immediate subordinates may be slight on the basis of the superiors' interpersonal participativeness, the cumulative impact of such participativeness could be substantial at the level of the plant—if large numbers of superiors behave in a given manner. The correlations are very noticeable, for example, when the *average* interpersonal participativeness of superiors in a plant is correlated with plant gradients.

While this potential effect should be of interest from a theoretical standpoint, it may or may not have corresponding value practically. Assuming that the climate of interpersonal leadership does have significant implications organizationally, how does one create the desired climate if it is not already there? Is the answer to be found in "human relations" and the psychological approach to organization development initiated in the early writings of Follett and Mayo and elaborated by contemporary behavioral scientists? Can it be achieved through selection procedures and training programs that focus on the interpersonal skills of leaders? Or is the answer to be found in political models and in the arguments of social scientists, including Marx, who attach primary importance to "the system"? Does it hinge on changes in the structure of the organization itself, including perhaps its structure of control?

These are long-standing questions and we cannot pretend to have found the answers to them here. But we shall touch on them in our concluding chapter, where we offer opinions concerning socialist and capitalist models of organization and how they approach the problem of mitigating the dysfunctional effects of hierarchy.

VII

HIERARCHY
IN SOCIALIST
AND CAPITALIST
SYSTEMS

The data of this research are relevant to social values and to political ideologies as well as to abstract theories of organization. We offer in this chapter interpretations of the data in the context of these theories, values, and ideologies, and the reader ought not to be surprised to find occasional disagreement between the authors concerning some of the interpretations. We came to this research with different points of view, and we still have differences that lead us occasionally to disagree about the broad implications of our findings. Nonetheless, we have been strengthened in our

207

conviction that the methods of science, which we have tried to apply in this research, are a unique tool for understanding people in organizations. We do not think the methods are infallible, but we share a reasonable confidence in the data we have presented so far. Caution is required, however, as we move from data about fifty organizations in five countries to principles about organizations in general. And controversy is inevitable as we go from descriptions of how organizations are to prescriptions about how they should be—which are among the issues we touch upon here.

We review in this chapter some of the facts and principles of hierarchy we have presented earlier. Hierarchy is designed to solve a universal problem of organization, the need for coordination. But hierarchy in turn creates problems of its own, division between persons of different rank, and the seeds of disaffection and conflict implicit in that division. The approach to understanding and solving these problems is different in the socialist and capitalist societies that we have studied, and we now consider the implications of our data in the context of these different approaches.

The Inevitability of Hierarchy

"The pyramid of hierarchical organizations represents a fusion of status, prestige, rewards, and power" according to Katz and Kahn (1966, p. 221). "As we ascend the pyramid all these increase and reach their maxima at the pinnacle of the hierarchy." But the gradients of authority and reward that accompany hierarchy differ in magnitude between systems, and hierarchy therefore expresses itself more definitively in some than in others. Hierarchy is a matter of degree, and the Italian, Austrian, and American plants are in this sense more hierarchical than the plants of kibbutzim and Yugoslavia.

Some functions associated with rank are the result of choices made by organization designers, and it is with respect to the distribution of these functions that the systems are most clearly distinguished from one another. For example, decisions are taken in Italian organizations that imply sharp gradients of salary and privilege. In kibbutz organizations the decisions are for flat distributions of these functions. But some functions are not readily subject to choice. Technology and administration affect substantially and differentially the quality of jobs at different ranks. Mass production requires repetitive work at lower levels, and the need for coordination in factories requires that upper personnel exercise more authority than those below. Effort to apply an equalitarian ideology—by rotating members from one rank to another or by selecting technologies and designing jobs that are rewarding in some measure to lower-ranking persons—may mitigate such differentials, even if this means a loss of efficiency or profit in some cases. And participation gives to lower-ranking persons some influence they might not otherwise have. But these solutions to the problems of hierarchy are compromises at best; they may reduce but they do not eliminate the effects of hierarchy. Few workers can be rotated into the job of engineer or of plant manager, and there is a limit on how much loss in efficiency an organization can sustain on behalf of rewarding jobs. Furthermore, although participativeness may increase the influence of lower-ranking members, it does not equalize power—it may in some cases actually increase the power of *top* personnel (Tannenbaum, 1968a; Mulder and Wilke, 1970; March and Simon, 1958; Rosner and others, 1973; Strauss and Rosenstein, 1970). Authority and influence are, therefore, inevitably hierarchical in the work organization, equalitarian ideology notwithstanding.

This assertion need not contradict the Marxist view of organizations, which acknowledges the inevitability of hierarchy. Specialized functions must be coordinated, and some persons must be assigned the responsibility and given the authority to expedite this coordination. Authority that is employed on behalf of the coordination function is therefore legitimate and to be expected. "Wanting to abolish authority in large scale industry" as Engels put it, "is tantamount to wanting to abolish industry itself" (Engels, 1959, p. 483). But a distinction is made in the Marxist view between this legitimate and universal function of hierarchy and a motivational or control function. Where workers own the means of production they will not need to be controlled hierarchically. Control (as distinguished from coordination), should it prove necessary, is exercised by peers, not by superiors. On the other hand, workers will not be motivated properly in systems based on wage labor, designed for the profit of an owner; such systems, therefore, require that members be controlled hierarchically, and the authoritarian character of hierarchy is reinforced by the rewards and privileges that distinguish upper from lower ranks.

Marxist and Capitalist Models of Organization

The kibbutz and Yugoslav plants illustrate the Marxist model, although they do not fulfill the model in all aspects. Nor are all of the negative implications concerning the non-Marxist organization that are suggested by the model apparent in the plants of the other systems, particularly the American. Nonetheless, the kibbutz and Yugoslav plants distinguish themselves from the others in a number of respects. They are clearly more participative than the others, at least formally. This difference between systems expresses itself first in formal ideology and in the charters that define decision making in plants. Structures consistent with a participative ideology (such as councils and other decision-making bodies) are found in each of these plants. Members in the kibbutz and Yugoslav organizations also express ideals that reflect the formal ideology, indicating preference for a more equalitarian and participative system than do members in the other places. Participativeness is, therefore, legitimated by members. Furthermore, respondents in the kibbutz and Yugoslav plants indicate, at least more than do respondents in the other places, that workers do participate in decisions affecting the plant, and control by peers is more likely here than elsewhere. Power equalization, a further criterion of the formal participative model, is more characteristic of kibbutz and Yugoslav plants than of the others according to our data, although this difference, like many of the differences between systems, is a matter of degree; none of the plants are fully equalized. These differences between systems imply a difference in emphasis on hierarchy. Consequently, we find flatter gradients of reward, and of reaction and adjustment, and a lesser desire among members to climb the hierarchy in the kibbutz and Yugoslav plants compared to the others. Hierarchy does not make as much difference to members in the first set of plants as in the second.

But differences between the two major systems are not consistent on all criteria; differences occur within the two systems as well as between them. For example, the interaction between superior and subordinate is characterized by *informal* participativeness in the American and kibbutz plants but not in the Yugoslav, Italian, or Austrian. And the American and kibbutz plants resemble each other more than they resemble the others in attitude of members toward the enterprise and in their sense of alienation and adjustment, members in the former plants showing more positive reactions than do members in the latter.

Thus some organizations appear to do "better" than others in terms of the variables considered in this research, although what is better in one system may not better in another. Values differ and the standards that define success vary from one place to another. International comparison adds perspective to the analysis of organizational effectiveness precisely because of these differences, which make apparent that the standards used to appraise organizations are not universal "givens" but are very much a matter of choice. If the efficient or profitable organization is said to be better than the less efficient or less profitable one it is only because we choose to evaluate organizations in these terms. Compelling arguments, of course, can be offered for such a choice in a competitive industrial world where efficiency and profitability can affect the standard of living of organization members. But standard of living, too, is a question of values, and the material and economic criteria that define this standard in some societies are not accepted unqualifiedly in all others. Furthermore, the definition of standard of living has been changing and is now being supplemented by notions of "quality of life" based on aesthetic and moral values. Human welfare, in the view of many persons, implies more than material and economic resources, and it may therefore call for organizations that are more than merely efficient.

The kibbutz and American plants differ radically from one another, yet each set of plants does well (and perhaps better than the plants in the remaining countries) in terms of standards that apply within their respective societies. In fact, the kibbutz and American plants seem relatively effective even in terms of a number of common standards, and each might be taken to illustrate successful features of socialist and capitalist forms of organization respectively. We do not mean to imply that the kibbutz plant is *the* model of socialism any more than the American plant is the only possible manifestation of a successful (in terms of the criteria considered in this research) capitalist organization. The kibbutz model obviously is not transferable in all aspects to other societies (although many features of the kibbutz organization fit the conditions of other socialist societies). Kibbutz plants are small and in a select set of industries, and it is not certain that they would maintain their distinctiveness were they to become larger and were they to be located in industries different from those studied here. But we do find in the kibbutz plant an organization that works well in terms of the standards that apply within a socialist society, and we see in the American plant an organization that meets the standards implicit in a capitalist framework. Success is worth noting, and Table 49 summarizes some of the features of the kibbutz and American plants that define them as successful examples within their respective societies.

The successful socialist plant looks different than the successful capitalist one, partly because success is defined differently in the two systems. But both systems place value on productive efficiency and in both there is a concern for morale and motivation and for the reduction of conflict that can impede efficient performance. Data from other research (Melman, 1970–1971) suggest that kibbutz plants are in general quite efficient (as, we assume, are the American), and both sets of plants look reasonably "good" in terms of morale and motivation. These data are, therefore, a reminder that radically different organizational forms—as radically different as the kibbutz

Table 49. Differences and Similarities between United States and Kibbutz Plants as Successful Examples of the Capitalist and Socialist Models

Organizational Features	United States Plants	Kibbutz Plants
Decisions regarding policy	Made at top of hierarchy	Made by membership as a whole (directly or indirectly)
Gradients of authority and reward	Substantial	Moderate; some rewards (for example, monetary) equalitarian
Agents of control	Primarily superiors, secondarily peers	Peers, as well as superiors
Main technique of control	Reward, punishment, criticism, approval	Social criticism, approval
Bases of superior's control	"Law of situation," expert, reward and coercion	"Law of situation" and expert
Superior-subordinate relations	Relatively supportive, informally participative	Same as the United States
Gradients of reaction and adjustment	Substantial	Moderate
Mobility opportunities	Moderately high	Very high
Mobility aspirations	High	Low
Bases for advancement	Rational-functional, e.g., competence, initiative, creativity vs. nepotism, favoritism	Same as the United States except greater attention apparently paid to experience as indicated by seniority
Psychological rewards to managerial personnel	Very high	Moderately high
Psychological rewards to workers	Moderate	Moderate
Morale-Motivation-Adjustment	Moderately positive	Moderately positive
Legitimacy of system and of managerial prerogatives	High	High

and American—can prove effective in terms of a number of criteria, at least among the kinds of small plants included in this research.*

While the two models, exemplified by the kibbutz plants on the one hand and by the American on the other, share some common values, they are sharply divided on a central value that is the basis for many differences between them—equality. Democracy and justice in the kibbutz conception hinge on equality of power and reward, and unlike the American system, the material rewards provided a member need not correspond to his ability or contribution. It is entirely equitable that a worker receive greater material support than a manager if the former has need for special services or goods. Thus equality, and the concepts of democracy and justice that are associated with equality, are important bases for organizing and evaluating kibbutz plants. American plants could, in principle, be organized and evaluated on the basis of these criteria, but they are not, and very few persons in industry (including workers) argue that they should be. Achievement rather than equality is the prepotent value here, and the organizing and functioning of American plants are expressions of this central value. The difference in values between the two systems is illustrated by the strong aspiration to move up the hierarchy expressed by members of American plants, and the very little desire on the part of kibbutz members to "advance" in this way. In a society

---

* We do not know how tolerant large organizations may be of the kinds of variation in formal structure included in this research, and we have seen evidence in earlier chapters suggesting a greater similarity among large organizations than among small, consistent with a "logic of industrialization" proposed by Kerr and others (1964). Large organizations face common administrative and technical imperatives, and they may, therefore, be subject more than small organizations to a common rationality. We are not likely to see this thesis proved or disproved by kibbutz plants simply because kibbutz plants are not likely to be much larger in the future than they are now. But data based on the questionnaire used in this research are being collected under the auspices of the European Coordination Centre for Research and Documentation in Social Sciences (Vienna) in a number of countries, including Bulgaria, Hungary, Poland, Roumania, West Germany, Ireland, Brazil, and Mexico; we hope, therefore, to have further evidence concerning large plants operating under different ideologies.

designed to function on the basis of individual achievement, as the American society is, aspiration to advance is functional because individual advancement is a source of motivation, and competition for leadership is presumably a way of assuring that the most highly qualified persons move into positions of responsibility. Upward mobility aspirations are therefore an essential ingredient in the American system. Not so in the kibbutz, however, where such aspirations might contribute to a struggle for power and might increase the tendency by leaders to protect their positions by authoritarian means. Michels' iron law of oligarchy (Michels, 1959) does not apply well to kibbutz plants simply because he assumes that persons have a strong motivation to climb into positions of great power and privilege. There is little motivation of this sort in kibbutz plants. On the contrary, many leaders must undergo considerable social pressure before they are induced to assume the responsibilities of the leadership role.

Achievement is not *entirely* insignificant in the kibbutz, however, any more than equality is unimportant in American plants. But these values are, relatively speaking, sublimated and secondary and they are defined differently in the respective systems. Achievement in the kibbutz is not individualistic and competitive, and high rank and the acquisition of material wealth are not criteria. Achievement means performing effectively in any role, and because members share a common interest and feel a sense of mutual identification, achievement by one is in some degree achievement by all. In American plants, equality as a value applies not so much to power or reward as to opportunity to acquire power and reward, consistent with the competitive-achievement value; and in fact, American respondents, more than respondents in other places (excepting kibbutzim), report that they have the opportunity to advance in their plant. Leadership which tends (within limits) to be supportive and informally participative, and which deemphasizes status differences, also introduces into American plants an element of equality in the relationship between superior and subordinate if not in the formal distribution of power and reward. Although substantial inequality exists, opportunity and reward are nonetheless reported by members to be high. This is not equality in the full sense, but it softens some of the negative psychological implications of inequality.

Mitigating the Effects of Hierarchy

We therefore see implicit in the American plants an approach, alternative to the Marxist, to mitigating the effects of hierarchy. The approach does not attempt to reduce substantially the gradients of power and reward themselves, as does the Marxist approach, but rather attacks some of the conditions which surround these gradients and which affect their effects. The "American approach" is therefore indirect. It is pragmatic in the sense of William James' notion that any difference that makes no difference is no difference, and it assumes that *depending on conditions,* some differences in power and reward do not make much difference.

Data from the American plants imply some of these mitigating conditions, although we find ourselves disagreeing in our speculations about them and especially about their value implications. We therefore suggest the following as hypotheses. One condition is the opportunity for upward mobility. A member at the bottom of a hierarchy will react differently to the deprivations of his position if he anticipates the possibility of moving into a better position, rather than seeing little possibility of change. The implications of this condition can be surmised by comparing the American and Italian plants. In both cases subordinates are disadvantaged compared to superiors in the rewards they receive. Members therefore want to move up the hierarchy in both sets of plants, but only in the American plants do members see some chance to move up. Upward mobility may not be great in American plants, but it is greater than in the Italian. The effect of inequality in reward on the reactions of members should therefore be less serious in the American plants than in the Italian.

A second condition concerns the character of interpersonal relations. Participativeness in a plant may be defined in terms of formal structures and procedures, such as workers' councils and the election of managers, or it may be defined informally, in terms of the day-to-day interaction between superiors and subordinates. Informal participativeness may mitigate the effects of hierarchy, especially where the organization is not formally participative. While the American plants are not formally participative, they show participativeness and support in the relationship of superior and subordinate. Relatively speaking, American superiors *treat* their subordinates as equals—even though they are not equal in power and reward.

A third condition is the absolute level as opposed to the relative distribution of reward in a system: where the absolute level is high, a given absolute differential will make less difference to members than where the level is low. A number of arguments can be offered for this hypothesis. The "law of diminishing returns," for example, suggests that when reward is great, increments of a given amount are likely to be less satisfying than when reward is low. If so, the distribution of reward is less important as a determinant of satisfaction when the level of reward is high than when it is low. The Weber-Fechner law of "just noticeable differences" (Garrett, 1941, Chapter 15) suggests that a small increment in the magnitude of a perceived stimulus is noticeable when the stimulus is weak, but not when the stimulus is strong. Given differences in reward therefore simply become less noticeable when reward is high than when it is low (if amount of reward is analogous to intensity of stimulus). Some theories of equity and of social comparison (Adams, 1965) imply, all other things being equal, that a given difference in reward between persons will be less important when the base is high than when it is low, since mathematically the ratio of the reward of one person to that of another approaches unity as the base increases. Such a conclusion is also consistent with the implications of Maslow's (1943) notion about the decreasing impact of specific rewards as the relevant needs are satisfied. These principles therefore suggest that the satisfaction and other reactions of members are a joint result of the distribution *and* the total amount of reward in a system, not one or the other exclusively. If the distribution cannot be changed—and there are limits on how equalitarian the distribution of some rewards can become—perhaps the total amount can be changed, although there are limits here, too.

The emphasis in organizational theory on the distribution or the allocation rather than the total amount of reward in a system is understandable, since distribution can be determined by decree; how much one group gets compared to another can be decided and enforced, at least within limits. The total amount of reward in an organization, however, is not so directly decided—if it is decided at all. It is obvious, nonetheless, that many rewards can increase in total amount. A profitable organization has a stock of disposable goods greater than a non-profitable one, and in principle everyone can acquire some incremental share without changing the distribution (gradient) of reward in the system. Organizations, however, dispense social and psychological rewards such as power, status, prestige, and approval in addition to material and economic ones, and the notion of an expandable "pie" of these rewards has been seriously neglected if not disputed in the literature. Power, for example, is said to be a fixed quantity in an organization and if one person increases his share another must decrease his (Dahrendorf, 1968). Similarly, status and prestige are said to be entirely relative. One person has great status only because another has little. Raising the status of one therefore automatically lowers that of another. The data of this research as well as of previous work, however, suggest that these social functions are indeed expandable (or contractable) in organizations.

Influence (or power) refers to the ability of persons to affect outcomes in intended ways and there is a good deal of logic and some evidence to suggest that organizations differ in the size of their "influence pie" (Tannenbaum, 1968a)—as the American and Italian plants do in this study, for example, even though the *gradients* of power are identical. It seems reasonable to think, furthermore, that a given gradient of power means something quite different to organization members when the total amount is high compared to when it is low. Economists long ago abandoned the notion of a fixed economic pie, and in so doing they have radically altered the nature of political and economic theory. But an expandable economic pie is simply a special case of an expandable pie of influence or power, since money is one (although not the only) source of power. The social and political implications of an expandable economic pie can therefore be understood in terms of the increased *power*—the ability to achieve intended ends—that individuals have, for example, under conditions of affluence compared to conditions of poverty. The economic pie concept is a familiar one. Some of the social and political implications of the power pie can therefore be inferred from what we already know of the expandable economic pie—although the former principle is the more general and its implications are therefore a good deal more extensive. The struggle for limited resources is not quite like the competition for goods that are plentiful.

Power is not the only social good that can grow or decline within organizations. The total amount of status and prestige, also, will vary in social systems, although status and prestige are not ordinarily understood in this way partly because they are often misconceived to mean something residing in and belonging to a person. The status of a person, however, is not so much in him as in an attitude of others toward him, in the regard or respect that others have for him. The respect may be accorded because of his rank, education, or performance on the job. Or it may grow out of an inclination on the part of others to respect a person as a person and to behave supportively toward another. But for whatever reason, a person has status only insofar as others attribute status to him and the attitude of respect that is the basis of status can grow or decline en masse in a system. In some systems persons have little regard for one another, while in others there is much respect and therefore much status. To assume that status and prestige, like power and material goods, can expand does not mean, however, that they *must* expand. They can also decline, or remain fixed, depending on conditions. Nor does an expandable system of status or prestige mean that some persons will not have more status or prestige than others, any more than an expandable economic or influence "pie" means that some persons will not have more

money or more power than others. A system in which the total
amount of status is high does not eliminate differentials in
status; it simply acts as a force in making these differentials in
status less important.

The above notions are consistent in a general way with
the data of this research, although they should be refined and
tested more precisely than we have been able to manage here.
In any event, their validity is subject to proof or disproof. The
value implications of these notions and the approach to hierarchy that they support, however, are likely to be a source of
controversy among some persons, as they are among the authors
of this volume. A position to which some of us subscribe, for
example, argues that the approach to hierarchy described above
supports techniques of "human relations" that maintain rather
than eliminate substantial hierarchical gradients of power and
reward. It therefore covers over and diverts attention from the
exploitation and injustice suffered by workers. Workers in the
American plants, for example, do not *feel* as alienated as workers elsewhere but in fact they *are* powerless with respect to basic
policy issues. Because of "human relations," a discrepancy exists
between the subjective and objective experience of alienation.
The Italian workers are more realistic and better adjusted in
this sense. Jobs are frustrating to them, opportunities for self
fulfillment or for achievement are sparse, and workers feel dissatisfied and poorly motivated. Italian workers *know* they are
without power and quite realistically, they *feel* alienated. This
realism is a symptom of good adjustment, not bad, although in
terms of our conventional measures the Italian worker looks
poorly adjusted. American workers, on the other hand, appear
well adjusted and they report high levels of opportunity and
satisfaction. Some actually feel a sense of responsibility in their
plant—at least more than do workers in other places. But this
is only because the "human relations" approach is so effective
in its manipulation. The approach no doubt works in mitigating some of the psychological effects of hierarchy, but it does
so without making any basic changes in hierarchy and, in the
view of some of us, it is therefore subject to question from a
moral standpoint.

Conditions Required for Worker Participation

For better or worse, organizations in the so-called capitalist or free enterprise system, broadly defined, have different effects on members depending on "conditions." American workers do not react in their privately owned plants like the Italian workers react in theirs. But the socialist system, too, has different effects depending on the version of socialism and on some of the conditions under which it is installed. In some respects, the reaction of the Yugoslav worker is as different from that of the kibbutz worker as the reaction of the kibbutz worker is from the reaction of the American. Models of organization, whether they be "socialist" or "capitalist," "human relations," or "bureaucratic," operate in a context, and conditions that define that context affect how well the system will achieve its objectives, whatever they may be.

The discrepancy between formal and informal participativeness in the Yugoslav plants illustrates the effect of such conditions. Formal participativeness is subject to legislation, and such participativeness has been mandated in the Yugoslav plants. These plants, therefore, are participative formally. But informal participation cannot be determined directly by law. It is subject to culture and tradition, to the habits, norms, and skills of members, as well as to other conditions that do not separate systems along ideological lines. Modern industry in Yugoslavia has grown out of a tradition based on hierarchy at least as extreme as that in Italy. Authoritarian hierarchical relations in prewar Yugoslavia were fostered by persistent unemployment, which led many persons to accept work under the harshest of conditions. The factory was a symbol of exploitation of which management was the most visible executor, and workers regarded authority figures with a mixture of hatred, fear, and reverence. These attitudes, which carried over into postwar Yugoslavia, were not conducive to participative relations. The peasants, too, many of whom were moving into industry, were in conflict with the ideology of self management by reason of their traditions. Private property, in the form of the peasant's little plot with a few pigs or chickens, was the core of his survival. The peasant understood and respected property of this kind, but he had little respect for public property, which did not belong to anyone (with whom he identified) and which he might therefore take for his own purposes, if he could. Individualistic and distrustful of strangers, the peasant had little regard for the social orientation of self management— or for any form of management for that matter. Although the system of ownership changed after the war along with the formal ideology of management, the attitudes of many workers and peasants remained essentially unchanged. Self management, insofar as it meant freedom from exploitation, was idealized by many workers to mean freedom from control. It meant opportunity to get and to do what one wants and workers had no problem, in principle, of accepting their role as controllers. But *being* controlled, the necessary counterpart of exercising control in any viable system of participation, did not fit their idealization or their inclination. The practice of participation therefore did not conform to the theory in the minds of many workers, and this unrealism represented an obstacle to the full development of participation in the plant. While workers may have expressed preference for the new participative system of organization, deeply ingrained habits of overt dependency on and covert resistance toward leadership could not be undone by edict or by act of individual will. Nor did the new manager have the skills or understanding to fulfill his role as participative leader. After all, his experience in organizations was like that of the workers under him, hierarchical and authoritarian. Furthermore, the war left Yugoslavia with a shortage of managers, and persons unqualified in technology were placed in leadership positions. Uncertain and insecure, they were more inclined to be directive and defensive, rather than receptive and open. Authoritarian reaction, rather than participative reaction, is the more natural under conditions of threat, and this, too, represented an obstacle to the full realization of the participative ideal. The relatively low level of education of the work force created additional conflict between the ideals of self management and the realities of industrial life, and the very sharp gradients of education in the Yugoslav plants (as in the Italian) indicate that poorly educated workers must discuss and decide issues with highly educated managers, if there is to be participation (Obradović, 1972). (Contrast this with the kibbutz, where workers have on the average as much formal education as managers.) The problem is exacerbated because education is a traditional basis of status in Yugoslavia, and the uneducated look with awe upon those who have education. *To increase the level of education of members would therefore be to increase the total amount of status in Yugoslav plants,* an increase that is now taking place. But because of the difference in education that still exists, there is an implicit but sharp difference in status between workers and managers, to say nothing about a difference in language facility and in the ability to use concepts.

Thus, the socialist system (like any system) faces conditions that may or may not be propitious for the realization of its precepts and the fulfillment of its goals. The average level of education of the work force is one such condition. Rotation among managers and workers, for example, which is one way of ensuring that many members play a formal role in management, as in the kibbutz plants, requires widespread qualification among members. But even in the absence of rotation, education contributes to the quality of collective decisions because it adds to the intellectual skills and knowledge of members. Decision makers must understand the meaning of a percentage or an average. Some sense of economics and mechanics, however rudimentary, are useful for participation. Education is also a basis of power for members and a basis for their understanding the larger system and their role in it. Education therefore is among the conditions that reduce the feeling of alienation, the sense of powerlessness and meaninglessness in socialist systems as in capitalist. But education does not make workers happy even though it may make them feel less alienated, because the skills they have acquired are not utilized in a factory and the aspirations that education instills are not fulfilled. A high average level of education in the work force, which is a condition for effective participation, therefore im-

poses its own conditions on the nature of work if the organization is to realize fully the participative ideal: the technology
must be appropriate to an educated work force.

Assembly lines and other technologies that are especially
frustrating to educated persons are not well suited to the participative enterprise. More suitable are industries such as
electronics, chemicals, and power. Size of organization may be
a related condition. (For a discussion of technology as related
to participation, see Woodward, 1965; Supek, 1972; Rus, 1972;
and Westley, 1972.) The data of this research suggest that large
organizations from different countries are more alike than are
small organizations because massive technology and administration impose requirements that supersede the ideological. If
this "logic of industrialization" is valid, there is no guarantee
that the technological and administrative inevitabilities of
massive industry will be conducive to the development of
workers' self management. We authors find ourselves in disagreement about the implications of this point, one of us argu-
ing that large organizations are indeed not adaptable to socialist
management. Large organizations are created because of the
drive for profit and they are an outgrowth, therefore, of capitalist values and modes of production. Large organizations need
not arise in the absence of the profit motive, and the subjugation
of man to machine, or what Marx called the "real submission
of Man to Capital," need not occur. In this view, massive
industry in socialist countries represents a compromise of socialism. The truly socialist enterprise will have to be small.

Success of the socialist model faces another condition.
The socialist organization implies a "way of life" that distin-
guishes it from other models, and the socialist enterprise will
not work well unless its way of life fits the preference and life
style of its members. This obvious condition has its parallel in
other models, too: a system works best when what it requires
of members is consistent with members' needs, habits, and
values. But there may be a special relevance of this condition
in a system that assumes a natural identity of interest between
man and organization—and such an identity is taken for
granted in the socialist system. Other models also make assump-

tions concerning common interest. "Human relations," for example, assumes that members *should* feel a common interest and that something is wrong if they do not. Conflict is a pathology that "human relations" attempts to cure by encouraging attitudes of cooperation and support for the organization. But there is no conflict in the classical socialist model, and hence there are no techniques to handle conflict (Zupanov, 1973). Nor is resort to coercion necessary to push workers or to keep them in line, because workers in the socialist system want to do what is right. The use of coercion would belie the assumption of common interest and would represent, therefore, a deviation from the socialist model. And there is little provision in the model for human relations procedures as a way of reducing conflict and encouraging cooperative attitudes— again for the reason that cooperative attitudes are taken for granted. A premium therefore exists on the assumption of common interest and of the natural desire of members in a socialist system to work cooperatively and to contribute to the goals of the enterprise. The socialist organization, perhaps more than other organizations, requires the condition of congenial values and prevailing "collective orientation" on the part of members, since in other systems, if members do not fit they might legitimtaely be coerced or manipulated into fitting. Coercion and manipulation can, of course, occur in systems guided by socialist principles, but to the extent that such techniques of control occur, the system, by definition, loses its socialist character.

Organizational Effectiveness

This research illustrates some of the variety that is possible in organizational design. Radically different organizational forms are possible and viable. An organization in which policy is decided by top personnel is quite workable, and so is one in which policy is established by the membership as a whole. Factories in which workers receive remuneration equal to that of managers can function effectively, just as can factories with substantial differences in reward between those at the top and those at the bottom. But the success of a system, however success may be defined, depends on "conditions," and ultimately on the definition of success itself; and the preference that we as observers may feel for one system or another will depend on our own values. For those of us who place great value on equality, the kibbutz system, and perhaps the Yugoslav, is the model of success. The American model looks better to those of us who value individual achievement. The choice is not simple, however, since we do not base our judgment on a single value. The American culture, for example, is ambivalent about achievement and equality (Seeman, 1953), and American organizations attempt to resolve this ambivalence by tempering inequality of power and reward with equalitarian human relations, and by softening the effects of competition by maintaining a high level of reward even for those who, relatively speaking, do not compete well. Persons at the bottom clearly get less than those at the top, but with respect to many rewards that are important to them they do not get less than do their counterparts in more equalitarian systems. The systems of formal participation that we have studied seem to say more about the distribution than about the total amount of reward in an organization.

The variety of organizational forms that we have observed, and the diversity of values that we might employ in appraising these forms, are indicative of a law of relativity that applies to understanding and evaluating organizations. Success depends on, and is therefore relative to, "conditions," and the definition of success itself is necessarily relative to the values of those who define it. We authors, for example, cannot agree as a group that one of the models we have studied is the best way of organizing and running a factory. It is true that all of the organizations can, in principle, be evaluated in terms of a common standard such as their productive efficiency, or the magnitude of their gradients, but we do not agree that either of these should be the ultimate criterion. What looks "effective" to one of us therefore does not necessarily look "effective" to all. But there is another vantage point which adds a dimension to the relativity of organizational life, and which may be helpful in our appraisal of organizational forms: the historical viewpoint.

Organizations change, and the forms that prevail and that seem appropriate at one point in time may not be appropriate at another. Marxists have stressed this developmental conception. Feudalism and capitalism, each with its own natural forms of organization, are stages in the development of political life. Capitalism will, in due time, be replaced because it contains the seeds of its own destruction, the inherent conflict created by owners who extract profit through the labor of others. We have seen symptoms of this conflict in the sharp gradients of power and reward and of reaction and adjustment among members in the capitalist plants. According to Marxists, this conflict grows with the inevitable concentration of capital and will lead inevitably to revolution, the abolition of private property, and the introduction of socialist, participative forms of organization.

Whether or not they are correct in their explanation, Marxists are not alone in predicting the development of participation in industry. Participation is the wave of the future in the view of many, and a variety of schemes including mitbestimmung, co-determination, Scanlon Plans, and behavioral science models are being introduced into industry, implying some movement in the direction of participativeness even if these variants fall short of the revolutionary ideal. In fact, some effort by industrial leaders to introduce participation may be designed to undercut the revolution by compromising in advance with the demands the revolution might make. But modifications on behalf of participativeness in privately owned plants can never, in the Marxist view, reach the level of participation possible under socialism. Participativeness in privately owned plants will always be a limited compromise within a basically authoritarian structure, rather than the central and guiding tenet of organizational management that it can be in socialist enterprises. The reason, in the Marxian view, is ownership. Workers, if they are to participate fully, must make decisions about the allocation of profit—decisions they cannot make under the private system. If they did, what would be left for the owners? Such decisions are essential for full participation because of their implication for decisions concerning investment, production planning, modernization, wages, and many other issues. Limiting the prerogatives of workers with respect to profit therefore limits them with respect to most important decisions.

The forms of participation found in the socialist plants therefore can not be adopted in private ones without substantial modification. But there is no reason why the techniques of human relations that seem to work in the private system can not be adopted as part of the approach to mitigating the effects of hierarchy in socialist organizations—except that the socialist model has traditionally assumed no need for such procedures. "Human relations" has been identified with capitalism, and to acknowledge the applicability of this tool in the socialist organization would seem an admission that ownership per se is not the whole answer to the problem of hierarchy. Nonetheless, principles of human relations are gaining recognition, and the implicit interdiction against this approach to improving the quality of participation will be less strict in future socialist organizations than in the past. Ironically, a serious limitation to full participation may be the orthodox emphasis in some versions of socialism on centralized planning and state control. The effect of such centralization is, in one respect at least, like that of private ownership: workers themselves cannot decide the allocation of profit or other basic issues. If it is to be participative in some degree, the centralized system, like the private, must rely on "human relations," allowing workers within a psychologically supportive context to make decisions that have only local significance.

We authors are not in full agreement on these points, and we disagree especially about the argument that centralized planning limits participation. Planning is designed to take into account the needs of the entire society, and in principle it represents the interests of all persons. Workers, therefore, participate indirectly if not directly in major decisions that affect society as a whole, and such participation is more extensive than that which is limited to decisions about a factory. These arguments, pro and con, are beyond the scope of the present research and we have little empirical basis here for providing a resolution, since all of the systems we have studied illustrate the decentralized model. In fact, the point of departure for the contemporary system of workers' self management in Yugoslavia is the break in 1949 from a highly centralized system of state control to a decentralized one in which plants have autonomy and in which members therefore can have authority with respect to all policy decisions.

Participativeness is a basis for minimizing the impact of hierarchy and for reducing the magnitude of gradients. The more participative, socialist plants, at least those of the type studied here, are likely to come closer to realizing an equalitarian ideal than the less participative privately owned plants. But the socialist organization does not eliminate gradients. Persons at the top have more authority and influence than do those at the bottom and they are more motivated, involved, and interested in their jobs than those below. Psychologically, at least, superiors in socialist plants, as in capitalist ones, are rewarded more than are subordinates. Hierarchical gradients of reaction and adjustment, insofar as we can tell, are universal.

Gradients are likely to be less sharp in the socialist than in the privately owned plants of the type studied here, yet there are differences in magnitude of gradient among socialist plants as among the capitalist, and some capitalist plants have gradients as flat as some socialist ones. Thus, while the two major systems are clearly distinguishable in formal plan, they do not differ so clearly in predicted outcome of the plan. Practice does not always correspond to theory, and facts do not always match ideals. There are just too many complicating "conditions." The systems are different, but given the overlap in some of their effects we might ask whether, in William James' terms, the difference makes a difference. The reader undoubtedly will have his own answer to this question.

REFERENCES

ADORNO, T. W., FRENKEL-BRUNSWICK, E., LEVINSON, D. J., AND SANFORD, R. N. *The Authoritarian Personality.* New York: Harper, 1950.

ADIZES, I. *Industrial Democracy: Yugoslav Style.* New York: The Free Press, 1971.

ALLPORT, F. H. "Individuals and Their Human Environment." *Proceedings of the Association for Research in Nervous Disorders,* 1933, *14,* 234–252.

ANDREWS, F., MORGAN, J. N., AND SONGQUIST, J. A. *Multiple Classification Analysis.* Ann Arbor: Institute for Social Research, 1967.

ANDREWS, I. R., AND HENRY, M. M. "Management Attitudes Toward Pay." *Industrial Relations,* 1963, *3,* 29–39.

ARGYRIS, C. *Personality and Organization.* New York: Harper, 1957.

ARGYRIS, C. *Integrating the Individual and the Organization.* New York: Wiley, 1964.

BACHMAN, J. G., BOWERS, D. G., AND MARCUS, P. M. "Bases of Supervisory Power: A Comparative Study in Five Organizational Settings." In A. S. Tannenbaum (Ed.), *Control in Organizations.* New York: McGraw-Hill, 1968.

BARKIN, S. "Trade Union Approach to Wage Incentive Plans." *Time and Motion Study,* June 1953, 24–29.

BARNOWE, J. T., MANGIONE, T. W., AND QUINN, R. P. "The Relative Importance of Job Facets as Indicated by an Empirically Derived Model of Job Satisfaction." Mimeo, May 1972.

BELL, D. "Two Roads from Marx." Paper presented at the International Seminar, Workers Participation in Management, under auspices of The Congress for Cultural Freedom. Vienna, September 19–25, 1958.

BENDIX, R., AND FISHER, L. H. "The Perspectives of Elton Mayo." Institute of Industrial Relations, University of California, Berkeley, Reprint No. 17, 1950.

230

BENDIX, R. *Work and Authority in Industry.* New York: John Wiley, 1956.

BENNIS, W. G., BERKOWITZ, N. AFFINITO, M., AND MALONE, M. "Authority, Power, and the Ability to Influence." *Human Relations,* 1958, *11,* 143–155.

BENNIS, W. G., AND SLATER, P. E. *The Temporary Society.* New York: Harper-Row, 1968.

BLAU, P. M. *The Dynamics of Bureaucracy.* Chicago: University of Chicago Press, 1955.

BLAUNER, R. "Work Satisfaction and Industrial Trends in Modern Society." In W. Galenson and S. M. Lipset (Eds.), *Labor and Trade Unionism.* New York: Wiley, 1960.

BLAUNER, R. *Alienation and Freedom.* Chicago: University of Chicago Press, 1964.

BLUMBERG, P. *Industrial Democracy.* London: Constable, 1968.

BRAYFIELD, A. H., AND CROCKETT, W. H. "Employee Attitudes and Employee Performance." *Psychological Bulletin,* 1955, *52, 5,* 396–424.

British Trade Union Congress. *Trade Unions and Productivity.* London: n.d.

BROWN, W. A. *Explorations in Management.* New York: Wiley, 1960.

BURNS, T., AND STALKER, G. M. *The Management of Innovation.* London: Tavistock, 1961.

BURT, W. J. "Workers' Participation in Management in Yugoslavia." *International Institute for Labor Studies Bulletin,* 1972 (9), 129–172.

CROZIER, M. *The World of the Office Worker.* Chicago: University of Chicago Press, 1971.

DAHRENDORF, R. "Class and Class Conflict in Industrial Society." Stanford, Calif.: Stanford University Press, 1968. (Originally published under the title "Soziale Klassen und Klassenkonflikt in der industriellen Gesellschaft." Stuttgart, 1957.)

DAHRENDORF, R. "On the Origin of Inequality Among Men." In E. O. Laumann, P. M. Siegel, and R. W. Hodge (Eds.), *The Logic of Social Hierarchies.* Chicago: Markham Publishing Co., 1970.

DAVIS, F. A., SPAETH, J. L., AND HUSON, C. A. "A Technique for Analyzing the Effects of Group Composition." *American Sociological Review,* Apr. 1961, *26,* 215–225.

DAVIS, K., AND MOORE, W. E. "Some Principles of Stratification." *American Sociological Review,* 1945, *10,* 2, 242–249.

DAVIS, K. "Reply to Tumin." *American Sociological Review,* 1953, *18,* 4, 394–397.

DEAN, D. G. "Alienation: Its Meaning and Measurement." *American Sociological Review,* 1961, *26,* 5, 753–758.

DUNLOP, J. T. *Industrial Relations Systems.* New York: Holt, 1959.

DUNN, J. T., AND COBB, S. "Frequency of Peptic Ulcer Among Executives, Craftsmen, and Foremen." *Journal of Occupational Medicine,* 1962, *4,* 7, 343–348.

DUNNETTE, M. D., CAMPBELL, J. P., AND HAKEL, M. D. "Factors Contributing to Job Satisfaction and Job Dissatisfaction in Six Occupational Groups." *Organizational Behavior and Human Performance,* May 1967, *2,* 2, 143–174.

ENGELS, F. "On Authority." In L. Fleuer (Ed.), *Marx and Engels: Basic Writings in Politics and Philosophy.* New York: Doubleday-Anchor, 1959.

FERRAROTTI, F. "Management in Italy." In F. Harbison and C. A. Myers, *Management in the Industrial World.* New York: McGraw-Hill, 1959.

FOLLETT, M. P. *Dynamic Administration.* In H. C. Metcalf and L. F. Urwick (Eds.), *Dynamic Administration, the Collected Works of Mary Parker Follett.* New York: Harper, 1942.

FORM, W. H. "Job Consciousness vs. Political Unionism: A Cross-National Comparison." *Industrial Relations,* 1973, *12,* 2, 224–238.

FRENCH, J. R. P., JR., AND RAVEN, B. H. *The Bases of Social Power.* In D. Cartwright (Ed.), *Studies in Social Power.* Ann Arbor: University of Michigan, Institute for Social Research, 1959.

FRENCH, J. R. P., JR. "The Social Environment of Mental Health." *Journal of Social Issues,* 1963, *19,* 4, 39–56.

GARRETT, H. E. *Great Experiments in Psychology.* New York: Appleton-Century, 1941.

GORUPIC, D., AND PAJ, I. *Workers' Management in Yugoslavia.* Geneva: ILO, 1962.

GOULDNER, A. *Patterns of Industrial Bureacuracy.* New York: Free Press, 1954.

GURIN, G., VEROFF, J., AND FELD, S. *Americans View Their Mental Health.* New York: Basic Books, 1960.

HAIRE, M., GHISELLI, E. E., AND PORTER, L. W. *Managerial Thinking: An International Study.* New York: Wiley, 1966.

HARBISON, F. H., AND BURGESS, E. W. "Modern Management in Western Europe." *The American Journal of Sociology,* July 1954, *60,* 1, 15–23.

HARBISON, F. H., AND MYERS, C. A. *Management in the Industrial World.* New York: McGraw-Hill, 1959.

HERZBERG, F., MAUSNER, B., PETERSON, R., AND CAPWELL, D. *Job Attitudes: Review of Research and Opinion.* Pittsburgh, Penn.: Psychological Service of Pittsburgh, 1957.

HOFFMAN, G. W., AND NEAL, F. W. *Yugoslavia and the New Communism.* New York: Fund for the Republic, 1962.

HULIN, C. H., AND BLOOD, M. R. "Alienation, Environmental Characteristics and Worker Responses." *Journal of Applied Psychology,* 1967, *51,* 284–290.

HULIN, C. H., AND BLOOD, M. R. "Job Enlargement, Individual Differences, and Worker Responses." *Psychological Bulletin,* 1968, *69,* 1, 41–55.

HUNNIUS, G. "Workers' Self-Management in Yugoslavia." In G. Hunnius, G. D. Garson, and J. Case (Eds.), *Workers' Control.* New York: Random House, 1973.

HUNT, S. M., JR., SINGER, K., AND COBB, S. "The Components of Depression Identified from a Self Rating Depression Inventory for Survey Use." *Archives of General Psychiatry,* 1967, *16,* 441–447.

INKELES, A. "Industrial Man: The Relation of Status to Experience, Perception, and Value." *The American Journal of Sociology,* 1960, *66,* 1–31.

JACKSON, E. "Status Consistency and Symptoms of Stress." *American Sociological Review,* Aug. 1962, *27,* 469–480.

KAHN, R. L. "Human Relations on the Shop Floor." In E. M. Hugh-Jones (Ed.), *Human Relations and Modern Management.* Amsterdam: North-Holland Publishing Co., 1958.

KASL, S., AND FRENCH, J. R. P., JR. "The Effects of Occupational Status on Physical and Mental Health." *Journal of Social Issues,* 1962, *17,* 3, 67–89.

KATZ, D. "Satisfactions and Deprivations in Industrial Life." In A. Kornhauser, R. Dubin, and A. M. Ross (Eds.), *Industrial Conflict.* New York: McGraw-Hill, 1954.

KATZ, D., AND GEORGOPOULOS, B. S. "Organizations in a Changing World." *Journal of Applied Behavior Science,* 1971, 7, 3.

KATZ, D., AND KAHN, R. L. *The Social Psychology of Organizations.* New York: Wiley, 1966.

KAVČIČ, B., RUS, V., AND TANNENBAUM, A. S. "Control, Participation, and Effectiveness in Four Yugoslav Industrial Organizations." *Administrative Science Quarterly*, 1971, *16*, 1, 74–87.

KERR, C., HARBISON, F. H., DUNLOP, J. T., AND MYERS, C. A. *Industrialism and Industrial Man*. London: Heinemann, 1964.

KOLAJA, J. *Workers' Councils, the Yugoslav Experience*. London: Tavistock, 1965.

KORNHAUSER, A. "Human Motivations Underlying Industrial Conflict." In A. Kornhauser, R. Dubin, and A. M. Ross (Eds.), *Industrial Conflict*. New York: McGraw-Hill, 1954.

KRALJ, J. "The New Management Systems in the Planned Economy —From the Point of View of Yugoslav Workers' Self Administration in Conditions of Planned Mixed Economy." Paper presented at the 15th Annual Meeting of the CIOS International Management Congress, Tokyo, 1969.

LAMMERS, C. J. "Power and Participation in Decision-Making in Formal Organizations." *American Journal of Sociology*, September, 1967, *73* (2) 201–216.

LAUMANN, E. O., SIEGEL, P. M., AND HODGE, R. W. (Eds.) *The Logic of Social Hierarchies*. Chicago: Markham, 1970.

LAWLER, E. E., III. *Pay and Organizational Effectiveness: A Psychological View*. New York: McGraw-Hill, 1971.

LAWLER, E. E., III, AND HACKMAN, J. R. "Corporate Profits and Employee Satisfaction: Must They Be in Conflict?" *California Management Review*, 1972, 46–55.

LAWLER, E. E., III, AND PORTER, L. W. "Predicting Managers' Pay and Their Satisfaction with Pay." *Personnel Psychology*, 1966, *19* (4), 363–374.

LEFKOWITZ, J. "Self-Esteem of Industrial Workers." *Journal of Applied Psychology*, 1967, *51*, 5, 521–528.

LENSKI, G. "Status Crystallization: A Non-Vertical Dimension of Social Status." *American Sociological Review*, 1964, 405–413.

LENSKI, G. *Power and Privilege: A Theory of Social Stratification*. New York: McGraw-Hill, 1966.

LEVIATAN, U. "The Industrial Process in Israeli Kibbutzim: Problems and Their Solutions." In M. Curtis and M. S. Chertoff (Eds.), *Israel: Social Structure and Change*. New Brunswick, N. J.: Transaction Books, 1973.

LIEBERMAN, S. "The Effects of Changes in Roles on the Attitudes of Role Occupants." *Human Relations*, 1956, *9*, 4, 385–402.

LIKERT, R. *New Patterns of Management.* New York: McGraw-Hill, 1961.

LIKERT, R. *The Human Organization.* New York: McGraw-Hill, 1967.

LIPSET, S. M., TROW, J. A., AND COLEMAN, J. S. *Union Democracy.* New York: Free Press, 1956.

MCCLELLAND, D. C., ATKINSON, J. W., CLARK, R. A., AND LOWELL, E. L. *The Achievement Motive.* New York: Appleton-Century-Crofts, 1953.

MCCLELLAND, D. C. *The Achieving Society.* Princeton: Van Nostrand, 1961.

MACLEAN, F. *Tito.* New York: Ballantine Books, 1957.

MCNEMAR, Q. *Psychological Statistics* (2nd edition). New York: Wiley, 1957.

MCVICKER, C. P. *Titoism: Pattern for International Communism.* London: Macmillan, 1957.

MAIER, N. R. F., HOFFMAN, L. R., HOOVEN, J. J., AND READ, W. H. *Superior-Subordinate Communication in Management.* New York: American Management Association, 1961.

MANN, F. C. "A Study of Work Satisfactions as a Function of the Discrepancy between Inferred Aspirations and Achievement." Unpublished doctoral dissertation. University of Michigan, Ann Arbor, 1953.

MAO TSE-TUNG. "Speeches, Directions, and Letters of Mao Tse-Tung." *New York Times,* March 1, 1970, p. 26.

MARCH, J. G., AND SIMON, H. A. *Organizations.* New York: Wiley, 1958.

MARENCO, C. *Employes de Banque.* Paris: Counseil Superior de la Recherche Scientifique, February 1959.

MARX, K. "Third Economic and Philosophical Manuscript." In K. Marx, *Early Writings.* New York: McGraw-Hill, 1963b. Quoted by Seeman, M., in "Alienation," *Psychology Today,* August 1971, *5*, 3, p. 83.

MARX, K. *Selected Writings in Sociology and Social Philosophy.* T. B. Bottomore and M. Rubel (Eds.). New York: McGraw-Hill, 1964.

MARX, K. *Capital, Vol. 1.* New York: International Publishing Co., 1967.

MASLOW, A. H. "A Theory of Human Motivation." *Psychological Review,* July 1943, *50*, 370–396.

MAYO, E. *The Social Problems of an Industrial Civilization.* Cambridge, Mass.: Divisions of Research, Graduate School of Business Administration, Harvard University, 1945.

MECHANIC, D. "Sources of Power of Lower Participants in Complex Organizations." *Administrative Science Quarterly,* December 1962, *7,* 3, 349–364.

MELMAN, S. "Managerial versus Cooperative Decision Making in Israel." *Studies in Comparative International Development,* 1970–1971, *6,* 3.

MICHELS, R. *Political Parties.* New York: Dover, 1959.

MILES, R. E. "Human Relations or Human Resources." *Harvard Business Review,* July–August, 1965, *43,* 4, 149–156.

MOZINA, S. Moutivisanost rukovodicik kadrova, sauremeno rukovodenje i samoupravljanje ("Motivation of Managerial Personnel"), Belgrade, 1969, pp. 170–180.

MORSE, N. *Satisfactions in the White Collar Job.* Ann Arbor: University of Michigan, Survey Research Center, 1953.

MORSE, N., AND REIMER, E. "The Experimental Change of a Major Organization Variable." *Journal of Abnormal and Social Psychology,* 1956, *52,* 120–129.

MULDER, M., AND WILKE, H. "Participation and Power Equalization." *Organizational Behavior and Human Performance,* 1970, *5,* 5, 430–448.

OBRADOVIC, J. "Distribution of Participation in the Process of Decision-Making on Problems Related to the Economic Activity of the Company." Proceedings, 1st International Conference on Participation and Self-Management, Dubrovnik, September 13–17, 1972, *2,* 137–164.

PARSONS, T. "An Analytic Approach to the Theory of Social Stratification." *In Essays in Sociological Theory.* Glencoe, Ill.: The Free Press, 1954.

PARSONS, T. *Structure and Process in Modern Society.* New York: Free Press, 1960.

PATCHEN, M. *The Choice of Wage Comparisons.* Englewood Cliffs, N.J.: Prentice-Hall, 1961a.

PATCHEN, M. "A Conceptual Framework and Some Empirical Data Regarding Comparisons of Social Rewards." *Sociometry,* June 1961b, *24,* 2, 136–156.

PATEMAN, C. *Participation and Democratic Theory.* London: Cambridge University Press, 1970.

PAUL, W. J., JR., ROBERTSON, K. B., AND HERZBERG, F. "Job Enrichment Pays Off." *Harvard Business Review,* March–April 1969, *47,* 61–78.

PERROW, C. *Organizational Analysis: A Sociological View.* Belmont, Calif.: Wadsworth, 1970.

PERROW, C. *Complex Organizations, A Critical Essay.* Glenview, Ill.: Scott, Foresman, 1972.

PORTER, L. W. "Job Attitudes in Management: I. Perceived Deficiencies in Need Fulfillment as a Function of Job Level." *Journal of Applied Psychology,* 1962, *46,* 6, 375–384.

PORTER, L. W., AND LAWLER, E. E., III. "Properties of Organizational Structure in Relation to Job Attitudes and Job Behavior." *Psychological Bulletin,* 1965, *64,* 1, 23–51.

QUINN, R. P. "What Workers Want: The Relative Importance of Job Facets to American Workers." Mimeo, May 1972.

REED, W. H. "Upward Communication in Industrial Hierarchies." *Human Relations,* 1962, *15,* 3–15.

RICHMAN, B. M. *Industrial Society in Communist China.* New York: Random House, 1969.

ROETHLISBERGER, R. J., AND DICKSON, W. J. *Management and the Worker.* Cambridge, Mass.: Harvard University Press, 1964.

ROSNER, M. "Principles, Types, and Problems of Direct Democracy in the Kibbutz." *New Outlook,* September 1965.

ROSNER, M. "Worker Participation in Decision-Making in Kibbutz Industry." In M. Curtis and M. S. Chertoff (Eds.), *Israel: Social Structure and Change.* New Brunswick, N. J.: Transaction Books, 1973.

ROSNER, M., KAVČIČ, G., TANNENBAUM, A. S., VIANELLO, M., AND WIESER, G. "Worker Participation and Influence in Five Countries." *Industrial Relations,* May 1973, *12,* 2, 200–212.

RUS, V. "Influence Structure in the Yugoslav Enterprise." *Industrial Relations,* February 1970, *9,* 2, 148–160.

RUS, V. "The Limits of Organized Participation." Proceedings, 1st International Sociological Conference on Participation and Self-Management, September 13–17, 1972, *2,* 165–188.

SEASHORE, S. E. *Group Cohesiveness in the Industrial Work Group.* Ann Arbor, Mich.: Institute for Social Research, 1954.

SEEMAN, M. "Role Conflict and Ambivalence in Leadership." *American Sociological Review,* 1953, *18* (4), 373–380.

SEEMAN, M. "On the Personal Consequences of Alienation in Work." *American Sociological Review,* Dec. 1959, *24,* 783–791.

SELZNICK, P. *TVA and the Grass Roots.* Berkeley: University of California Press, 1949.

SHEPARD, J. M. "Functional Specialization, Alienation, and Job Satisfaction." *Industrial and Labor Relations Review,* January 1970, *23,* 2, 207–219.

SIMON, H. A. *Administrative Behavior.* New York: The Free Press, 1965.

SKINNER, B. F. *Beyond Freedom and Dignity.* New York: Knopf, 1971.

SMITH, C. G., AND TANNENBAUM, A. S. "Organizational Control Structure: A Comparative Analysis." *Human Relations,* 1963, *16,* 4, 299–316.

STAGNER, R. "Union-Management Relations in Italy: Some Observations." *Current Economic Comment,* May 1957.

STANTON, A. A., AND SCHWARTZ, M. S. *The Mental Hospital.* New York: Basic Books, 1954.

STOTLAND, E., AND KOBLER, A. L. *Life and Death of a Mental Hospital.* Seattle: University of Washington Press, 1965.

STOUFFER, S., SUCHMAN, E. A., DEVINNEY, L. C., STARR, S. A., AND WILLIAMS, R. M., JR. *Studies in Social Psychology in World War II, Vol. II, The American Soldier: Adjustment During Army Life.* Princeton: Princeton University Press, 1949.

STRAUSS, G. "Some Notes on Power-Equalization." In H. Leavitt (Ed.), *The Social Science of Organizations: Four Perspectives.* Englewood Cliffs, N.J.: Prentice-Hall, 1963.

STRAUSS, G., MILES, R., AND TANNENBAUM, A. S. (Eds.). *Organizational Behavior: Research and Issues.* Madison, Wis.: Industrial Relations Research Association, 1974.

STRAUSS, G., AND ROSENSTEIN, E. "Workers' Participation: A Critical View." *Industrial Relations,* Feb. 1970, *9* (2), 197–214.

STURMTHAL, A. *Workers' Councils.* Cambridge, Mass.: Harvard University Press, 1964.

SUPEK, R. "Two Types of Self-Managing Organizations and Technological Processes." Proceedings, 1st International Sociological Conference on Participation and Self-Management, Dubrovnik, September 13–17, 1972, *1,* 15–173.

SYKES, G. M. *The Society of Conflicts.* Princeton, N.J.: Princeton University Press, 1958.

TALMON-GARBER, Y. "Differentiation in Collective Settlements." *Scripta Hicrosolymitana, 3,* Jerusalem: Hebrew University, 1956.

TANNENBAUM, A. S. "An Event-Structure Approach to Power and

to the Problem of Power Comparability." *Behavioral Science,* July 1962a, 7, 3, 315–331.

TANNENBAUM, A. S. "Control in Organizations: Individual Adjustment and Organizational Performance." *Administrative Science Quarterly,* 1962b, 7, 2, 236–257.

TANNENBAUM, A. S. "Reactions of Members of Voluntary Groups: A Logarithmic Function of Size of Groups." *Psychological Reports,* 1962c, *10,* 113–114.

TANNENBAUM, A. S. "Unions." In J. March (Ed.), *Handbook of Organizations.* Chicago: Rand McNally, 1965.

TANNENBAUM, A. S. *Social Psychology of the Work Organization.* Belmont, Calif.: Brooks/Cole Publishing Co., 1966.

TANNENBAUM, A. S. *Control in Organizations.* New York: McGraw-Hill, 1968a.

TANNENBAUM, A. S. "Leadership: Sociological Aspects." *International Encyclopaedia of the Social Sciences, Vol. 9.* Crowell, Collier and Macmillan, Inc., 1968b, 101–107.

TANNENBAUM, A. S. "Systems of Formal Participation." In G. Strauss, R. Miles, and A. S. Tannenbaum (Eds.), *Organizational Behavior: Research and Issues.* Madison, Wis.: Industrial Relations Research Association, 1974.

TANNENBAUM, A. S., AND KAHN, R. L. *Participation in Union Locals.* Evanston, Ill.: Row, Peterson, 1958.

TAYLOR, D. W. "Decision Making and Problem Solving." In J. G. March (Ed.), *Handbook of Organizations.* Chicago: Rand McNally, 1965.

TRIST, E. L., HIGGIN, G. W., MURRAY, H., AND POLLOCK, A. B. *Organizational Choice.* London: Tavistock, 1963.

TUMIN, M. "Some Principles of Stratification: A Critical Analysis." *American Sociological Review,* 1953, *18* (4), 387–394.

TUMIN, M. *Social Stratification, Forms and Functions of Inequality.* Englewood Cliffs: Prentice-Hall, 1969.

TURNER, A. M., AND LAWRENCE, P. R. *Industrial Jobs and the Worker: An Investigation of Response to Task Attributes.* Boston: Harvard University, Graduate School of Business Administration, 1965.

U.S. BUREAU OF THE CENSUS. *Annual Survey of Manufacturers.* Washington, D.C., 1971.

VERTIN, P. G. "Bedryfsgeneeskundige aspecten van het ulcus pepticum" (Occupational Health Aspects of the Peptic Ulcer). Thesis, Groningen, 1954. As cited in French, J. R. P., Jr.,

"Social Environment of Mental Health." *Journal of Applied Psychology,* 1963, *19,* 4, 39–56.

WALKER, C. R., AND GUEST, R. H. "The Man on the Assembly Line." *Harvard Business Review,* 1952, *30,* 71–83.

WERNIMONT, P. F. "Intrinsic and Extrinsic Factors in Job Satisfaction." *Journal of Applied Psychology,* 1966, *50,* 41–50.

WESOLOWOSKI, W. "The Continuing Debate on Equality." In R. Bendix and S. M. Lipset (Eds.), *Class, Status, and Power.* Glencoe, Ill.: The Free Press, 1966.

WESTLEY, W. "An Evaluative Model for Worker Participation in Management." Proceedings, 1st International Sociological Conference on Participation and Self-Management, Dubrovnik, September 13–17, 1972, *2,* 199–210.

WHISLER, T. L. "Measuring Centralization of Control in Business Organizations." In W. W. Cooper, H. J. Leavitt, and M. W. Shelly, Jr. (Eds.), *New Perspectives in Organization Research.* New York: Wiley, 1964.

WHYTE, M. K. "Bureaucracy and Modernization in China: The Maoist Critique." *American Sociological Review,* April 1973, *38,* 2, 149–163.

WILENSKY, H. "Human Relations in the Workplace: An Appraisal of Some Recent Research." In C. Arensberg, S. Barkin, W. Chalmers, H. Wilensky, J. Worthy, and B. Dennis (Eds.), *Research in Industrial Human Relations—A Critical Appraisal.* New York: Harper, 1957.

WOODWARD, J. *Industrial Organization: Theory and Practice.* London: Oxford University Press, 1965.

YUCHTMAN, E., AND SEASHORE, S. E. "A System Resource Approach to Organizational Effectiveness." *American Sociological Review,* 1967, *32,* 891–903.

ZUPANOV, J., AND TANNENBAUM, A. S. "The Distribution of Control in Some Yugoslav Industrial Organizations as Perceived by Members." *Ekonomski Pregled,* God 1966, *17,* Broj. 2–3, 115–132. Also in Tannenbaum, A. S. *Control in Organizations.* New York: McGraw-Hill, 1968.

ZUPANOV, J. "Two Patterns of Conflict Management in Industry." *Industrial Relations,* May 1973, *12,* 2, 213–223.

NAME INDEX

241

SUBJECT INDEX